Sixty Second Sermons

By
Bobby G. Roberts, Sr., D. Min.

Copyright © 1988 by Christian Foundations of Faith, Inc.

All rights reserved. No part of this book may be reproduced if the reproduction will be sold or used in any manner for profit. However, you are encouraged to use this material in sermons, on radio, television or any other method in order to further the gospel of Jesus Christ, as long as these avenues of ministry are presented to the public without charge. If you have questions concerning the use of this copyrighted material, please contact the author for permission. Please provide complete details along with your written request.

Library of Congress Catalog Number: 88-71153

ISBN: 0-9620462-0-5

PRINTED IN THE UNITED STATES OF AMERICA

Reproduction Of Cover Artwork Is Available

Art quality, lithographic prints of the cover of *Sixty Second Sermons* are available for purchase. They are printed on acid neutral 100% rag paper with ultra violet resistant ink. These prints are suitable for framing. Print size is 16 × 22½". If you desire one of these beautiful prints please contact Dr. Bob Roberts at the address below for complete ordering information. No reproduction of cover artwork or lithographic print is authorized in any form.

Cover Art & Design by Paul Annan.

Printed by Faith Press International, Inc., 3710 West Way, Tyler, Texas 75703

Typography by Creative Typography, P. O. Box 296, Tyler, Texas 75710

Scripture quotations are from the *King James Version*. Public domain.

Published by
Christian Foundations of Faith, Inc.
Dr. Bob Roberts
P. O. Box 130252
Tyler, Texas 75713

Table of Contents

	Acknowledgements	iv
	Foreword	vi
	Introduction	vii
	A Note About The Author	xiv
Chapter 1	Faith's Foundations	1
Chapter 2	Life and Living	35
Chapter 3	Moving Toward Maturity	75
Chapter 4	Thoughts That Triumph	101
Chapter 5	Death and Dying	128
Chapter 6	Caring and Sharing	139
Chapter 7	Hope For The Home	154
Chapter 8	Comfort and Cheer	165
Chapter 9	Conquering Circumstances	193
	Bibliography	207
	Index	208

Acknowledgements

It would be impossible to more than scratch the surface in the form of acknowledgments to the many individuals who have helped me through the years realize the fulfillment of my calling through the pastorate, evangelism, missions, and the outreach ministry of Christian Foundations of Faith Inc. It has been through the ministry of the latter that the sixty second sermons in this book have been presented hundreds of times on radio and television.

Surely, none deserve more recognition than my wife, Gay, of thirty-five years and our four lovely Children. Sandra, our oldest daughter set such a wonderful precedent for our other children to follow. She cut a good path for them to follow and we shall ever be grateful to her for it. Bob Jr., early gave his life to Christ and has been a true disciple and discipler of others. He has brought much joy to my heart as a son, a student, and a preacher of God's Word. Mark has been a constant minister to me. He dared do what others would not. He questioned me and helped me discover much about myself that needed perfecting. His high aspirations will not go without reward. Sheila has helped us realize the depth of God's Grace, the grace she continues to grow and develop in herself. We are pleased that all have now graduated from college and some have gone beyond. The achievements of the children are largely due to their mother who remained at home to make a home for the family. She instilled in them character, desires and aspirations that has caused them all to be achievers. It is to my family who knew me at my best and loved me at my worst that this book is dedicated. They knew me as many never shall know me and loved me in spite of my short comings.

Words could never express the gratitude I have for Mr. and Mrs. Bud Morriss who first encouraged me to begin a radio ministry and offered the financial support needed for it to begin and continue. Because of the radio ministry that was begun, Christian Foundations of Faith Inc., was begun as a non-profit organization to carry on this ministry of outreach. It is to the many who have served on the Board of Christian Foundations of Faith Inc. over the years that we express gratitude . These individuals knew my heart best and helped me to dream dreams and realize their fulfillment.

Space would not permit the listing of all who have given prayerfully and financially to undergird this ministry. The first contributors were largely members of the First Baptist Church of Lindale, Texas where I pastored for eight years. It was this good Church that allowed me to carry on the outreach ministry of Christian Foundations of

Faith along with my pastoral duties until I was called into full time Mission Evangelism. All other support has been received from former Church Members and friends whom we have met out here in Evangelism along with the Churches who have been gracious enough to invite us for revival crusades.

Surely, you would not be reading this had it not been for the assistance of Mrs. Gloria Peggram, Mrs. Lynda Rozelle, and Mrs. Linda Porche. They spent much time proof reading these messages and correcting them grammatically. Gloria was ever ready to offer a listening ear and give advice and insight that has been most valuable.

Credit must be given to Artist Paul Annan for the format and art work found in the book. Paul has been a true yoke fellow. No man ever sought to make available his gifts to the cause of Christ in a greater way than Paul.

In 1978 I resigned the pastorate of the First Baptist Church of Lindale, Texas to enter full time evangelism. The radio ministry immediately became in jeopardy. David Wilkerson, author of *The Cross and The Switchblade* and president of World Challenge, stepped to my side as he did for young men from the asphalt jungles of New York City. He enabled us to carry on the radio ministry for over a year. During much sickness and trouble, he stood by us as a true friend and brother and fellow evangelist. We shall never forget the encouragement and help he has given this ministry over the years.

Surely only heaven will reveal the influence my mother and father have had on my life. It was through their sickness and suffering and death that God taught me much about death and dying and allowed me to communicate this truth to others.

I owe much to Mr. and Mrs. Bill Parrot who enabled me to do additional studying through The Luther Rice Seminary while engaged in mission evangelism. It was through Luther Rice Seminary that I was brought in contact with Dr. Paul Enns, my advisor in the Doctor of Ministry program. It has been through his permission and direction that these sermons have been finally brought to book form.

Finally the publication of this book is made possible because of the financial assistance of Mr. and Mrs. Kyle Greer who share with us a burden for missions and a desire to get God's word out to men where they are. They are faithful members of the First Baptist Church of Canton, Texas and board members of Christian Foundations of Faith Inc. Because of their encouragement this book is sent forth with a burning desire to meet the needs of men where they are.

Foreword

I believe Bob Roberts is one of the finest Baptist preachers I have ever heard. His messages are quick, sharp, and as powerful as a two-edged sword. He cuts to the marrow of the bone and then pours in the balm of Gilead.

His sixty second sermons are the best I've heard. It is difficult to say a lot in such a short time, but he manages to do it. The messages are clear, scriptural, and very meaningful. They are the result of much study, research, and preparation.

Our ministry has been honored to be one of his friends and a regular supporter of his dynamic ministry.

In Christ,
David Wilkerson

Introduction

Sir Frederick the Great said to his chaplain during a crucial moment in his life, "Doctor, if your religion is a true one, it ought to be capable of very brief and simple proof. Will you give me evidence of its truth in one word?" The chaplain responded quickly with the word, "Israel." The answer was self explanatory, for nations come and go but Israel remains on the world scene.[1]

The sixty second sermons in this book were first prepared and presented over the radio in an effort to give brief and simple proof of the Gospel and the claims that God makes on all of our lives. It is my firm conviction that while many people may not go to the traditional church in an effort to seek answers to life's perplexing problems, that they are concerned about what God and the Bible has to say concerning them. It then becomes our responsibility to be innovative enough to find ways to communicate the Gospel to them. I have discovered that one of the most effective ways today is through the presentation of these sixty second sermons through the medium of radio. In the past I taught the Sunday School lesson on the radio and preached various messages. However, I was disappointed to find out that it was mostly friends and fellow church members who listened to me. I began to evaluate new approaches that would enable me to reach a greater cross section of the community. The Lord inspired me to purchase small segments of time on the more popular radio stations and present the Gospel in a simple and brief manner.

I did this and immediately the response became obvious and rewarding. Now instead of being on the radio once a week at a given time, I was on the radio five times a day and seven days a week, with the cost being little more than it was for a thirty minute or hour program, The format was simple. I simply would read a scripture and find some illustration close to life to offer explanation.

During the past years many have written and wanted copies of particular messages. Others have encouraged us to put them in a book. I have sought to do this with the desire that others might use them in a similar fashion as I have used them. I send them forth with full permission to be used on the radio, television, local newspapers, church bulletins, or as a devotional to be shared with a friend who needs a fresh word from God. It would be an impossibility for me to give proper credit to all who have shared some of the illustrations with me. I have gleaned them from thirty-five years in the ministry. Some I have heard, and some I have read from books. I cannot fully

---

[1] W. E. Blackstone, *Jesus Is Coming*, (Old Tappan, New Jersey: Flemming H. Revell, 1898), p. 161.

document the original source, but I have sought to provide a bibliography that will reveal where many of them found original inspiration with me. I do not feel I need to offer any defense for them. They have been tried in the very crucible of life. All of them have been written, evaluated and used on the radio many times. There are some principles that I discovered in the preparation and presentation of these sixty second sermons that I would share with you by way of introduction which would hopefully help you in your preaching, teaching, or witnessing. Consider with me first of all the principle of simplification.

The Principle Of Simplification

Haddon W. Robinson in his book, *Biblical Preaching*, says, "a sermon should be a bullet and not buckshot. Ideally each sermon is the explanation, interpretation, or application of a single dominant idea supported by other ideas, all drawn from one passage or several passages of scripture,"[2] Public speaking students learn early that effective speaking centers on one specific thing or central idea. It is the idea that we must concern ourself with. The word "idea" comes from a Greek word EIDO which means "to see," and therefore "to know." An idea then enables us to see what was previously unclear. Donald G. Miller has said, "any single sermon should have just one major idea..."[3] J. H. Jowett states, "I have a conviction that no sermon is ready for preaching, not ready for writing out, until we can express its theme in a short, pregnant sentence as clear as crystal."[4] Abraham Lincoln once commented that one should speak, "so that the most lowly can understand you, and the rest will have no difficulty."[5] This single and central idea can most easily be presented by using short words and phrases. George G. William maintains that, "... from 70 to 78 per cent of the words used by W. Somerset Maugham, Sinclair Lewis, Robert Louis Stevenson and Charles Dickens have only one syllable. Seventy-three percent of the words in Psalm 23, seventy-six percent of the words in the Lord's Prayer and eighty per cent of the words in I Corinthians 13 are one syllable words."[6] The success of these sixty second sermons rests largely upon their truthfulness and simplicity. In homiletics one is taught to make it warm, make it simple and make it Biblical. I have sought to do this with each message contained in

---

[2] Haddon W. Robinson, *Biblical Preaching*, (Grand Rapids, Michigan: Baker Book House, 1980), p. 33.
[3] Ibid., p. 34.
[4] Ibid., p. 35.
[5] Ibid., p. 182.
[6] Ibid., p. 182.

this book.

I am aware of the danger of over simplification. I know we have over-used the word, "relevant," and some have suggested in some circles that a fad has almost developed called, "making the church relevant." Peter Wagner, in his book, *A Turned on Church in an Uptight World*, says that this futile attempt to make salvation more palatable to sinners through the use of simplicity is as old as the Corinthians. Harold Lindsell says, "ultimately the Gospel is relevant to the true needs of men and for us to try to debase the good coinage of the Gospel by vitiating it so that we can make it more attractive to men is to lose the Gospel and to make it irrelevant."[7] The simplicity by which we have sought to present these sixty second sermons has in no way cheapened the Gospel. They have simply made the Gospel applicable and understandable.

The Principle of Illustration

There is another principle that I discovered in the process of writing these messages and that is the principle of illustration. I discovered that people can more easily understand the scriptures if they have something to relate them to. It is said that when the people heard Jesus that they heard him gladly. They had never heard anyone speak with such clarity and simplicity. What was the secret behind it all? It was no secret at all. He simply spoke with simplicity. He took full advantage of parables, metaphors and stories as means of explaining Biblical truth, It has been estimated that more than one half of His public instructions were given in the form of parables or comparisons. One scholar found 164 metaphors in the synoptic Gospels. There have been as many as 56 metaphors found in the sermon on the mount. No wonder the common man heard Him gladly. No wonder His words were alive. Kipling said in reference to the words of Christ, "They walked up and down the hearts of the hearers."[8] By means of the principle of illustration Jesus was able to give immediate understanding to His listeners.

Is this not the purpose of illustration? The very word itself means to make clear, to illuminate, to throw light upon a subject. It is like the picture on television that makes clear what the speaker is explaining. Illustrations apply ideas to experience. They aid memory, stir emotions, create need and hold attention. They help the listener not only

---

[7] C. Peter Wagner, *A Turned On Church in An Uptight World*, (Grand Rapids, Michigan: Zondervan, 1971), p. 105.

[8] Ilion T. Jones, *Principles and Practice of Preaching*, (Nashville: Abingdon Press, 1956), p. 137.

to understand but to accept a concept. Illustrations cannot stand as proof, but they can psychologically work with argument to gain acceptance. John A. Broadus quotes Bryan Dawson as saying, "... the preacher cannot rely upon his gift of lucidity and power in exposition, reasoning and persuading; he must make truth interesting and attractive by expressing it in transparent words and using it in revealing metaphor and story and picture. The necessity of illuminating the sermon properly is found in the mental attitude of the people. Whether we like it or not, most of us preach to the moving picture mind. It is the mind accustomed to images, pictures, scenes, rapidly moving. It certainly is not accustomed to deep thinking or long sustained argument. Current magazines, billboards, novels, drama, rapid transit all aid to this popular method of visual thinking. We as ministers may not approve of the daily fare of the people; we may wish them to prefer theoretical reasoning. But whatever our wishes, we must recognize that they regard thinking which is not imaginary and concrete as dull and uninteresting."[9]

Now once again a word must be said about the danger of illustrations. There is the danger of allowing the illustration to draw attention to itself instead of the Gospel truth one is seeking to present. Phillip Brooks says there is a test that we must always apply to the use of an illustration and it is; will it call attention to or away from the truth? If it takes away it must be abandoned. You must remember that it should be true and have real relations to the subject it illustrates. The illustrations used with these sixty second sermons in this book have been but a simple vehicle to bear the truth of the Gospel upon.

The Principle of Identification

I discovered also another principle in the preparation and presentation of these sixty second sermons and that is the principle of identification. David Wilkerson relates that as he was sitting on the platform of a church filled to capacity in Colorado that the pastor turned to him and said, "Do you know why these people are here? They are here because during the week I go out and mix and mingle with them and discover where they are hurting. I then get in my study with God's Word and seek to find answers for their hurts. On Sunday I simply give them the Biblical answers and they come to hear." John A. Broadus says, "Communicative preaching is dialogical and always has been. It is characterized by the preacher's concern for the attitudes and experiences and needs of his people. In every aspect of his

---

[9] John A. Broadus, *On The Preparation and Delivery of Sermons*, (San Francisco: Harper and Row, 1870), p. 179.

ministry he must listen to them and respond appropriately to their needs and feelings."[10]

Leslie Tizard said, "whosoever will become a preacher must feel the needs of men until it becomes an oppression of his soul."[11] We live today in a world where people are hurting and God's man must have something to say to these hurts. They shall surely be tossed to and fro with every wind and doctrine in search of an answer, if he does not. This demands that God's man be among the people; that he identify with them in their hurts and trials; that he, as Ezekiel, go and sit where they sit. I discovered after a series of three surgical operations in a period of six weeks, that people going through trials listened to me more intently afterwards. This is what the Apostle Paul meant in II Corinthians 1:34 when he said, "Blessed be God, even the Father of our Lord Jesus Christ, the Father of mercies, and the God of all comfort; who comforteth us in all our tribulations, that we may be able to comfort them which are in trouble, by the comfort wherewith we ourselves are comforted of God." The presentation and proclamation of the Gospel is largely dependent upon our identification with the people and their needs. This is why Phillips Brooks said, "The man whose eye is set upon the souls of men and whose heart burns with the desire to save them, chooses with an almost unerring instinct what figure will set the truth more clearly before their minds, what form of appeal will bring it most strongly to their sluggish wills. He takes those and rejects every other."[12] W. M. MacGregor stated that it was indispensable for a preacher to know men, what they are and how they think and feel. It was said of Phillip Henry that he did not shoot the arrow of the word over the head of his audience in effectual rhetoric, not under their feet by homely expression but to their heart in close and lively application.[13]

Many if not most of the sixty second sermons found in this book were born out of real life situations. It was while pastoring the First Baptist Church of Lindale, Texas for eight years that most of them were prepared. It was as I went in and out of their homes; as I prayed with them in the hospitals; as I went with one after the other to and from the funeral home and cemetery; as I visited with them on the

---

[10] Ibid., p. 306.
[11] Lloyd M. Perry, *Biblical Preaching For Today's World*, Chicago: Moody Press, 1973), p. 105.
[12] Phillips Brooks, *Lectures on Preaching*, (Grand Rapids, Michigan: Baker Book House, 1969), p. 267.
[13] Perry, Op. Cit., p. 104.

streets and counseled with them in my office that I discovered their hurts and sought to address myself to them through God's Word.

The Principle of Communication

The principle of communication was another principle that I rediscovered in the preparation and presentation of these brief messages. Phillips Brooks says that, "preaching is the communication of truth by man to men. It has in it two essential elements, truth and personality."[14] Andrew W. Blackwood stated that, "preaching is divine truth voiced by a chosen personality to meet human needs."[15] All of these capable and able men would agree that preaching is the presentation of truth through human personality. God could have chosen a multitude of means and methods to communicate truth, but He chose man, a human personality with a voice to sound forth God's message. It is true that God often chose writers to convey His truth, but more often it was one who would stand and speak the truth. Though the canon was closed long ago, with God not adding any new books to the Bible, He continues to redeem and forgive fallen men and command them to, "Go home and tell . . ." Whenever and wherever men take that command seriously and lift up their voices to bear witness of God's love and grace, hearts are warmed and lives are changed. The sermon spoken through human personalities to men has but one supreme purpose and that is the persuasion and moving of men's souls. That purpose must never be lost sight of. The sermon must be recognized as a medium of conveying the truth of God to the hearts of men. While the sermons of men may vary they must all achieve the goal of explaining, illustrating and applying God's word to the lives of men in today's world while there is still time. This leads me to the final principle that I wish to discuss. It is the principle of obligation.

The Principle of Obligation

The Biblical basis for this principle is best set forth in Paul's book to the Romans where he says, ". . .I am debtor both to the Greek, and to the Barbarian; both to the wise and to the unwise, so much as in me is, I am ready to preach the Gospel to you that are at Rome also" (Rom.1:14). He reveals the method he used in seeking to fulfill this

---

[14] Perry, Op. Cit., p. 15.
[15] Perry, Op. Cit., p. 14.

obligation in I Corinthians 9:22 when he says, "To the weak became I as weak, that I might gain the weak; I am made all things to all men, that I might by all means save some."

We too are under the same obligation and time is running out for us. In Lloyd Perry's book on *Biblical Preaching for Today's World* he gives us some alarming facts and figures. He states, "It has been said that the world is growing pagan at the rate of 38 million souls a year. Only 3 per cent of the lost ever attend church. Only 5 per cent of those who come to Christ come without a personal invitation. In 1850, it took five Christians to lead one soul to Christ. It now takes an average of 1,000 laymen and six pastors to lead one soul to Christ in 365 days. Eighty per cent of those who will be saved will be younger than 25 years of age. Seventy-five per cent of our Sunday School students leave the Sunday School by the time they are 18 years of age. We have 400 million more in the world today without the Gospel than we had thirty years ago. Billy Graham stated at the World Congress of Evangelism that the population was increasing at the rate of 40 million people a year. This would mean that 110,000 people a day, or 4,500 an hour, or 75 every minute would have to be won to Christ just to keep up with the population increase. We dare not just stand here. We must do something."[16]

We are ambassadors of the King (II Cor. 5:20). We have a message from Heaven to earth desperately needed, and the King's message must get through. One morning in January, 1930, King George was to speak to the London Naval Conference. Just moments before his speech was to be delivered and broadcast by the Columbia Broadcasting Company, Mr. Walter Vivian, an official of the company, discovered that a wire connection had been severed. The repair would take thirty minutes, but the time was not available. To meet the crisis, he gripped the broken wire, one end in each hand, and thereby restored the current. In doing so, his body was shocked and his hand severely burned by the 250 volt charge. He endured the pain because the King's message had to get through. Our King, Jesus Christ, has gone to Heaven and He has left us with a message. May God help us to get the message through.

These sixty second sermons are brief and simple, but they come from a heart that is burning to get the King's message through. May God help us to use whatever means is available to us to reach men, where ever they are, with the Gospel. Remember that preaching is not just standing in a pulpit at 11:00 A.M. on Sunday morning, but preaching is the communication of truth by man to men. Therefore; wherever you go, go preaching the message of Christ the King.

---

[16] Perry, Op. Cit., p. 151.

A Note About The Author

Dr. and Mrs. Bob Roberts are engaged in full time Mission Evangelism and reside in Tyler, Texas where he serves as president of Christian Foundations of Faith Inc., a non-profit organization he founded that is committed to evangelism and missions. He and His wife Gay have been married for thirty-four years and are the parents of two sons and two daughters. One of their sons is pastor of a Baptist Church. Another son is in law school. One daughter is a nurse and one a school teacher. They have spent all of their married life in the ministry. He pastored Southern Baptist Churches in Texas for the first twenty-six years of his ministry and for the last nine years has devoted himself to full time evangelism. Much of his time is devoted to preaching revivals and conducting Bible Conferences in the States and doing extensive mission work in the Country of Belize Central America.

He has worked closely with Southern Baptist Missionaries in Belize helping to establish churches, to build buildings, to provide leadership training programs, to provide scholarships for some of the youth, to provide resource teams for the Baptist Mission in Belize, and to carry on an extensive program of evangelism. He is widely known and well received in the country due to the many revivals he has conducted there and to an extensive television ministry that He has maintained for nearly four years. He is heard three times daily in Belize city, the primary city of Belize, where one third of the population lives. His wife Gay, equally committed to the work, gives direction to a Bible Correspondence Course that is primarily concerned with follow-up evangelism. They are members of The Green Acres Baptist Church of Tyler, Texas

Dr. Roberts was saved and converted at the age of ten. He felt the call to preach at age seventeen and shortly after graduating from Beaumont High School in Beaumont, Texas entered into Bible College. He graduated from Baylor University in 1956 with a Bachelor of Arts Degree in Religion. He later did graduate work at Southwestern Baptist Theological Seminary in Fort Worth, Texas and Luther Rice Theological Seminary in Jacksonville, Florida. It was at the latter that he received both the Master of Divinity and Doctor of Ministry Degrees.

Chapter 1
Faith's Foundations

Doctrine
Hebrews 13:9

The Bible says: "BE NOT CARRIED ABOUT WITH DIVERS AND STRANGE DOCTRINES." Several years ago one of the breakfast cereal companies had a commercial on television advertising Malt-O-Meal. They showed the picture of a person eating a bowl of Malt-O-Meal and then the person would fly off like Superman. One little boy in the church I pastored suddenly insisted that his mother buy some Malt-O-Meal. She did and prepared it for his next breakfast. As he was eating, she went about her work and was surprised to suddenly hear screaming. She ran into the den to discover him completely disappointed. She asked him what was wrong. He told her that he had eaten the Malt-O-Meal but that when he jumped off the chair instead of flying like Superman, he hit the floor. We are not only plagued by many foolish commercials on television, but also by many strange doctrines coming from many people in the religious world of today. God's Word warns us not to be carried about with strange doctrines that promise everything but produce nothing. A study of God's Word will help us to be stable in an unstable world.

Spiritual Mirages
Jeremiah 2:13

The Bible says: "FOR MY PEOPLE HAVE COMMITTED TWO EVILS; THEY HAVE FORSAKEN ME THE FOUNTAIN OF LIVING WATERS, AND HEWED THEM OUT CISTERNS, BROKEN CISTERNS, THAT CAN HOLD NO WATER." Conchy, the cartoon character, is making his way through the desert and is completely exhausted. Suddenly, he sees a water hole, but really it is just a mirage. In desperation, he makes his way toward it and in the last picture we find him under the water saying, "it's actually quite difficult to tell a mirage from the real thing until you crawl up close." The world in which the believer lives is like a spiritual desert. There are thirsts that the spiritual man has that can only be satisfied by God, and yet, so often man crawls up to every mirage in an effort to satisfy that thirst. It is often difficult to tell the real water from the mirage until you crawl up close and then often it is too late. The Bible warns us against substituting the real water of life with the various mirages with which Satan confronts us. Our Lord says: "LET HIM THAT IS A THIRST COME..."

Building On Proper Foundations
I Corinthians 3:11

The Bible says: "FOR OTHER FOUNDATION CAN NO MAN LAY THAN THAT IS LAID, WHICH IS IN JESUS CHRIST." Foundations are important for great buildings. When a skyscraper is built the builders dig down deeply into the earth and pour cement piers and footings that will support the building. The Christian life is like that. The Christian life must be built upon a proper and secure foundation. Sometimes people build lives upon prosperity, position, and the material things of this world, and then they wonder why, when the storms of life come against them, they fall. The great earthquake of San Francisco illustrates what I am saying. San Francisco is built upon the fault line that earthquakes follow. Therefore; when the tremor struck the garbage gave way, and the city was destroyed. The Bible says that Jesus Christ is the only sure foundation. Don't build your life upon the garbage of this world that will give way when trouble strikes.

The Book That Changes Lives
Romans 15:4

The Bible says: "FOR WHATSOEVER THINGS WERE WRITTEN AFORETIME WERE WRITTEN FOR OUR LEARNING, THAT WE THROUGH PATIENCE AND COMFORT OF THE SCRIPTURES MIGHT HAVE HOPE." It was time for a commercial on the local television station, and the announcer came on with his plastic smile. Holding a small green book in his hand, he said, "I want to tell you about a book that can change your life. That's right. When you open a savings account at your local savings and loan association, the contents of this little book will change your life." While money may be important to live and achieve in this world, it cannot change the inward depraved nature of man. However, there is another book that has been responsible for the changing and transformation of millions of lives, and that book is the Bible. In Romans 15:4 we are told that it was written that we might have hope. When did you last read it?

The Book You Can Trust
II Peter 1:21

The Bible says: "FOR THE PROPHECY CAME NOT IN OLD TIME BY THE WILL OF MAN: BUT HOLY MEN OF GOD SPAKE AS THEY WERE MOVED BY THE HOLY GHOST." Multitudes of God-denying and God-defying men have, through the years, denied that the Bible is the Word of God. They have denied that God was its author and that its Biblical accounts were valid. However, archaeological discoveries continue to confirm its reality. On November 4, 1976 the Dallas Times Herald carried the discovery story of 17,000 clay tablets excavated from an ancient site in northwestern Syria. It is interesting to note that Sodom and Gomorrah, the Biblical sin cities often considered more legendary than real, are mentioned in one of these clay tablets. Biblical scholars were also excited to find that names and places like Jerusalem, Gaza, Abraham and David were also found in these tablets. Giovanni Rettinato, one of the two University of Rome professors in charge of the excavations said the tablets reveal that the heaven, earth, sun, and moon were created as the Genesis account states. The Bible is God's Word and it can be trusted.

The Book That Won't Burn
Psalm 119:130

The Bible says: "THE ENTRANCE OF THY WORDS GIVETH LIGHT; IT GIVETH UNDERSTANDING UNTO THE SIMPLE." On one occasion in a land where the Word of God was not revered or respected, the commanding general of the army was ordered to gather all copies of the Word of God and burn them together in one large bonfire. Years later a missionary went to the community where the Bibles were burned and found a church that had been founded and was being pastored by that commanding general. His story revealed that as the Bibles were being burned, one of the pages ablaze was caught by the wind and blown into a field. Later as he was walking across that field, he found the page and read the words: "HEAVEN AND EARTH SHALL PASS AWAY, BUT MY WORD SHALL ABIDE FOREVER." The Holy Spirit through God's Word used that to convict him of his sins and bring him to salvation and to organize a church where others could learn of Jesus Christ. Take time for God's Word today.

Sanctification
Ephesians 5:25-26

The Bible says: "HUSBANDS, LOVE YOUR WIVES, EVEN AS CHRIST ALSO LOVED THE CHURCH, AND GAVE HIMSELF FOR IT; THAT HE MIGHT SANCTIFY AND CLEANSE IT WITH THE WASHING OF WATER BY THE WORD." The Bible is a mirror. A woman looks into the mirror and sees her wrinkles, and immediately she does something about it. Likewise, we should look into the Word of God and see our sin and confess it to God. If we would search God's Word more, we would sin against God less. A woman one day was dusting her books, one of which was her Bible. Her little girl saw the Bible and said, "Mother, is that God's Book?" The mother answered, "Yes." "Well," said the little girl, "why don't we send it back to God? We never use it." No one will ever grow in grace and live a cleansed life who does not read and study God's Word. The Bible says we are cleansed and sanctified by the washing of Water by the Word. Study it today!

How To Understand The Bible
I Corinthians 2:14

The Bible says in I Corinthians 2:14: "BUT THE NATURAL MAN RECEIVETH NOT THE THINGS OF THE SPIRIT OF GOD: FOR THEY ARE FOOLISHNESS UNTO HIM: NEITHER CAN HE KNOW THEM, BECAUSE THEY ARE SPIRITUALLY DISCERNED." In a certain college there was a professor who did not understand or believe the Bible and sought to persuade others to share his convictions. One day as class was beginning for a new term he asked all who believed the Bible to stand. Several stood. Then he said, "All who really believe those fables and fairy tales remain standing." All but two sat down. He then said to the two, "I intend to free you from these superstitions this semester." One of the two left standing said tactfully, "Sir, undoubtedly you did not read far enough; for if you had, you would have discovered the Bible is God's Word to Christians, and that's what you get from reading someone else's mail." The Bible becomes a new book when you become a new person in Jesus Christ. Trust Him today!

Understanding The Bible
I Corinthians 2:14

The Bible says: "BUT THE NATURAL MAN RECEIVETH NOT THE THINGS OF THE SPIRIT OF GOD: FOR THEY ARE FOOLISHNESS UNTO HIM: NEITHER CAN HE KNOW THEM, BECAUSE THEY ARE SPIRITUALLY DISCERNED." A lot of people often complain that they read the Bible but cannot understand it. Why is it? The answer is simple. The Bible is a book different from all other books. It is a spiritual book. It is God breathed. The Spirit of God impressed Holy men of Old (II Peter 1:21), and they wrote what they were instructed to write. Since it is a spiritual book, one must have the Spirit of God to understand it, and the way to have the Spirit of God is to be born again. When a man is truly saved and born again, God's Holy Spirit moves into his life (Romans 8:9), and he is able to understand spiritual things. That is why I Corinthians 2:14 says the natural man or the unsaved man understandeth not the things of God for they are spiritually discerned. It is amazing how the Bible comes alive when a person is truly saved.

The Ten Commandments
Matthew 5:17

The Bible says: "THINK NOT THAT I AM COME TO DESTROY THE LAW, OR THE PROPHETS: I AM NOT COME TO DESTROY, BUT TO FULFIL." Years ago a man and one of his helpers went deep sea fishing one night. Late that night as they were returning, the man became sleepy and turned the wheel over to the helper. He told him to keep his eye fixed on the North Star and he would find his way home. Pretty soon the helper woke the man up and said, "Boss, wake up and show me another star. I have done run clean past that one." Many people feel that way about the Ten Commandments. They feel they are no longer valid and consequently, misconstrue the teachings of law and grace by saying they are no longer under law but grace. However, the poet Lowell put it rather well when he said, "In vain we call old notions fudge and bend our conscience to our dealing; the Ten Commandments will not budge, and stealing will continue stealing." Jesus did not come to destroy the Law, but fulfill them by giving them their proper interpretation.

The Christ Who Dewells Within
Galatians 2:20

The Bible says: "I AM CRUCIFIED WITH CHRIST: NEVERTHELESS I LIVE; YET NOT I, BUT CHRIST LIVETH IN ME: AND THE LIFE WHICH I NOW LIVE IN THE FLESH, I LIVE BY THE FAITH OF THE SON OF GOD, WHO LOVED ME, AND GAVE HIMSELF FOR ME." A little girl came home from church one Sunday and cried, "Mama, come see this beautiful rainbow that God has drawn with his left hand!" The mother ran out on the front porch and said, "What do you mean sugar?" The little girl said, "Oh, Mother, I know that He could not have drawn it with His right hand because our preacher said this morning that Jesus was sitting on God's right hand." To some, Jesus or God is someone who is ten trillion miles out in outer space, He is in heaven, or somewhere else. However, to the believer, God is not only in HEAVEN BUT ALSO IN OUR HEARTS. It was the Apostle Paul who said, "CHRIST LIVETH IN ME," It was Jesus himself who said, "I WILL NEVER LEAVE THEE." A study of God's Word will make the God of heaven real in your own heart.

Worship
Deuteronomy 26:10

The Bible says in Deuteronomy 26:10: "AND NOW, BEHOLD, I HAVE BROUGHT THE FIRSTFRUITS OF THE LAND, WHICH THOU, O LORD, HAST GIVEN ME. AND THOU SHALT SET IT BEFORE THE LORD THY GOD, AND WORSHIP BEFORE THE LORD THY GOD." Worshiping God is important to every believer and it was so with the true Israelite. He was instructed to take a basket and pick of the first-fruit all that God had blessed him with and bring it as a gift to the Lord in worship. Worship then involves giving, yet too many worshipers suffer from a disease known as the "gimmies." They come to God saying, "Give me this and give me that," but God says we are to give. A little girl illustrates the spirit each worshiper should have. She came in one day from her play, sat down on a chair, and watched her mother as she ironed. Her mother inquired, "What do you want, dear?" The child replied, "I don't want anything Mother. I just want to sit here and look at you and love you." This is true worship and the kind that pleased God.

Have Faith In God
Mark 11:22

The Bible says: "AND JESUS ANSWERING SAITH UNTO THEM, HAVE FAITH IN GOD." Hudson Taylor, once speaking in the saintly F. B. Meyer's church, opened his Bible and said, "Friends, I will give you the motto of my life, and he turned to Mark 11:22 and read, "HAVE FAITH IN GOD." Now, if you will note in the margin of your Bible, it reads, "Have the faith of God." How encouraging it is to realize that "The faith of God," like "The love of God," is a gift from God. God, then, is the source of our faith, but He is not only the source of our faith but the support and strength of our faith. If we put our faith in money; if we put our faith in man; if we put our faith in the strength of these things, we are sure and certain to fall and know failure. What multitudes of people need to learn to do is to put their faith in God, who is faithful and never fails us. To have the faith of God is to have a faith that has God as both its source and support. What does your faith rest in today?

Building Faith In Others
Philippians 1:14

The Bible says in Philippians 1:14 "AND MANY OF THE BRETHREN IN THE LORD, WAXING CONFIDENT BY MY BONDS, ARE MUCH MORE BOLD TO SPEAK THE WORD WITHOUT FEAR." There is hardly a power greater than the power of influence. We can influence people to have faith or to be faithless. Through Paul's faithfulness to Christ during adverse circumstances while in prison, he became an influence and encouragement to others that resulted in their faith being expressed without fear. Several years ago I heard of an atheist who spoke to a large gathering of people in Philadelphia. When he was through he said, "Now if there is anyone here who still believes in God let him speak." There was not a word uttered; but then, way up in the balcony a little girl stood and began to sing, "STAND UP, STAND UP FOR JESUS, YE SOLDIERS OF THE CROSS, LIFT HIGH HIS ROYAL BANNER, IT MUST NOT SUFFER LOSS." Then in only seconds, people all over the auditorium stood up and joined in the song. Because one little girl exercised faith, others were influenced to do likewise. Do you have this kind of faith?

Facing Evidence
John 12:10-11

The Bible says: "BUT THE CHIEF PRIESTS CONSULTED THAT THEY MIGHT PUT LAZARUS ALSO TO DEATH; BECAUSE THAT BY REASON OF HIM MANY OF THE JEWS WENT AWAY, AND BELIEVED ON JESUS." The Sadducees did not believe in the resurrection and felt after Lazarus' death and resurrection they must put him to death or have their belief destroyed. Many people are like that. In the days after Charles Darwin made public his conception of evolution, many men thought the new concept meant man was sprung from and akin to the beasts. H.G. Wood relates the story of two old ladies who had been exposed to this early Darwinism. They were heard to say, "Let's hope it's not true, and if it is, let's hush it up!" When a man has to support a position by destroying the evidence which threatens it, it means that he is prepared to use dishonest methods to support a lie. Christianity is not to be defended by destroying atheism, but by demonstrating the life of the Christ of Christianity.

Who Is Worse
Romans 2:21

The Bible says: "THOU THEREFORE WHICH TEACHEST ANOTHER, TEACHEST THOU NOT THYSELF?..." There are a lot of people today who would not classify themselves as an atheist, or one who does not believe there is a God, and yet they live as though there is no God. Now, really who is worse? One who does not believe in God, or one who believes in Him but does not serve Him? One who does not believe the Bible, or one who believes the Bible, but does not read it? One who does not believe in prayer, or one who believes in prayer, but never prays? One who does not believe in the Church, or one who believes in it but never attends, doesn't support it regularly, doesn't pray for it and very often criticizes it? WHO IS WORSE? (Selected) The tragedy of today is that too many talk better than they walk. They talk cream and live skimmed milk. The Bible says: "THOU THEREFORE WHICH TEACHEST ANOTHER, TEACHEST THOU NOT THYSELF?"

Witnesses Of His Grace
Acts 4:33

The Bible says: "AND WITH GREAT POWER GAVE THE APOSTLES WITNESS OF THE RESURRECTION OF THE LORD JESUS:..." As witnesses of Jesus Christ, we are not to be arguing and debating religion, but rather we are to be testifying what we simply know to be so. Many years ago, Charles Bradlaugh, an atheist, challenged Hugh P. Hughes, a consecrated man of God, to debate with him concerning the reality of the Christian faith. The challenge was accepted with these words: "I will bring with me, to the debate, one hundred men and women who have been saved from lives of sin by the gospel of Christ. They will give their evidence and you will be allowed to cross-examine them. I will ask that you bring with you one hundred men and women who have been similarly helped by the gospel of infidelity which you preach." The atheist backed down and the debate was never held. The unbeliever had no evidence. Does your life testify of the saving grace of Christ?

Believing Is Seeing
Hebrews 11:1

The Bible says: "NOW FAITH IS THE SUBSTANCE OF THINGS HOPED FOR, THE EVIDENCE OF THINGS NOT SEEN." The great preacher, F.B. Meyer said: "Faith is the faculty of realizing the unseen. The maxim of human experience runs thus: Seeing is believing; but with the child of God the reverse is true: Believing is seeing. We are as sure of what God has promised as we would be if we saw it already before our eyes." God promised to Moses and the Israelites that He would open up the Red Sea. They believed it, acted on the basis of that belief and saw it open up before their eyes. God promised to Joshua that the walls of Jericho would fall. He acted on the basis of that belief and saw them fall. God promises salvation to all. When we believe and act on the basis of that belief we appropriate that promise with all that it includes. It is true with the child of God: "Believing is seeing."

History's Greatest Failure
John 6:70-71

The Bible says: "JESUS ANSWERED THEM, HAVE NOT I CHOSEN YOU TWELVE, AND ONE OF YOU IS A DEVIL? HE SPAKE OF JUDAS ISCARIOT THE SON OF SIMON: FOR HE IT WAS THAT SHOULD BETRAY HIM, BEING ONE OF THE TWELVE." Of all the prominent men that history records as failures, Judas stands out to me above them all. He could have been remembered for his FAITH, but we remember him for his FAILURE. He betrayed the Lord for thirty pieces of silver. I have often thought that perhaps Judas really did not believe that men could or would kill Jesus. When he saw that they were, he sought to undo his crime, only to find out it was too late. From him we learn that human sin is infinitely more serious than you and I want to believe it is in the moment we are tempted to commit it; that a person cannot sin, walk out and leave his sin behind; and that one cannot undo his sins by his own efforts. Live that men may remember your faith, not your failures.

Escaping God
Amos 9:2

The Bible says: "THOUGH THEY DIG INTO HELL, THENCE SHALL MINE HAND TAKE THEM; THOUGH THEY CLIMB UP TO HEAVEN, THENCE WILL I BRING THEM DOWN." Whatever this verse may mean, it suggests that man cannot escape or get away from God. A pastor recently told of a young man in his church who had been saved by God's grace, forgiven of his sins, and was seeking to live for Christ. However, one night he called the pastor and told him of how he had committed a very grievous sin. He felt that God had forsaken him and that he was running away from God. The pastor said, "Son, your problem is not that you are running away from God as much as you are running into God." The reason that man feels conviction and condemnation when he sins is because of a Holy God in whose presence no sin can stand unconvicted and uncondemned. If you have sinned and feel this awful condemnation, it is altogether possible that you have "run into God" who wants you to confess that sin and know forgiveness.

Forms Of Religion
II Timothy 3:1-5

The Bible says: "THIS KNOW ALSO, THAT IN THE LAST DAYS PERILOUS TIMES SHALL COME. FOR MEN SHALL BE LOVERS OF THEIR OWN SELVES, COVETOUS, BOASTERS, PROUD, BLASPHEMERS, DISOBEDIENT TO PARENTS, UNTHANKFUL, UNHOLY, WITHOUT NATURAL AFFECTION, TRUCEBREAKERS, FALSE ACCUSERS, INCONTINENT, FIERCE, DESPISERS OF THOSE THAT ARE GOOD, TRAITORS, HEADY, HIGHMINDED, LOVERS OF PLEASURES MORE THAN LOVERS OF GOD; HAVING A FORM OF GODLINESS, BUT DENYING THE POWER THEREOF..." Voltaire, the atheist, was walking one day in Paris with a friend when a religious procession passed them, carrying a crucifix. Voltaire lifted his hat. "What?" said his friend, "have you too found God?" "Ah," said Voltaire sadly and bitterly, "we salute, but we do not speak." Is not a good deal of present day religion of that same kind – men saluting the cross but not speaking, and acknowledging God's Christ, but having no personal relationship with Him? The Bible says one of the marks of the last days will be that man will have a form of religion, but will deny the power thereof...

Self Sufficiency
1 Corinthians 10:12

The Bible says: "WHEREFORE LET HIM THAT THINKETH HE STANDETH TAKE HEED LEST HE FALL." Many who boast of their self sufficiency and who reject any idea of their need for God and religion, need to take seriously the testimonies of others who shared such a common belief but who found out too late how wrong they had been. M. F. Rich, an atheist, said on his deathbed, "I would rather be on a stove and broil for a million years than to go into eternity with the eternal horrors that hang over my soul! I have given my immortality for gold, and its weight sinks me into an endless, hopeless, helpless hell." Sir Thomas Scott, on his deathbed, said, "Until this moment I thought there was neither a God nor a hell. Now I know and feel that there are both, and I am doomed to perdition by the just judgment of the Almighty." To the self-willed and self-sufficient the Bible says: "LET HIM THAT THINKETH HE STANDETH TAKE HEED LEST HE FALL."

In The Image Of God
Genesis 1:26-27

The Bible says: "AND GOD SAID, LET US MAKE MAN IN OUR IMAGE, AFTER OUR LIKENESS:...SO GOD CREATED MAN IN HIS OWN IMAGE, IN THE IMAGE OF GOD CREATED HE HIM; MALE AND FEMALE CREATED HE THEM." There are others, however, who say that life was formed from a chemical reaction resulting from lightning passing through poisonous gasses. Professor Edwin Conklin, the great Princeton University Biologist, said in the "Readers Digest" some time ago, "The probability of life beginning from an accident is comparable to the probability of the unabridged dictionary resulting from an explosion in a printing factory." Man is more than an animal. He is a creation of God whose image he reflects. A study of God's Word will reveal his importance, and the love that God has for him.

Creation
Genesis 1:1

The Bible says: "IN THE BEGINNING GOD CREATED THE HEAVEN AND THE EARTH." Many reject the Biblical account of creation and say that life came to pass because of a spontaneous generation. They say life began with a green scum. However, Louis Pasteur demonstrated once and for all that there is no such thing in this life as life coming from anything but antecedent life. If a thing is sterile, it is sterile forever. When the earth was formed it was around 1600 degrees. We boil and sterilize at 212 degrees. Even Charles Darwin himself admits the difficulty of life in any form existing on this earth at its formation. It is difficult to know what one is doing on this earth and where he is going if he does not understand where he came from. The Bible says man is God's creation. Believe it!

The Soul Of Man
Genesis 2:7

The Bible says: "AND THE LORD GOD FORMED MAN OF THE DUST OF THE GROUND, AND BREATHED INTO HIS NOSTRILS THE BREATH OF LIFE; AND MAN BECAME A LIVING SOUL." A medical doctor once trying to destroy this truth asked a noted preacher if he had ever seen, tasted, smelled or heard a soul. The preacher said, "no." The doctor then asked if he had ever felt a soul. To this the preacher replied, "yes." The doctor then said, "Four of the five senses are against there being a soul." The preacher then asked the doctor if he had ever seen, tasted, smelled or heard a pain. The doctor replied, "no." He then asked the doctor if he had ever felt a pain. The doctor replied, "yes." The preacher then said, "Doctor, four of the five senses say there is no pain, but you and I both know that pain is real and so is the soul of man." It is worth enough that Christ came to redeem it.

Nature And God
Romans 1:18-20

The Bible says: "FOR THE WRATH OF GOD IS REVEALED FROM HEAVEN AGAINST ALL UNGODLINESS AND UNRIGHTEOUSNESS OF MEN, WHO HOLD THE TRUTH IN UNRIGHTEOUSNESS; BECAUSE THAT WHICH MAY BE KNOWN OF GOD IS MANIFEST IN THEM; FOR GOD HATH SHEWED IT UNTO THEM. FOR THE INVISIBLE THINGS OF HIM FROM THE CREATION OF THE WORLD ARE CLEARLY SEEN, BEING UNDERSTOOD BY THE THINGS THAT ARE MADE, EVEN HIS ETERNAL POWER AND GODHEAD; SO THAT THEY ARE WITHOUT EXCUSE." The man who rejects God's offer of salvation will one day stand before God's judgment without excuse. Nature itself attests to the fact of God's reality. The visible things of the world only prove there is an invisible God. The sun, the moon, the stars testify: "God is real." Astrologers tell us that the sun is 93 million miles away from the earth. If it were one third closer we would be burned to death, and if it were one third further away we would be plunged into an ice age. Only God could be so precise in putting this vast universe together. Preparation for meeting this God must be made today.

The Name Of God
Exodus 20:7

The Bible says: "THOU SHALT NOT TAKE THE NAME OF THE LORD THY GOD IN VAIN; FOR THE LORD WILL NOT HOLD HIM GUILTLESS THAT TAKETH HIS NAME IN VAIN." Travelers in heathen lands tell us that one never hears the name of pagan gods used carelessly. Their worshipers fear them too greatly for such use. A missionary was returning from India on board a ship, with his son. The little boy had never been to America. One day an American on deck was indulging in profuse profanity. The missionary went to him and said, "Sir, my little boy was born and brought up in a heathen land, a land of idolatry, but in all of his life he has never heard a man blaspheme his Maker until now." What a sad commentary that is! How sad it is that the heathen have a greater reverence for their false gods than many here in America have for the true God. What does the name of God mean to you? God says: "THOU SHALT NOT TAKE THE NAME OF THE LORD THY GOD IN VAIN, FOR THE LORD WILL NOT HOLD HIM GUILTLESS THAT TAKETH HIS NAME IN VAIN."

Making Vows To God
Deuteronomy 23:21

The Bible says: "WHEN THOU SHALT VOW A VOW UNTO THE LORD THY GOD, THOU SHALT NOT SLACK TO PAY IT: FOR THE LORD THY GOD WILL SURELY REQUIRE IT OF THEE; AND IT WOULD BE SIN IN THEE." People often, when facing crisis, make vows to God to the effect that if He will help them, then they will live for Him. Far too often they forget these vows when the crisis passes. They are like the young man I once heard of that was giving an infidel lecture. An old man came upon the scene and stepped forward and said, "I will not argue with this young man, but I will tell you that two days ago I was walking by the Niagara River when I heard a cry for help. I saw a young man caught in the current and being carried toward the falls. He was calling upon God and promising to live for God if He would save him. I went to his rescue – I risked my own life to save his life. This man who called upon God two days ago is the same man who speaks to you today." God will not take lightly the man who breaks an honest vow. What about you my friend?

Worthy Of Praise
Psalm 139:14

The Bible says: "I WILL PRAISE THEE; FOR I AM FEARFULLY AND WONDERFULLY MADE: MARVELLOUS ARE THY WORKS; AND THAT MY SOUL KNOWETH RIGHT WELL." One cannot consider the human body that God has made without praising Him and knowing that He is God. Who, but God, could put together a body with a heart that beats 103,680 times each 24 hours and circulates the blood every 23 seconds, traveling 43 million miles; that causes us to breathe 23 thousand times and inhale 438 cubic feet of air; that causes us to digest 3¼ pounds of food and assimilate over a half gallon of liquid; that causes us to evaporate 2 pounds of water by perspiration and generates 98.6 degrees of heat and generates 450 tons of energy; that gives to us 750 muscles and 7 million brain cells to use? It is little wonder, then, that David says in Psalm 100:3 : "KNOW YE THAT THE LORD HE IS GOD..." and in Psalm 139:14: "I WILL PRAISE THEE, FOR I AM FEARFULLY AND WONDERFULLY MADE . . ." A study of God's Word will lead us to a greater appreciation of the human body and the God who made it.

Acceptance Of Self
Ephesians 2:10

The Bible says: "FOR WE ARE HIS WORKMANSHIP, CREATED IN CHRIST JESUS UNTO GOOD WORKS . . ." Among the many problems with which man is daily confronted, not one, perhaps, gives him more trouble than the problem of his learning to accept himself. Many people are unsatisfied with their personality, their looks, their family, and a thousand other insignificant things. What is the solution to the problem? There are a multitude of answers, but a good place to begin is to realize what Paul says in Ephesians 2:10. There he says that we are God's workmanship. Just as a parent is not happy when a son or daughter has a low self concept, neither is God. God made us and it displeases Him when we criticize his workmanship. Several years ago during a crusade in London, England, someone asked why Dr. Graham was getting such a tremendous response from thousands upon thousands of Britons. Ethel Waters just smiled and said, "Honey, God don't sponsor no flops." We might add, neither does He make junk! A realization of this will result in the complete acceptance of oneself.

Every Man Counts With God
Hebrews 2:6

The Bible Says: "... WHAT IS MAN, THAT THOU ART MINDFUL OF HIM? OR THE SON OF MAN, THAT THOU VISITEST HIM?" They say that once when Sir Michael Costello was conducting a great orchestra rehearsal with hundreds of instruments, the man playing the flute, feeling that his flute could not be heard, decided to stop playing. Then all of a sudden the great orchestra leader threw up his hands and stopped the mighty rehearsal and said, "I miss the flute. The one who plays the flute is silent." Suddenly the man playing the flute realized that his instrument was as important as the largest and loudest of all instruments. In this busy world we live in, we too often think that we are not needed and insignificant. Then God has to allow the powers and forces of life to come upon us so that we are reminded that He is conscious of every step we take and every word that we speak. God's estimate of man is summarized in the words of the writer of Hebrews when he says, "... WHAT IS MAN THAT THOU ART MINDFUL OF HIM?..." Mindful enough that He gave His Son to redeem us.

Predestination
Romans 8:29

The Bible says: "FOR WHOM HE DID FOREKNOW, HE ALSO DID PREDESTINATE TO BE CONFORMED TO THE IMAGE OF HIS SON, THAT HE MIGHT BE THE FIRSTBORN AMONG MANY BRETHREN." Predestination is a precious doctrine in the Bible that many people shun because they do not understand it and feel they never can. As a result, they miss one of the great blessings of God. The real aim of predestination is not to make people go to hell or to heaven but to make them like God's son, Jesus Christ. God was so well pleased with his first Son that He wanted to make more sons like Him. This is part of what is involved in salvation. God is not just concerned that we be saved and stay out of hell. He wants us to be like His Son and is working in us to achieve this goal and promise. It takes nine months for a baby to be born, but a lifetime to become fully grown. Dear friend, if you find a Christian who disappoints you, just remember that God is working in that Christian to conform him to the image of Christ. This is the image that God has predestinated us all to be conformed to.

The Ultimate Purpose Of God
Romans 2:4

The Bible says: "OR DESPISEST THOU THE RICHES OF HIS GOODNESS AND FORBEARANCE AND LONGSUFFERING; NOT KNOWING THAT THE GOODNESS OF GOD LEADETH THEE TO REPENTANCE?" Too often we take the blessings of God for granted without seeing the ultimate purpose that God has in mind. Let me illustrate what I mean. A father went outside to call his young son to go to town with him. When the son came, he was muddy, for he had fallen down in the mud. After the father cleaned him up and changed his clothes, the little fellow became attached to a new toy he had just received. He became so engrossed with it that he forgot the original intent of the father. He now insisted that his father let him stay home. Too often we accept and enjoy the grace and blessings of God without realizing that the purpose of it all is to lead us to repentance and a closer walk with God. This is the ultimate purpose of God in blessing us from time to time.

Getting Rid Of Jesus
Matthew 23:37-38

The Bible says: "O JERUSALEM, JERUSALEM, THOU THAT KILLEST THE PROPHETS, AND STONEST THEM WHICH ARE SENT UNTO THEE, HOW OFTEN WOULD I HAVE GATHERED THY CHILDREN TOGETHER, EVEN AS A HEN GATHERETH HER CHICKENS UNDER HER WINGS, AND YE WOULD NOT! BEHOLD YOUR HOUSE IS LEFT UNTO YOU DESOLATE." Someone tells the story of a missionary who had to use crude and primitive methods to get his message across to the primitive tribe he had gone to. He had a chart painted which showed the progress of the man who accepted Christ and was on his way to heaven, and the man who rejected Christ and was on his way to hell. The whole message disturbed the tribe. They did not want it to be true so they simply burned the chart and thought that eliminated the entire matter. Jesus speaks of people who killed the prophets because they did not like their message. Man must know that he may refuse to listen to the message of Jesus Christ, but he cannot eliminate that message from this universe or even his life.

Discovering The Reality Of Christ
1 John 1:3

The Bible says: "THAT WHICH WE HAVE SEEN AND HEARD DECLARE WE UNTO YOU, THAT YE ALSO MAY HAVE FELLOWSHIP WITH US: AND TRULY OUR FELLOWSHIP IS WITH THE FATHER, AND WITH HIS SON JESUS CHRIST." E. Stanley Jones tells of a little boy, the son of missionary parents, who was in school in the United States during Christmas. One day when a teacher asked him what he wanted most for Christmas, he looked at a framed picture of his father on his desk and replied, "I want my father to step out of that frame." To many Christ is out of reach and untouchable. However, the Apostle John declares that Jesus Christ came into the world that we might know him in a personal way. He is within reach and touch of every man who by simple faith will trust Him. A study of God's Word will help us to know how to know Him better.

Where Is God.
Matthew 2:1-2

The Bible says in Matthew 2:1-2: "NOW WHEN JESUS WAS BORN IN BETHLEHEM OF JUDEA IN THE DAYS OF HEROD THE KING, BEHOLD, THERE CAME WISE MEN FROM THE EAST TO JERUSALEM, SAYING, WHERE IS HE THAT IS BORN KING OF THE JEWS?..." Today there is no question asked perhaps any more by an unbelieving world than that of the wise men, "WHERE IS HE," or "Where is God?" One little boy came to his father on one occasion and said, "Daddy, is God dead?" The father replied, "Well, no, son, but why do you ask such a question?" The little fellow said, "Well, I never hear His name mentioned around our home anymore and so I thought He must be dead." When people hear you speak and observe your life, what do they learn about God? I want to ask every father and mother this question today. "Do your children see in your home the evidence of a dead God or a God that is very much alive?" The world is asking: "WHERE IS HE THAT IS BORN KING OF THE JEWS?" Don't give the wrong answer. Help the world to discover the Christ of Christmas in and through your life.

Beholding Christ
John 19:5

The Bible says: "THEN CAME JESUS FORTH, WEARING THE CROWN OF THORNS, AND THE PURPLE ROBE. AND PILATE SAITH UNTO THEM, BEHOLD THE MAN!" I want to use the words of Pilate to challenge you to behold the man, Jesus Christ. Behold His birth, His life, His death, His resurrection, His ascension, and His return. Someone has declared that there may be another Homer, another Virgil, another Dante, another Milton, another Alexander, another Caesar, another Shakespeare, another Raphael, but there will never be another Jesus. We see in Jesus a priest greater than Moses, a king greater than David, a commander greater than Joshua, a philosopher greater than Solomon, and a prophet greater than Elijah. Children cluster at His knee; womanhood places a crown on His brow; youth forsake all to follow Him; and culture whispers, "We know thou art a teacher come from God." During this Christmas season I challenge you to behold Him whose birthday we seek to celebrate.

The Light Still Shines
John 1:1-5

The Bible says: "IN THE BEGINNING WAS THE WORD, AND THE WORD WAS WITH GOD, AND THE WORD WAS GOD. THE SAME WAS IN THE BEGINNING WITH GOD. ALL THINGS WERE MADE BY HIM; AND WITHOUT HIM WAS NOT ANYTHING MADE THAT WAS MADE. IN HIM WAS LIFE; AND THE LIFE WAS THE LIGHT OF MEN. AND THE LIGHT SHINETH IN DARKNESS; AND THE DARKNESS COMPREHENDED IT NOT." One Christmas, one business establishment sent to all its customers a solid black greeting card with a star of bethlehem right in the center and underneath the star the words, "HIS LIGHT STILL SHINES." There have been many attempts to extinguish the light and life of Christ. Philosophers and even some theologians have tried to put His light out, but all have failed. We can join with John the Apostle in saying, "THE LIGHT SHINETH IN DARKNESS; AND THE DARKNESS COMPREHENDED IT NOT", or in our modern vernacular, "THE DARKNESS COULD NOT PUT IT OUT." That light wants to light your pathway. Why not let Him?

Entertaining Angels
Hebrews 13:1-2

The Bible says: "LET BROTHERLY LOVE CONTINUE. BE NOT FORGETFUL TO ENTERTAIN STRANGERS: FOR THEREBY SOME HAVE ENTERTAINED ANGELS UNAWARES." Edwin Markham tells the story of Conrad, a shoe cobbler who dreamed one Christmas Eve that Christ would visit his home the next day. The next day he arose early and prepared his home and then began to wait and watch. That day three people came to his door: an old man, hungry and cold, whom he took in and gave a pair of shoes to; an old woman, struggling under a heavy load, whom he gave shelter and warmth to; and a little child, lost, that he carried home. However, at the end of the day Christ had not come, and as he was closing the day with disappointment the Lord seemed to say to him, "I came to you and you recognized me not for I was the old man, the old woman, and the lost child. Do you not remember that I said, INASMUCH AS YOU HAVE DONE IT TO THE LEAST OF THESE MY BRETHREN YOU HAVE DONE IT UNTO ME." Helping others is sometimes like helping angels unawares.

The Wise Men
Matthew 2:11

The Bible says: "AND WHEN THEY WERE COME INTO THE HOUSE, THEY SAW THE YOUNG CHILD WITH MARY HIS MOTHER, AND FELL DOWN, AND WORSHIPPED HIM: AND WHEN THEY HAD OPENED THEIR TREASURES, THEY PRESENTED UNTO HIM GIFTS; GOLD, AND FRANKINCENSE, AND MYRRH." From the story of the Wise men we learn many things. We learn that wise men seek God; that wise men follow God's instructions; that wise men not only receive from God but give to God. A businessman recently sent a Christmas message to his friends that I thought was very meaningful. He told the story of a young man whose brother gave him a new car for Christmas. When he showed it to a friend, the friend said, "I wish...", but before he could finish the sentence the owner of the new car knew what he was thinking and offered to carry him for a ride. The friend asked to be driven to his home. When they arrived, the friend went in and brought out a crippled brother to show him the car. Then he said to his brother, "I wish that one day I could be that kind of a brother." This truly is the spirit of Christmas. It is not what or how much we get but what we are able to give.

The Unspeakable Gift
II Corinthians 9:15

The Bible says: "THANKS BE UNTO GOD FOR HIS UNSPEAKABLE GIFT." Christmas is a time of giving; a time in which we exchange gifts to reveal our love one to another. This Christmas you may receive many wonderful gifts, but God says the greatest gift, the unspeakable gift, is the gift of salvation. I wonder this Christmas if you will receive that gift or if you will allow it to go unclaimed and unwrapped? Some time ago I had a friend whose wife died. After the funeral he said to me, "Brother Bob, the night we put our Christmas tree up she wanted to open her present, but I told her she would have to wait until Christmas morning. Now I guess I will have to open it myself." As he told me that I thought of how one day in heaven, after the earth is no more, God will have to open many unclaimed and unwrapped gifts of salvation. Will one of them have your name on it? What have you done or what will you do with God's unspeakable gift this Christmas?

Knowing Christ Personally
John 4:29

The Bible says: "COME SEE A MAN, WHICH TOLD ME ALL THINGS THAT EVER I DID: IS NOT THIS THE CHRIST." One of the mistakes of modern man is that while he has heard often of Christ, in reality he has too often neglected to seek Him out, find Him, and know Him personally. Clovis G. Chappel tells an imaginary story of one of the shepherds who had been present as a youth the night the angels appeared, but who now is an old man. His grandson sits on his knee as he tells the story. He tells of the angels' appearance, of their message and the place where Christ could be found. Then he pauses, and the young boy asks, "But Grand-daddy, is that all? Was what the angels said really true? Was the Christ child really born?" The old shepherd sadly shakes his white head and answers, "I never knew. I never went to see." What about you? The challenge of the woman who found Christ in John 4:29 is "COME SEE . . . IS NOT THIS THE CHRIST." A study of God's Word will help you to know Him personally.

The Difference Christ Makes
I John 4:4

The Bible says: "YE ARE OF GOD, LITTLE CHILDREN, AND HAVE OVERCOME THEM: BECAUSE GREATER IS HE THAT IS IN YOU, THAN HE THAT IS IN THE WORLD." In the spring of 1924, Negro troops were stationed in Germany, and there was a great deal of resentment against them. Roland Hayes, the American Negro tenor, was touring Europe and had scheduled a concert in Berlin. When he appeared to sing, the audience hissed and booed. Hayes waited until they were quiet and then sang Schubert's, "Thou Art My Peace." The audience listened in hushed silence. After it was over, Roland Hayes said that this was not a personal victory but the victory of a force that sang within him and subdued the hatred of the audience. This power, the power of Jesus Christ, can be known of all men, who by simple faith will come to Him and repent of their sins. The Christ who came into the world in the form of man nearly 2,000 years ago is prepared to come into your heart today. Will you let Him?

God's Love Demonstrated
John 3:16

The Bible says: "FOR GOD SO LOVED THE WORLD, THAT HE GAVE HIS ONLY BEGOTTEN SON, THAT WHOSOEVER BELIEVETH IN HIM SHOULD NOT PERISH, BUT HAVE EVERLASTING LIFE." When I was a lad, about nine or ten years of age, I sold enough cloverine salve to buy my mother a new set of dishes. I remember the day they arrived at the depot station. It took me almost a half a day to carry them from the station to our house. I could not wait to get home. My mother did not know! I had a gift for her that I had sacrificed to get and it would be a total surprise. You can imagine the joy when she opened that box to discover those beautiful dishes. With joy she hugged me and thanked me, and I felt so good. However, the greatest gift that any person can ever receive is the gift of eternal life in the person of Jesus Christ. It is a gift that required the sacrifice of God's Son. I have often thought how it must grieve the heart of God to know that after making such a sacrifice, many people reject it altogether. What have you done with this gift?

No Room In The Inn
Luke 2:7

The Bible says: "AND SHE BROUGHT FORTH HER FIRSTBORN SON, AND WRAPPED HIM IN SWADDLING CLOTHES, AND LAID HIM IN A MANGER; BECAUSE THERE WAS NO ROOM FOR THEM IN THE INN." Two thousand years ago Christ was born in a stable because there was no room in the inn. Really there was no room for Him anywhere. There was no room for Him in His own synagogue and they drove Him out (Lk. 4:29). There was no room for Him in Jerusalem and they tried to stone Him (John 8:34). There was no room for Him permanently anywhere and He said, "FOXES HAVE HOLES AND THE BIRDS OF THE AIR HAVE NESTS BUT THE SON OF MAN HATH NOT WHERE TO LAY HIS HEAD." Two thousand years later there is still little room for Christ. Some time ago a ruling by a United States Court outlawed the display of the manger scene depicting the birth of Christ, which had regularly been shown in Washington during the Christmas tree lighting ceremony. What about you? Will there be any room in your life for Christ this Christmas?

The Risen Christ
I Corinthians 15:3-4

The Bible says: "FOR I DELIVERED UNTO YOU FIRST OF ALL THAT WHICH I ALSO RECEIVED, HOW THAT CHRIST DIED FOR OUR SINS ACCORDING TO THE SCRIPTURES;...AND THAT HE ROSE AGAIN THE THIRD DAY ACCORDING TO THE SCRIPTURES!" There is nothing more certain about the Christian faith than the resurrection of Christ. One year at the World's Fair in Chicago, Illinois, representatives from many foreign religions were brought in to speak for their religion. In the United States, a brilliant and spiritual man by the name of David Cook was chosen to represent Christianity. The panel sat and discussed their religions before a large audience. David Cook said the man we worship and trust for salvation is Jesus Christ. Each of the other speakers gave their leaders as Buddah, Mohammed, Confucius and etc. They each spoke of the book left by the one they worshipped. Then David Cook stated that our Lord not only died for us, but arose from the dead. The others replied that they knew nothing of their prophet's existence. The difference between Christianity and other religions is that we believe in a LIVING, RISEN CHRIST WHO IS ALIVE TODAY.

Where Is Christ?
Luke 24:6-7

The Bible says: "HE IS NOT HERE, BUT IS RISEN: REMEMBER HOW HE SPAKE UNTO YOU WHEN HE WAS YET IN GALILEE, SAYING, THE SON OF MAN MUST BE DELIVERED INTO THE HANDS OF SINFUL MEN, AND BE CRUCIFIED, AND THE THIRD DAY RISE AGAIN." John Masefield, the British Poet Laureat, relates a conversation between Pilate's wife and the centurion who was in charge of the crucifixion. Pilate's wife asked him, "Do you think He is dead?" The centurion replied, "No lady, I do not," "Then where is He?" she asked. He exclaimed, "Let loose in the world lady – let loose in the world, where neither Roman nor Jew can stop His truth!" Our Lord and Saviour is a living Christ and we can say with the poet:

> The stars shine over the earth,
> The stars shine over the sea,
> The stars look up to the Mighty God,
> The stars look down on me.
> The stars shall live for a million years...
> For a million years and a day;
> But God and I will live and love
> When the stars have passed away.

Is Death All?
John 14:19

The Bible says: "YET A LITTLE WHILE, AND THE WORLD SEETH ME NO MORE; BUT YE SEE ME: BECAUSE I LIVE, YE SHALL LIVE ALSO." The age old question, "If a man dies will he live again?" is answered by Jesus himself when He says, "BECAUSE I LIVE YE SHALL LIVE ALSO." The mystery of the resurrection is illustrated through many natural forms. A caterpillar is formed and begins spinning a small silk thread around itself until it soon becomes encased and enclosed by a cocoon. Now if one did not know better he would think that the caterpillar is done for: but then, out of that cocoon, by a mysterious miracle, comes a butterfly that goes forth to be born upon the wind and light upon the flower. Many thought with Christ's death that He was done for, but then came the resurrection. Because He lives, we can live too, as we place our faith in Him and experience the new birth. Visit a Bible teaching church this Sunday and learn of this living Christ.

A Comforting Promise
I Thessalonians 4:16-18

The Bible says: "FOR THE LORD HIMSELF SHALL DESCEND FROM HEAVEN WITH A SHOUT, WITH THE VOICE OF THE ARCHANGEL, AND WITH THE TRUMP OF GOD: AND THE DEAD IN CHRIST SHALL RISE FIRST: THEN WE WHICH ARE ALIVE AND REMAIN SHALL BE CAUGHT UP TOGETHER WITH THEM IN THE CLOUDS, TO MEET THE LORD IN THE AIR: AND SO SHALL WE EVER BE WITH THE LORD. WHEREFORE COMFORT ONE ANOTHER WITH THESE WORDS." A little girl and her father were swimming in the ocean when the tide changed. The father realized he could not save them both so he gave the girl instructions as to how to float, and went for help. The girl was saved hours later and people tearfully rejoiced. They asked the girl, "How did you do it? How did you swim for four hours?" She said, "My father said he would return for me and I knew I could believe him." 318 times in the New Testament Jesus says He will return. Trusting Him is essential for preparing to meet Him.

Coming Again
John 14:1-3

The Bible says: "LET NOT YOUR HEART BE TROUBLED: YE BELIEVE IN GOD, BELIEVE ALSO IN ME. IN MY FATHER'S HOUSE ARE MANY MANSIONS: IF IT WERE NOT SO, I WOULD HAVE TOLD YOU. I GO TO PREPARE A PLACE FOR YOU. AND IF I GO AND PREPARE A PLACE FOR YOU, I WILL COME AGAIN, AND RECEIVE YOU UNTO MYSELF; THAT WHERE I AM, THERE YE MAY BE ALSO." No one can possibly go through the Christmas season without coming to have a greater love for God who first loved us and gave His only begotten Son to come into the world to live and die and redeem us from our sins. However, the Bible emphatically declares that He not only came once, but that He shall return again one day to carry us all to heaven with Him. The Bible speaks of this as a blessed hope, and what a hope it is. However, all do not share it. Some time ago while traveling in Israel, our guide, who was not a Christian said, "The only difference between me and you Christians is the word AGAIN. We believe He is yet to come." One can never be ready for His second coming until they acknowledge the first. This truly is what Christmas is all about.

Preparing For The Final Event
Acts 1:11

The Bible says: "...YE MEN OF GALILEE, WHY STAND YE GAZING UP INTO HEAVEN? THIS SAME JESUS, WHICH IS TAKEN UP FROM YOU INTO HEAVEN, SHALL SO COME IN LIKE MANNER AS YE HAVE SEEN HIM GO INTO HEAVEN." The times that we live in are dark, dismal, and often discouraging. Many are saying that we have passed beyond the mark of no return. Messages of doom are being heard from every corner. Politics has failed us; education has fooled us; our economy frightens us. But thank God there is hope. We can say with the Apostle Paul, "IF IN THIS LIFE WE HAVE HOPE ONLY WE ARE OF ALL MEN MOST MISERABLE." The hope of the saved and forgiven – the hope of the lost and doomed rests in the second coming of Jesus Christ. He who came to die for us will soon come to deliver us from this wicked and perverse world. His coming demands preparation. Have you prepared for this great event in history?

Falling Leaves And A Coming King
Luke 21:31

The Bible says: "SO LIKEWISE YE, WHEN YE SEE THESE THINGS COME TO PASS, KNOW YE THAT THE KINGDOM OF GOD IS NIGH AT HAND." Jesus has just declared that the age in which we live will be one characterized by false prophets, wars, violence, conflicts among nations, earthquakes, famines, disloyalty both in the church and home: but the real sign of His coming soon will be seen in regard to trouble in Jerusalem and His working among the Jewish people. One cannot observe what God is doing at this point without knowing that Jesus is coming soon. I sometimes feel like the little boy whose father was leaving for the entire summer. His small son wanted to know when he would return. The father, wanting to give him an answer he could understand, said, "When you see the leaves falling I will return home." At the end of September the nurse saw the little fellow kicking in the leaves one day and asked what was wrong. "Nothing," he replied, "I just know Father is coming home." Friend, THE LEAVES ARE FALLING AND CHRIST IS ABOUT TO RETURN.

The Signs Of The Times
Matthew 11:16

The Bible says, "BUT WHEREUNTO SHALL I LIKEN THIS GENERATION? IT IS LIKE UNTO CHILDREN SITTING IN THE MARKETS, AND CALLING UNTO THEIR FELLOWS..." One of the signs of the end time preceeding the second coming of Jesus Christ is the over emphasis on recreation and having a good time. Jesus likens it to little children playing in the market places. As I read of all that happened following Super Bowl XII held in New Orleans, I thought of this verse of scripture. The Associated Press reported that thirty million dollars was spent; that four hundred tons of trash, or seven to eight times the normal amount was hauled off; that street sweepers, at 3:00 in the morning, could not tell where they had swept; and that a total of 4.6 million dollars in bets were handled, which broke a 105 year old record of 2 million dollars. Surely, these signs along with many others tell us that Christ is coming soon. The Bible admonishes us to prepare for this great confrontation.

Famine
Luke 21:11

The Bible says: "AND GREAT EARTHQUAKES SHALL BE IN DIVERS PLACES, AND FAMINES, AND PESTILENCES; AND FEARFUL SIGHTS AND GREAT SIGNS SHALL THERE BE FROM HEAVEN." Jesus declares that one of the characteristics of the age just preceding His coming, the age in which you and I live, will be that of famine. It has been a long time since America knew famine, but how far away from a famine are we? Climatologists tell us a major drought appears to be overdue in the United States Great Plains raising the threat of a situation perhaps more serious than that in sub-saharan Africa. Helmut Landsburg, a university of Maryland climatologist, says that a drop of one or two degrees in the average temperature above the 40th parallel could completely eliminate wheat and corn production in some major growing districts of Canada. Every 20-22 years the area of Dodge City, Kansas to Abilene, Texas, or the area west of the 100th meridian has suffered drought. If this pattern continues, one is overdue now. These things only serve to remind us to get ready for the coming Christ.

The Church, Love It
Ephesians 5:25

The Bible says in Ephesians 5:25: "HUSBANDS, LOVE YOUR WIVES, EVEN AS CHRIST ALSO LOVED THE CHURCH, AND GAVE HIMSELF FOR IT;" I read once of two young men who grew up together and graduated from school. One became a Christian and a preacher of the Gospel, and the other a lawyer and an agnostic. The agnostic decided to go out West and find a community where there were no churches and there set up practice. After one year he wrote his preacher friend that he had been saved and wanted him to come out West, bring some Bibles and begin a church. He stated that a place without churches was the closest thing to hell he had ever found. Would you choose to live in a city without churches? Of course not. But do you often find yourself among those who cast their vote against the Church? The vote may be cast in many ways! A game of golf, mowing the lawn, a fishing trip, or entertaining guests. They all add up to the same thing – a vote against the Church. Let Jesus be your example. He loved the Church and gave Himself for it.

What's Right With The Church?
Acts 20:28

The Bible says: "TAKE HEED THEREFORE UNTO YOURSELVES, AND TO ALL THE FLOCK, OVER THE WHICH THE HOLY GHOST HATH MADE YOU OVERSEERS, TO FEED THE CHURCH OF GOD, WHICH HE HATH PURCHASED WITH HIS OWN BLOOD." Today there are many people who are talking about what is wrong with the Church. I think it is time for us to speak about what is right with the Church. I am confident that if one will seriously seek to answer this question, he will find there is more right with the Church than is wrong with it. Let me suggest to you today that there are five things right with the Church: the founder, the foundation, the framework, the function, and the future. Some who criticize the Church would not live where there was no church. One agnostic went into an area where there were no churches but soon wrote a young preacher to come and bring Bibles. He then helped to organize a church. Some people wait too late in life to discover the true value of the Church that Jesus purchased with his blood.

Making The Church
Luke 19:46

The Bible says: "...MY HOUSE IS THE HOUSE OF PRAYER: BUT YE HAVE MADE IT A DEN OF THIEVES." Daniel Webster, the great statesman of other years, was once asked, "Mr. Webster, what is the most sobering, searching thought that ever entered your mind?" Without hesitancy, the staunch statesman replied, "My personal accountability to God!" It is sobering to realize that one day we must give and account to God for what we have done with our soul, our life, our money, our talents, our family, our world, and yes, the Church. Jesus said His house was a house of prayer but He rebuked some for making it a den of thieves. They had made it what it was not to be. When you find a church that is spiritual, that is missionary, that is compassionate, that is prayerful, and that is friendly, just remember that someone MADE it that way. How sobering to realize that we MAKE the Church what it is or what it is not. Just what is your life making the church to be?

Giving
II Corinthians 9:7

The Bible says: "EVERY MAN ACCORDING AS HE PURPOSETH IN HIS HEART, SO LET HIM GIVE; NOT GRUDGINGLY, OR OF NECESSITY: FOR GOD LOVETH A CHEERFUL GIVER." Dr. Allen Redpath tells the story of a person who once complained that the church cost too much, and that they always talked about money. A friend of the critic said, "Some time ago a little boy was born in our home. He cost us a lot of money. He had a big appetite, he had to have clothes, toys, and even a dog. Then he went to school and cost even more. And when he started dating he cost a small fortune. However, during his senior year at college he took sick and died, and since the funeral he hasn't cost us a penny." The friend then said, "Now which situation do you think we had rather have?" The critic paused and then replied, "As long as this church is alive it will cost, and when it dies for want of support it won't cost us anything." The church has a vital message for the world, and we must give to get that message out.

Christian Example
Matthew 5:16

The Bible says: "LET YOUR LIGHT SO SHINE BEFORE MEN, THAT THEY MAY SEE YOUR GOOD WORKS, AND GLORIFY YOUR FATHER WHICH IS IN HEAVEN." There is no command for the Christian that is more imperative than this. The Christian is to live such a life that Jesus can be revealed through him. A Missionary in China once told of Jesus for the first time to a group of people in an inland town. When he finished someone said, "We knew Him, He used to live here." Somewhat surprised, the missionary said, "No, He lived centuries ago in another land." The native insisted that Jesus had lived in his town, and he had seen Him. Seeking to prove it, he led the missionary to the village cemetery and showed him the grave of a medical missionary who had lived, served, healed and died in that community. This is what Jesus means when He says: "LET YOUR LIGHT SO SHINE BEFORE MEN, THAT THEY MAY SEE YOUR GOOD WORKS, AND GLORIFY YOUR FATHER WHICH IS IN HEAVEN."

Spiritual Castaways
I Corinthians 9:27

The Bible says: "BUT I KEEP UNDER MY BODY, AND BRING IT INTO SUBJECTION: LEST THAT BY ANY MEANS, WHEN I HAVE PREACHED TO OTHERS, I MYSELF SHOULD BE A CASTAWAY." Many have interpreted this verse to mean that the Apostle Paul feared that after preaching the Gospel to others the time might come in his life when God would cast him away as though He never knew him. It is not salvation that Paul speaks of here but service. Paul feared that unless he lived a cautious, careful and circumspect life, the time might come when God would have to put him on the shelf. Those who sometimes fear God might want to use them should learn an important lesson from one who was afraid that God might not use him. While God keeps those whom He saves, He does not always use all that He saves. Sin keeps Him from using a believer. What is your relationship to God? Are you on the shelf or in His service?

Moral Decay
Deuteronomy 4:25-26

The Bible says: "WHEN THOU SHALT BEGET CHILDREN, AND CHILDREN'S CHILDREN, AND YE SHALL HAVE REMAINED LONG IN THE LAND, AND SHALL CORRUPT YOURSELVES. . . . AND SHALL DO EVIL IN THE SIGHT OF THE LORD THY GOD, TO PROVOKE HIM TO ANGER: I CALL HEAVEN AND EARTH TO WITNESS AGAINST YOU THIS DAY, THAT YE SHALL SOON UTTERLY PERISH FROM OFF THE LAND . . . BUT SHALL UTTERLY BE DESTROYED." Here is an Old Testament warning that is as new as it is old and as relevant now, as when it was first given. Is America living in light of this warning? Let's see!! In September of 1976, Washington D.C. reported two alarming statistics: More abortions than births out of wedlock than in (9,819 compared to 9,746), and more births out of wedlock than in (4,998 compared to 4,758). How much longer can our sick society, with its decadent moral values and disrespect for human life, exist. It is knee time in America! It is time to repent lest we be utterly destroyed.

Chapter 2
Life and Living

You Have The Key To Life Or Death
Deuteronomy 30:19

The Bible says: "I CALL HEAVEN AND EARTH TO RECORD THIS DAY AGAINST YOU, THAT I HAVE SET BEFORE YOU LIFE AND DEATH, BLESSING AND CURSING: THEREFORE CHOOSE LIFE, THAT BOTH THOU AND THY SEED MAY LIVE:" I read the story once of an old man who lived in Venice, Italy. He was a genius. Legend had it, he could answer any question anyone might ask of him. Two little boys figured out how they could fool him, so they caught a small bird and headed for his residence. One of the little boys held the bird in his hands and asked the old man if the bird was dead or alive. Without hesitation the old man said, "Son, if I say alive, you will close your hands and crush him to death. If I say the bird is dead, you will open your hands and he will fly away. You see, son, in your hands you hold the power of life and death." It is true spiritually! Each man, in a real sense, holds in his hands his destiny. The Bible asks: "Will it be life or death?"

Don't Waste Your Life – A Loss You Cannot Afford
Matthew 10:28

The Bible says: "AND FEAR NOT THEM WHICH KILL THE BODY, BUT ARE NOT ABLE TO KILL THE SOUL: BUT RATHER FEAR HIM WHICH IS ABLE TO DESTROY BOTH SOUL AND BODY IN HELL." A young boy, who sold newspapers, would get on a street car in his city, hawk his newspapers, and get off a few blocks down. One day there was a man who sought to make sport of him. He took from his pocket a 25 cent piece and said, "Son, I am going to flip this coin. You call it and if you win you get the quarter and if not, I get the newspaper for nothing." The young boy refused, to which the man increased his offer to fifty cents, and then, in desperation, went up to a dollar. But still the boy refused. The man said, "Son, I don't understand. You have the opportunity of making one dollar, and if you loose, you only loose a dime." The young boy replied, "But sir, I cannot afford the loss." Yet millions of people gamble with their souls each day failing to realize that they only have one, and if it is lost, it is an eternal loss; one that no man can afford.

Short Beds And Narrow Cover
Isaiah 28:20

The Bible says: "FOR THE BED IS SHORTER THAN THAT A MAN CAN STRETCH HIMSELF ON IT: AND THE COVERING NARROWER THAN THAT HE CAN WRAP HIMSELF IN IT." As a youngster I remember going to some of the relatives' homes during a death. Many of my cousins were there. When bedtime would come, we would have to sleep cross ways on the bed in order for everyone to have a place to sleep. I can still remember those cold nights waking up with cold feet because of short beds and pulling for covering that was not big enough to cover everyone. The prophet Isaiah, in chapter 28, uses this simple but vivid illustration to show that when a man sins and tries to cover that sin up, it is like sleeping on a short bed and trying to cover with narrow covering. He says that sin cannot be covered but ultimately is exposed leaving the sinner in a miserable condition. A study of God's Word will help one to see that "...HE THAT COVERETH HIS SINS SHALL NOT PROSPER BUT WHOSO CONFESSETH THEM SHALL HAVE MERCY."

The Reality Of Sin
James 1:15

The Bible says: "...WHEN LUST HATH CONCEIVED, IT BRINGETH FORTH SIN: AND SIN, WHEN IT IS FINISHED, BRINGETH FORTH DEATH." Someone once asked the famed Dr. Sir John Simpson what the greatest thought he had ever had was, and he replied, "The greatest thought that I ever had was that I was a sinner and that Jesus Christ saved me." It seems rather strange to me that men not nearly as great or scholarly deny the reality of sin and simply suggest that sin only exists as it exists in the mind of man. Many modern psychologists even call it, "an evolutionary legacy, a moral hangover from our alleged animal ancestry, good in the making, the growing pains of the human race." Yet God declares sin to be the evil working of Satan springing forth from a polluted heart and that its' wages is death. God's answer for sin is life that is found through faith in Jesus Christ. Why not carry your sins to Him today?

What God Does With Our Sins
Psalm 103:12

The Bible says: "AS FAR AS THE EAST IS FROM THE WEST, SO FAR HATH HE REMOVED OUR TRANSGRESSIONS FROM US." One of the most difficult things for a person to do to be saved is to accept the forgiveness of God. Some find it almost inconceivable that a Holy God can forgive them of the most wicked of sins, and yet He does. The Bible, in seeking to prove that God does forgive us of our sins and that He does not hold them either over our heads or against us, uses four illustrations to show what He does with our sins when we come to Christ for salvation and forgiveness. The Bible says, in Psalm 103:12, that He casts our sins as far as the east is from the west; in Micah 7:19, He casts our sins into the depth of the sea; in Isaiah 38:17, He casts our sins behind His back; and in Isaiah 44:22, the Bible says He casts them behind the clouds. The Bible does not say He casts our sins in a ditch, a creek, or even a river, for all of these things may go dry, but He casts our sins in the depth of the sea that never goes dry. He puts our sins out of His sight. Accept His forgiveness today.

Just As You Are
Romans 5:1

The Bible says: "THEREFORE BEING JUSTIFIED BY FAITH, WE HAVE PEACE WITH GOD THROUGH OUR LORD JESUS CHRIST..." While justification is an act whereby a Holy God judicially declares a believing sinner to be righteous and acceptable before Him, it means more than that. In justification, God not only pardons the sinner, but looks upon him as though he had never sinned. The President may pardon a man guilty of murder, but he can never remove the crime. However, a Holy God not only pardons a believing sinner, but looks upon him as though he never committed the sin. That is why someone has defined that word justify as "JUST AS IF I NEVER SINNED." That is what Christ will do with your sins, if you, by faith, will bring them to Him. An artist once sought to find a man to pose as the prodigal son. He found one and asked him to come to his office the next day. He did, but he came cleaned and all dressed up, and was sent away because he did not look like a prodigal. God wants you, as you are, to forgive and justify.

The Atonement
Romans 5:11

The Bible says: "... BUT WE ALSO JOY IN GOD THOUGH OUR LORD JESUS CHRIST, BY WHOM WE HAVE NOW RECEIVED THE ATONEMENT." The word atonement is a word used only one time in the New Testament, but the entire Christian faith hinges upon it. The word means a covering and describes what God does with our sins when by faith we come to Him – He covers them with His blood. Dr. R.G. Lee says that as he, Mel Trotter, and F.B. Meyer were walking across a burned prairie, they came to a dead bird with its' wings out-stretched and as they turned the bird over, four little birds opened their mouths for something to eat. Suddenly, they realized that the mother bird had saved the baby birds lives by spreading her wings over them and protecting them from the blazes of the burning prairie. Dr. Meyer turned to R.G. Lee and said, "Lee, that is what Christ did for me when He died on the cross of Calvary. He covered my sin debt by dying in my stead." And that, my friend, is what the word atonement means.

Believing God
Acts 16:31

The Bible says: "... BELIEVE ON THE LORD JESUS CHRIST, AND THOU SHALT BE SAVED, ..." Today there is so much "easy believism" being taught. People are saying, "Believe, believe and you will be saved." The question is, "What kind of believing is it that really saves?" The Bible says, "The devil believes and trembles." Now is the devil saved because he believes? Of course not! The kind of believing that saves is the kind that commits oneself totally to Christ as Lord and Saviour. Many people believe with the mind but not the heart. Faith is not believing that Christ can, but that He will. Some people with this "easy believism" approach remind me of the people who believed a certain tight rope walker could push a wheelbarrow across Niagara Falls, but when he asked someone who said they believed, to sit in the wheelbarrow, he had no takers. It is true, "BELIEVE ON THE LORD JESUS CHRIST, AND THOU SHALT BE SAVED," but please remember, this kind of faith commits all to Christ. Have you made this commitment?

Faith
Hebrews 11:1-2

The Bible says: "NOW FAITH IS THE SUBSTANCE OF THINGS HOPED FOR, THE EVIDENCE OF THINGS NOT SEEN. FOR BY IT THE ELDERS OBTAINED A GOOD REPORT." The maxim of human experience leads one to believe that "seeing is believing." Man says, "You show me and then I will believe it." However, with the child of God the reverse is true. The believer who has learned to walk by faith knows that "believing is seeing." As a believer we do not see and then believe, but rather we believe and then we see. One does not wait until he can "see" salvation and then believe it, but rather on the authority of God's Word he believes and then he sees or experiences and has the assurance of salvation. Perhaps you are saying "If I ever see this bit about Christianity I am going to be saved!" You will never be saved if you wait to see. You must first believe, and then you will receive. The Bible says Abraham believed God and it was counted unto him for righteousness. Remember that "BELIEVING IS SEEING." Why not believe Him today?

Put That On My Account
Philemon 1:18-19

The Bible says: "IF HE HATH WRONGED THEE, OR OWETH THEE OUGHT, PUT THAT ON MINE ACCOUNT . . . I WILL REPAY IT." Onesimus was a runaway slave who heard Paul preach and was saved. He illustrates God's offer of salvation to all. As a slave the Roman law gave him no right of asylum but granted him the privilege of making an appeal; it gave him the privilege of fleeing to his master's best friend – not for concealment but for intercession; it gave him the privilege of being adopted by his owner and then freed. In light of this we were God's property and ran away. Our sin was against God, and nothing but Christ's death could atone for it. The law gave us no right of appeal, but grace stepped in and enabled us to flee to Jesus whom God counted as a partner and through faith in Him we were begotten as a son. In this new relation we were set free from the penalty of sin and death. You need not be a slave to sin any longer. Place your faith in Him who says "PUT THAT ON MINE ACCOUNT."

A Testimony From The Grave
Luke 16:30-31

The Bible says: "AND HE SAID, NAY, FATHER ABRAHAM: BUT IF ONE WENT UNTO THEM FROM THE DEAD, THEY WILL REPENT. AND HE SAID UNTO HIM, IF THEY HEAR NOT MOSES AND THE PROPHETS, NEITHER WILL THEY BE PERSUADED, THOUGH ONE ROSE FROM THE DEAD." Recently I learned of a psychiatrist who was an agnostic, but who had become a firm believer in life after death as a result of working with dying patients in a hospital. The testimonies of several who were brought back to life after being pronounced clinically dead convinced her of the reality of life after death. It seems a little strange to me that scholarly and intelligent beings would put more confidence in the testimonies of man than of Jesus Himself. Jesus lived a sinless life for thirty-three years and was condemned to die for crimes He was not guilty. After three days in the grave, He arose victoriously. The next forty days He went everywhere preaching the Gospel to those to whom He appeared. Why not believe His testimony today and give your heart to Him? Believe Him who lives forever.

Believing
Acts 16:31

The Bible says: "... BELIEVE ON THE LORD JESUS CHRIST, AND THOU SHALT BE SAVED..." What kind of a belief is it that saves, for after all does not the Bible also say that the devil believes in the Lord and trembles? Does that mean that since Satan believes in God that he is saved? Of course not. There are three elements in saving faith, two of which most people are ignorant. There is the intellectual, the emotional, and volitional element. One affects the mind, the other the heart and the other the will. The mind gives ASSENT, THE HEART GIVES ASSURANCE, AND THE WILL GIVES ACCEPTANCE. With the mind I assent to the fact that Jesus died for me; with the heart I have ASSURANCE that He died for me, and with my will I ACCEPT Him as my Saviour. Thus the kind of belief that saves is the kind that affects the mind, the heart and the will. There are only six inches between heaven and hell – that is the distance between the head and the heart. What kind of faith is yours?

The Love Of God
John 3:16

The Bible says: "FOR GOD SO LOVED THE WORLD, THAT HE GAVE HIS ONLY BEGOTTEN SON, THAT WHOSOEVER BELIEVETH IN HIM SHOULD NOT PERISH, BUT HAVE EVERLASTING LIFE." Someone has said, "The love of God is an ocean and no line can sound its depths; it is a sky of unknown dimensions, and no space craft can reach its heights; it is a continent of unexplored distance and no tape can measure its length; it is a width of unsurpassed country and no survey can find its boundary; it is a mine of wealth and no archaeologist can estimate or exhaust its riches; it is a pole of attraction, which no explorer can discover; and it is a forest of beauty, and no botanist can find and describe its variety and glory." Thus, we must conclude that God's love cannot be apprehended, only appreciated; it cannot be explained, only experienced; it cannot be written out on paper, but worked out in God's people. God's love becomes real in our hearts when we accept God's Son as our Saviour through faith.

Man's Worth To God
Matthew 16:26

The Bible says: "FOR WHAT IS A MAN PROFITED, IF HE SHALL GAIN THE WHOLE WORLD, AND LOSE HIS OWN SOUL?. . ." In these busy commercial days we are always talking about the value of things and how much things cost. Maybe it would be good after all if we sought to answer this question, "How much is the soul worth?" Chemically man is worth about $6.50. Spiritually he is worth enough that God sent His only begotten Son all the way from heaven to this earth to be born of a virgin, live a sinless life, that would qualify Him to die a sinful death and then be raised by the power of God to enable me to be everything. He created me to be in the first place. While many do not feel they are worth much to themselves or others, they need to see what they are worth to God. You may not count with others, but you do count with Him. Your soul is worth everything to God. Don't lose it. Trust God today to redeem it.

Depravity

Romans 3:23

The Bible Says: "FOR ALL HAVE SINNED, AND COME SHORT OF THE GLORY OF GOD;" One of the most difficult things to get an unsaved man to do is to admit his need for Christ and salvation. Man wants to believe that he is basically good, even though the evidence is all against him. Read the Bible, even listen to atheistic philosophers, and study the main characters in the novels being produced today and you will get some picture of the corruption of mankind. Somerset Maugham, when past seventy, wrote in *Summing Up,* "It seems incredible that I ever believed in the progress of man... man makes no progress... in fact, he goes backward." When Eugene O'Neal was asked why man behaves like an animal he replied, "Why? Man is born broken, needs constant mending and I suppose God is the glue." The Bible not only tells us that all have sinned and come short of God's glory, it also tells us that Jesus Christ came into this world to die for man's sinfulness and lead him back to God. You can know true forgiveness and restoration by trusting Gods's Son today.

The Name That Saves

Romans 10:13-14

The Bible says: "FOR WHOSOEVER SHALL CALL UPON THE NAME OF THE LORD SHALL BE SAVED. HOW THEN SHALL THEY CALL ON HIM IN WHOM THEY HAVE NOT BELIEVED? AND HOW SHALL THEY BELIEVE IN HIM OF WHOM THEY HAVE NOT HEARD? AND HOW SHALL THEY HEAR WITHOUT A PREACHER?" Dr. Jackie Stephenson of the Lower Rio Grande Valley with the help of Senator John Tower made legal arrangements for a Vietnamese doctor, Doctor Vu Thien Long, and his family to be evacuated before Saigon fell to the Communists. There was one problem however, they did not know how to contact Dr. Long and tell him the good news. It may well be that the good doctor and his family died at the hands of the Communists because they never heard. God has promised salvation from sin and hell to all who call upon Him. Read Romans 10:13 today and claim this promise. (SOURCE: *Tyler Morning Telegraph*, April 23, 1975).

Without Excuse
Romans 1:20

The Bible says: "FOR THE INVISIBLE THINGS OF HIM FROM THE CREATION OF THE WORLD ARE CLEARLY SEEN, BEING UNDERSTOOD BY THE THINGS THAT ARE MADE, EVEN HIS ETERNAL POWER AND GODHEAD: SO THAT THEY ARE WITHOUT EXCUSE:" Man uses many excuses for not coming to Christ, but the most frequently one used is, there are too many hypocrites in the church. This excuse was used over and over by a certain farmer until one day he saw the fallacy of it. The pastor who had been trying to win him to the Lord came for dinner after which the farmer carried him out to the hog pens to show him a new litter of pigs. The pastor noticed one was in a pen by itself and when he asked why, he was informed it was the runt. The farmer tried to get the pastor to go look at the others, but he insisted on looking at the runt. Finally, when the farmer became perturbed, the wise pastor said, "Jim, for several years this is exactly what you have been doing. You have been looking at the hypocrites instead of the real saints." That day the farmer saw his mistake and gave his heart to Christ.

The Way To Life
John 5:39-40

The Bible Says: "SEARCH THE SCRIPTURES; FOR IN THEM YE THINK YE HAVE ETERNAL LIFE: AND THEY ARE THEY WHICH TESTIFY OF ME. AND YE WILL NOT COME TO ME, THAT YE MIGHT HAVE LIFE." Recently I discovered that in 1974 Americans made over a million visits to the doctors' offices. According to the World Health Organization Journal, almost fifty percent of the American people are on medication of some type at any given point in time. This does not necessarily mean that fifty percent of the American people are sick, but that Americans are using drugs for help in coping with reality! Many who have left God out of their lives are seeking to quench the inner thirst of their soul by drinking from polluted streams, and in the words of the prophet Jeremiah, ". . . HEWING THEMSELVES OUT CISTERNS, BROKEN CISTERNS THAT CAN HOLD NO WATER." What is the solution to man's problems? Christ is the answer, and yet we hear Christ saying: ". . . AND YE WILL NOT COME TO ME THAT YE MIGHT HAVE LIFE." The waiting Christ waits for you to come to Him today for help only He can give.

The New Birth
John 3:3

The Bible says: "JESUS ANSWERED AND SAID UNTO HIM, VERILY, VERILY, I SAY UNTO THEE, EXCEPT A MAN BE BORN AGAIN, HE CANNOT SEE THE KINGDOM OF GOD." Recently I read of a man who had the following inscribed on his tombstone when he died: "JOHN EVANS – BORN 1850 – DIED 1915 – AGE 2 YEARS." I looked at that and at first I did not understand, for a little simple arithmetic would indicate the man was not two years of age but sixty-five years of age. Suddenly it dawned upon me what the inscription was really saying. It was really saying that physically John Evans was sixty-five years of age, but spiritually he was only two years of age. The most important thing to John Evans was not when he was born physically into the world, but when he was born again spiritually. Moses P. Timms once said, "He that is born once dies twice, but he that is born twice dies once; and if a man is not born twice it would be better for him not to be born at all." Have you been born again? How old are you spiritually?

Too Late
Jeremiah 8:20

The Bible says: "THE HARVEST IS PAST, THE SUMMER IS ENDED, AND WE ARE NOT SAVED." Charles Lamb tells the story of a certain man called Samuel LeGrice. In his life there were three stages. When he was young, people said of him, "He will do something." As he grew older and did nothing, people said of him, He could do something if he tried." Toward the end of his life, they said of him, "He might have done something if he had tried." His whole life was the tale of a promise that was never fulfilled. How tragic it is indeed, for a man to spend his life without taking advantage of the opportunities that came his way. How tragic indeed, it is for a person to go through all of life without ever coming to know the forgiveness that comes through salvation in Jesus Christ. It is not just to nations, but to individuals that the prophet speaks when he says: "THE HARVEST IS PAST, THE SUMMER IS ENDED, AND WE ARE NOT SAVED." Don't let this happen to you.

Revealed By Fire
I Corinthians 3:11-15

The Bible says: "FOR OTHER FOUNDATION CAN NO MAN LAY THAN THAT IS LAID, WHICH IS JESUS CHRIST. NOW IF ANY MAN BUILD UPON THIS FOUNDATION GOLD, SILVER, PRECIOUS STONES, WOOD, HAY, STUBBLE; EVERY MAN'S WORK SHALL BE MADE MANIFEST: FOR THE DAY SHALL DECLARE IT, BECAUSE IT SHALL BE REVEALED BY FIRE; AND THE FIRE SHALL TRY EVERY MAN'S WORK OF WHAT SORT IT IS. IF ANY MAN'S WORK ABIDE WHICH HE HATH BUILT THEREUPON, HE SHALL RECEIVE A REWARD. IF ANY MAN'S WORK SHALL BE BURNED, HE SHALL SUFFER LOSS: BUT HE HIMSELF SHALL BE SAVED; YET SO AS BY FIRE." Several years ago, I stood one morning, around two o'clock, with a family in the church I pastored and saw their house as it was burned to the ground. They were grief stricken, but received some comfort in knowing that the house was insured and could be replaced. Many people however, one day will stand before the judgment of God and see their life's work burned up without any hope of restoration. They built their life on temporal things instead of eternal things. What are you building your life on? Where are your values being placed?

Counting The Cost
Luke 14:28

The Bible says: "FOR WHICH OF YOU, INTENDING TO BUILD A TOWER, SITTETH NOT DOWN FIRST, AND COUNTETH THE COST, . . ." Jesus says that making the decision to live the Christian life is like making a decision to build a tower – the cost must be determined. It is said that when a man wishes to become a member of the great Benedictine Order of monks, he is accepted for a year on probation. During that time his clothes, which he wore in the world, hang in his cell. At any time he can put off his monk's habit, put on his worldly clothes, and walk out, and no one will think badly of him. Only at the end of the year are his clothes finally taken away. He must know what he is doing and make a definite, intelligent decision. So it is with Christianity. Jesus does not want followers who have not counted the cost, who have joined Him on waves of emotionalism, but ones who have joined Him with eyes wide open to the demands of discipleship which He makes of each who follow Him.

Forsaking The World
I John 2:15-17

The Bible says: "LOVE NOT THE WORLD, NEITHER THE THINGS THAT ARE IN THE WORLD. IF ANY MAN LOVE THE WORLD, THE LOVE OF THE FATHER IS NOT IN HIM. FOR ALL THAT IS IN THE WORLD, THE LUST OF THE FLESH, AND THE LUST OF THE EYES, AND THE PRIDE OF LIFE, IS NOT OF THE FATHER, BUT IS OF THE WORLD. AND THE WORLD PASSETH AWAY, AND THE LUST THEREOF: BUT HE THAT DOETH THE WILL OF GOD ABIDETH FOR EVER." The world that the believer is commanded not to love is not the world that God made but the one that man has corrupted. A man once reasoned that since all that God made was good and since corn liquor comes from corn, that liquor must be good. That man failed to see that God made the corn but man took it and misused it because of sin, and it is this world of sin we must separate ourselves from. A person once replied to a missionary who had given his testimony, "I would give the world to have that experience." The missionary said, "That's exactly what it cost me."

Second Hand Religion
John 4:42

The Bible says: ". . . NOW WE BELIEVE, NOT BECAUSE OF THY SAYING: FOR WE HAVE HEARD HIM OURSELVES, AND KNOW THAT THIS IS INDEED THE CHRIST, THE SAVIOUR OF THE WORLD." Today I want to ask you a question, "Do you have a hand-me-down religion? Are you living off a mother's, or a father's, or a friend's religion? Once John Wesley had this kind of religion until one day the ship he was on was caught in a storm and fear got hold of him. He noticed the only people not afraid were a little group of Moravian missionaries. When the storm was abated he asked them, "Were you not afraid?" "Afraid?" said the Moravian, "Why should I be afraid, I know Christ," and looking at Wesley with disconcerting frankness said, "DO YOU KNOW CHRIST?" It was the first time John Wesley had realized that he did not, and as a result of this discovery he came to trust Him. Let me ask you again, "Do you know Christ or are you living with a hand-me-down religion?"

Everlasting Life
John 3:36

The Bible says: "HE THAT BELIEVETH ON THE SON HATH EVERLASTING LIFE: AND HE THAT BELIEVETH NOT THE SON SHALL NOT SEE LIFE; BUT THE WRATH OF GOD ABIDETH ON HIM." The Bible makes it clear that the man who does not know Jesus and is unsaved is spiritually dead and for his dead condition Christ offers him everlasting life. What is everlasting life? Some say that it is a life that goes on forever and forever, a life without end. But what kind of an offer is that to a person who is sick, in pain and dying with a dreaded disease? Surely no person in that condition would want life to go on forever for them. I have heard many in that condition pray that God would let them die. Thus, we see the life that is everlasting is a certain kind of life. It is different from anything else for it is the very life of God Himself. This kind of life knows no sickness, pain, suffering or termination, and this kind of life God offers to you. The way to have it is to believe and so the Bible says: "HE THAT BELIEVETH ON THE SON HATH EVERLASTING LIFE."

Almost But Lost
Acts 26:27-29

The Bible says: "KING AGRIPPA, BELIEVEST THOU THE PROPHETS? I KNOW THAT THOU BELIEVEST. THEN AGRIPPA SAID UNTO PAUL, ALMOST THOU PERSUADEST ME TO BE A CHRISTIAN. AND PAUL SAID, I WOULD TO GOD, THAT NOT ONLY THOU, BUT ALSO ALL THAT HEAR ME THIS DAY, WERE BOTH ALMOST, AND ALTOGETHER SUCH AS I AM, EXCEPT THESE BONDS." This verse of scripture tells us about a man who was almost saved yet who died lost. He is a perfect picture of many. Recently I heard the story of a young man who ran the twenty-six mile marathon race at the Olympics. He ran into the stadium at Montreal and collapsed. He got up and started again sixteen times. Finally, he crawled on his hands and knees to what he thought was the finish line and collapsed again. When he regained consciousness, he found he was one-hundred and fifty yards from the finish line. He almost won the race. Don't let this happen to you at heaven's gate. It is not enough to be almost saved; one must be altogether saved.

The Light Of Jesus
John 1:4-5

The Bible says: "IN HIM WAS LIFE; AND THE LIFE WAS THE LIGHT OF MEN. AND THE LIGHT SHINETH IN DARKNESS; AND THE DARKNESS COMPREHENDED IT NOT." Recently I read the story of a lighthouse that had burned. When the ones who operated the lighthouse arrived to survey the ruins, they found that only the house had burned. The light was still intact since it was fireproof. The Bible says that Jesus is the Light of the world and that we are only lighthouses that house the light. The world may destroy us; death may claim our bodies, but the light is fireproof. It is indestructible. It is eternal. It shall never be extinguished. This is what John meant when he said Jesus, the Light of the world, shineth in darkness, but the darkness comprehended it not. Literally, the darkness could not extinguish it. Today God's light is a beacon to lead every soul into the safe harbor of salvation. Why not look to this light for life's direction?

The Shut Door
Matthew 25:10-13

The Bible says in Matthew 25:10-13: "AND WHILE THEY WENT TO BUY, THE BRIDEGROOM CAME; AND THEY THAT WERE READY WENT IN WITH HIM TO THE MARRIAGE: AND THE DOOR WAS SHUT. AFTERWARD CAME ALSO THE OTHER VIRGINS, SAYING, LORD, LORD, OPEN TO US. BUT HE ANSWERED AND SAID, VERILY I SAY UNTO YOU, I KNOW YOU NOT. WATCH THEREFORE, FOR YE KNOW NEITHER THE DAY NOR THE HOUR WHEREIN THE SON OF MAN COMETH." When Christ returns some are going to be as unprepared as were those five foolish virgins who had no oil in their lamps. They tried to make last minute preparation by going and buying some, but found when they returned, the door was shut. A couple of years ago as I stood at the airport one night waiting for my wife to arrive, I saw a man and woman running down one of the concourses trying to get to a plane before it left. However, only seconds before they got there the door was shut and the ramp pulled away from the plane. Some are going to miss heaven, not by years, but seconds. What about you? Are you ready should Christ come today?

Urgency Of Salvation
Proverbs 27:1

The Bible says: "BOAST NOT THYSELF OF TOMORROW; FOR THOU KNOWEST NOT WHAT A DAY MAY BRING FORTH." One of the biggest lies that Satan has a lot of people believing is that they have plenty of time to be saved. It is a proven fact that the older a person becomes the more difficult it becomes for them to give their hearts to Christ. It has been suggested that one out of ten thousand people that are twenty-five years of age get saved; that one out of fifty thousand people thirty-five years of age get saved; that one out of two-hundred thousand people forty-five years of age and older get saved; that one out of three-hundred thousand people fifty-five years of age and older get saved; that one out of five-hundred thousand people sixty-five years of age and older get saved. This is why the Bible warns us against hardening our hearts and encourages a person to give his heart to Christ while in his youth.

Life's Great Choice
Deuteronomy 30:19

The Bible says: "... I HAVE SET BEFORE YOU LIFE AND DEATH, BLESSING AND CURSING: THEREFORE CHOOSE LIFE, THAT BOTH THOU AND THY SEED MAY LIVE:" To the agnostic who scoffingly says, "If God is a God of love then why does He send anyone to hell?" I always respond by saying, "God doesn't send anyone to hell, man chooses to go to hell of his own free will." Have you heard the story of the wise old man who lived on the mountain who told the little boy what hand he held a bird in and even the kind of bird he held? You remember the little boy thought he figured out a way to catch him. He thought that he would take a live bird in his hand and ask him if it was alive or dead, and if he said dead, he would free it, and if he said alive, he would squeeze it to death. So he made his way up the mountain, but when he asked the wise old man the question, the wise old man said, "Son you only have the answer to that question, for the bird is in your hands." You too have the answer to where you will spend eternity. The Bible challenges you to choose life.

Facing The Future
Matthew 27:22

The Bible says: "PILATE SAID UNTO THEM, WHAT SHALL I DO THEN WITH JESUS WHICH IS CALLED CHRIST?..." You know the Bible is filled with many questions, and there are many questions that man needs to answer. For instance, "Where will you be ten million years from today?" "When you get where you are going where will you be?" These questions can be answered intelligently. One young man graduating from school was asked what he intended to do. He replied, "I intend to go to college, get my law degree, become a successful lawyer, become wealthy, and then retire and travel over the world." He was then asked, "What then?" "I suppose then I will die and my friends will come and mourn my passing." He was then asked, "What then?" "What then? Sir, I know not what then!" What you do with Jesus Christ, God's Son, determines what will happen then and where you will be ten million years from today.

Redemption
Galatians 3:13

The Bible says: "CHRIST HATH REDEEMED US FROM THE CURSE OF THE LAW, BEING MADE A CURSE FOR US: FOR IT IS WRITTEN, CURSED BE EVERY ONE THAT HANGETH ON A TREE:" When the Bible says Christ hath redeemed us, what does it mean? The word redemption means to buy back; to purchase in a market place; to loose and set free. It means we all were created by God but because of disobedience became slaves to sin. Christ came into the world, the slave market, and bought us with His death and set us free. Let me illustrate. A little boy built a boat once; and as he played with it in a stream of water, it got away from him and was lost. Later he found it in a curio shop where someone had sold it. He went into the store and paid the man two dollars for it and carried it home. Then he took the little boat and held it close to his bosom and said, "ONCE I MADE YOU AND NOW BOUGHT YOU, YOU ARE MINE ALL MINE." This is what the Bible means by redemption.

Defiled Hearts
Matthew 15:18-20

The Bible says: "BUT THOSE THINGS WHICH PROCEED OUT OF THE MOUTH COME FORTH FROM THE HEART; AND THEY DEFILE THE MAN. FOR OUT OF THE HEART PROCEED EVIL THOUGHTS, MURDERS, ADULTERIES, FORNICATIONS, THEFTS, FALSE WITNESSES, BLASPHEMIES; THESE ARE THE THINGS WHICH DEFILE A MAN!..." A Jewish Rabbi once asked his scholars what was the best thing a man could have in order to keep him in the straight path. One said "A good companion," another said, "Wisdom," and the last replied, "A good heart." To the last the Rabbi replied, "You have comprehended all that the others have said for he that hath a good heart will have a good disposition, and will be a good companion and a wise man." The Bible declares that the things that defile the man come not from the mouth but the heart. That is why Jesus is more concerned that a man have a new heart than a new start. The way to have this new heart is through faith in Jesus Christ, God's Son.

The Judgment Of God
Romans 2:2

The Bible says: "BUT WE ARE SURE THAT THE JUDGMENT OF GOD IS ACCORDING TO TRUTH AGAINST THEM WHICH COMMIT SUCH THINGS." Several years ago I pastored a church in a county in which the District Judge was blind. He was a highly respected judge and had a colorful life even though he was blind. It is said that a particular woman in the city was brought to trial in his court. Since she was not able to afford a lawyer for herself, the court appointed her one, and one that she did not altogether trust. Just before the judge sent the jury out to reach a verdict, he turned to this woman and asked if she had any comment, to which she replied, "Yes sir! I would like to ask this jury to have mercy on me because I have a blind judge and a crooked lawyer!" While there is a bit of humor here, there is a serious truth to be seen. God reminds us that when we stand, some day, before the judgment that it will be according to truth, the real truth about ourselves. Let us live our lives in view of this great truth.

Don't Sell Out Too Cheaply
I Corinthians 3:15

The Bible says: "IF ANY MAN'S WORK SHALL BE BURNED, HE SHALL SUFFER LOSS!..." The Bible reveals that a man can build his life upon temporal things or upon eternal things, and that the judgment seat of Christ will reveal where he has placed his true values. If he placed them on eternal things he will be rewarded, but if upon temporal things he will suffer loss. I had a friend once whose parents died when he was a young boy. The parents had left the children some property that seemed to be of little value, and in the years that followed they sold the land for practically nothing. However, many years later, an oil company discovered oil on that property and later built a refinery. Many times I have heard my friend say to me, "Oh, if we only had not sold out so cheaply I would be wealthy today." I believe when people stand before the judgment seat of Christ and see what they could have had, they will cry out, "Oh, if I had only not sold out so cheaply." That is why the Bible exhorts us to build our lives on things that are of eternal value.

Shooting Holes In Darkness
John 1:4-5

The Bible says in John 1:4-5: "IN HIM WAS LIFE; AND THE LIFE WAS THE LIGHT OF MEN. AND THE LIGHT SHINETH IN DARKNESS; AND THE DARKNESS COMPREHENDED IT NOT." There is no word that better describes God than light. John tells us that Christ came into a world filled with darkness. That darkness tried to extinguish His light, but His light expelled the darkness. Robert Louis Stevenson best describes what I am seeking to say. He tells the story of a lamp lighter in the days of old who would go each night and light the lamps along the streets. One night as he lit the lamps a little boy saw the circle of light that would appear above each lamp in the darkness. He was so amazed by what he saw that he ran home and said, "Mama, come see this man that is shooting holes in the darkness." That is precisely what Jesus, the light of the world, did to this world of darkness.

Peace With God
Romans 5:1

The Bible says in Romans 5:1: "THEREFORE BEING JUSTIFIED BY FAITH, WE HAVE PEACE WITH GOD THROUGH OUR LORD JESUS CHRIST:..." In this verse the Apostle Paul tells us three things: he tells us that all men need peace; he tells us how to have this peace; and he describes the kind of peace that God gives. Paul tells us that men have peace with God when they are justified by faith in Jesus Christ. The word justify is a legal term. It means to declare just; to render acceptable; to pardon, but it means more than that. A criminal may be pardoned from the penalty of a crime committed but never from the guilt. In justification God frees us from the penalty and the guilt. He looks upon us as someone has said, "JUST AS IF I NEVER SINNED." The result of being justified by faith is that, "... WE HAVE PEACE WITH GOD THROUGH OUR LORD JESUS CHRIST."

The Word Of God
II Timothy 3:16

The Bible says: "ALL SCRIPTURE IS GIVEN BY INSPIRATION OF GOD, AND IS PROFITABLE FOR DOCTRINE, FOR REPROOF, FOR CORRECTION, FOR INSTRUCTION IN RIGHTEOUSNESS:" Recently I read in a newspaper that of the fifteen hundred daily newspapers in America, 1,250 of them carry an astrology column. It is estimated that fifty million people read their horoscopes every day. This all illustrates that man is frantically trying to find the answer to many questions and problems. The answers are not to be found in a fortune teller but a fortune giver; not in a book but in the Bible. Astrology has never led anyone to a saving faith in the Lord Jesus, but instead has led millions away. And yet the only book that offers hope for tomorrow is neglected by the millions. God's Word is true; it is inspired; it is infallible; it will help you not only to know how to get to heaven but how to live on earth before you get there. Why not read it every day and attend church where it is taught?

Spiritual Values
Matthew 6:19-20

The Bible says: "LAY NOT UP FOR YOURSELVES TREASURES UPON EARTH, WHERE MOTH AND RUST DOTH CORRUPT, AND WHERE THIEVES BREAK THROUGH AND STEAL: BUT LAY UP FOR YOURSELVES TREASURES IN HEAVEN..." Some people live their lives contrary to what Jesus teaches here, failing to realize that one day the record will reveal where their real values were placed in this life. There is a story of a woman who lived a life of luxury with little thought of God. She died, and when she arrived in heaven an angel was sent to conduct her to her house. They passed down the main streets and by all the great mansions, and just outside of the town they came to a shack that the angel said was hers. "What," said the woman, "I cannot live in that." "I am sorry," replied the angel, "That is all we could build for you with the materials you sent up." Jesus said, "LAY UP FOR YOURSELVES TREASURES IN HEAVEN." Such a person will surely meet the Lord with full confidence.

When Jesus Wiped The Mud Off
Titus 3:4-6

The Bible says: "BUT AFTER THAT THE KINDNESS AND LOVE OF GOD OUR SAVIOUR TOWARD MAN APPEARED, NOT BY WORKS OF RIGHTEOUSNESS WHICH WE HAVE DONE, BUT ACCORDING TO HIS MERCY HE SAVED US, BY THE WASHING OF REGENERATION, AND RENEWING OF THE HOLY GHOST; WHICH HE SHED ON US ABUNDANTLY THROUGH JESUS CHRIST OUR SAVIOUR;" Dr. E.J. Daniels tells the story of a little boy who came up to him at the close of a service once and said, "Preacher do you know me? You wiped the mud off me one day." Then the preacher remembered the day the little boy was passing his house and fell down in the mud. He picked him up and carried him into his house and washed him and carried him to school. That little boy had remembered that preacher as the one who wiped the mud off. One day, in our sins, you and I were like that little boy, but Jesus came and forgave us of our sins and wiped the mud off. One day we too shall gather round the crystal throne and bow before the Lord and say, "Thank you, Jesus, for wiping the mud off."

World Destruction
II Peter 3:10

The Bible says: "BUT THE DAY OF THE LORD WILL COME AS A THIEF IN THE NIGHT; IN THE WHICH THE HEAVENS SHALL PASS AWAY WITH A GREAT NOISE, AND THE ELEMENTS SHALL MELT WITH FERVENT HEAT, THE EARTH ALSO AND THE WORKS THAT ARE THEREIN SHALL BE BURNED UP." Just as God destroyed the earth once with water when man sinned, so He has declared He will destroy it the last time with fire. II Peter 3:7 says the earth is storing the fire that shall be used to destroy it. The earth is one big fire bomb that is twenty-five thousand miles in circumference and eight thousand miles in diameter. It is formed like a hollow ball with an outer crust and a hot molten liquid as its core. Geysers, eruptions of volcanos, and earthquakes all prove this. Peter says that not only will the earth be destroyed by fire, but the elements will melt with a fervent heat. Once, men denied this, until the Atomic bomb weighing six hundred pounds was dropped and exploded fifteen hundred feet above Hiroshima leaving one hundred thousand dead and dying. The only way to escape this judgment brought about because of sin is to trust Jesus Christ, God's Son.

Broken Cisterns
Jeremiah 2:12-13

The Bible says: "BE ASTONISHED, O YE HEAVENS, AT THIS, AND BE HORRIBLY AFRAID, BE YE VERY DESOLATE, SAITH THE LORD. FOR MY PEOPLE HAVE COMMITTED TWO EVILS; THEY HAVE FORSAKEN ME THE FOUNTAIN OF LIVING WATERS, AND HEWED THEM OUT CISTERNS, BROKEN CISTERNS, THAT CAN HOLD NO WATER." Some time ago I was in a department store, and as I passed the jewelry department I glanced over and saw some beautiful diamond rings. However, as I came closer to the counter I saw a sign under them that said, "SIMULATED." They were not real diamond rings but only appeared to be. They were artificial and at their very best only a substitute. That day as I walked away from the counter I thought of the many people who have a seemingly "SIMULATED RELIGION." They become satisfied to turn the real thing down for substitutes. The prophet Jeremiah saw this also and said, "MY PEOPLE HAVE . . . FORSAKEN ME THE FOUNTAIN OF LIVING WATERS AND HEWED THEM OUT CISTERNS BROKEN CISTERNS THAT CAN HOLD NO WATER." Don't be satisfied with substitutes.

The Absurdity Of Excuses
Luke 14:17-18

The Bible says: ". . . COME; FOR ALL THINGS ARE NOW READY. AND THEY ALL WITH ONE CONSENT BEGAN TO MAKE EXCUSE . . ." People use all kinds of excuses for not coming to Christ, but the most frequently used one is, "There are too many hypocrites in the church." This is such an absurd excuse. It is absurd for four reasons. First, it is absurd because while some profess to be loyal to Christ and are not, that this does not give you a right to be disloyal. Secondly, it is absurd because usually it is only in the church that people refuse to identify with the hypocrites that are found. Thirdly, it is absurd because while there are hypocrites in the church there are some of the most Godly people in the world there also. And fourth, it is absurd because unless the hypocrites repent they will spend eternity in hell, and unless you repent you will spend eternity in hell with them. I decided a long time ago that I had rather go to church with the hypocrites than to hell with them. What about you?

The Last Days
Luke 17:26-27

The Bible says: "AND AS IT WAS IN THE DAYS OF NOE, SO SHALL IT BE ALSO IN THE DAYS OF THE SON OF MAN." Jesus tells us that if we want to know what the world is going to be like when He returns in the air for the saved, then we must understand what it was like in the days of Noah. How strange it seems that the same signs that preceded the destruction of the world by water will precede the destruction of the world by fire. It would appear to me that in the six thousand years of human history that man still has not learned from his mistakes. What was the world of Noah like? Genesis chapter six tells us. It was a world in which marriage was abused, revelation was rejected, violence prevailed, a world in which the people were sensual, a world under the inspection of God and threatened by destruction, and a world experiencing rapid growth. These things describe our world today with masses of people starving to death and little hope in sight! What is the answer? The ark of safety offered Noah only speaks of Jesus Christ our only hope today.

God's Wrath
John 3:36

The Bible says: "HE THAT BELIEVETH ON THE SON HATH EVERLASTING LIFE: AND HE THAT BELIEVETH NOT THE SON SHALL NOT SEE LIFE; BUT THE WRATH OF GOD ABIDETH ON HIM." John states that those who receive Christ receive light and life while those who reject Him continue in darkness and under the wrath of God. God's wrath is his opposition to sin. John saw God's wrath like a fire sweeping across a dry desert with snakes and other creatures fleeing before it. Where can you flee to safety from the fire – only where fire has already burned. Where is that? At Calvary. There God's fiery fury erupted like a volcano and was poured out without measure upon His Son. In Him were satisfied all of the demands of God's Holy and Righteous nature and only there can the sinner find eternal security from God's abiding universal opposition to sin. Today there is refuge at Calvary. Discover it for yourself.

What Is A Christian?
Acts 26:28

The Bible says: "THEN AGRIPPA SAID UNTO PAUL, ALMOST THOU PERSUADEST ME TO BE A CHRISTIAN." A little boy once asked his father what a Christian was. The father did such a good job explaining to the young fellow what a Christian, according to the scripture, should be that when he had finished the little fellow looked up into his father's face and said, "Have I ever seen a Christian?" Now a person must have real sympathy for that little fellow, because the word Christian has been so misused and even abused by those who claim to be Christian, that the world must often wonder what a Christian really is. The word Christian is used only three times in the Bible: in Acts 26:28; Acts 11:26; and Peter 4:16. As the word Christ means anointed one, so the word Christian means anointed ones. A Christian then should be one who truly reflects the life and character of Jesus Christ. In light of this truth, are you a Christian?

Coming To Christ
Matthew 11:28

The Bible says: "COME UNTO ME ALL YE THAT LABOUR AND ARE HEAVY LADEN, AND I WILL GIVE YOU REST." No word more adequately expresses the concern of Christ for men lost in their sins than the word "come." It was to drunkards, gamblers, prostitutes, thieves, and murderers that Jesus' invitation to come to Him for salvation was issued. So many feel they must change their ways and get good enough to come to Him, and so they fail to see He wants them just as they are. I heard one prominent doctor in Tyler, Texas testify that when he first read in Ephesians that we are saved by grace and not by works, he couldn't believe it. He thought he had to get good enough to achieve salvation. However, he did come to Christ by faith and learned as Charlotte Elliott learned, that Christ takes us just as we are. When she saw that, she wrote, "JUST AS I AM WITHOUT ONE PLEA, BUT THAT THY BLOOD WAS SHED FOR ME, AND THAT THOU BIDEST ME COME TO THEE, OH LAMB OF GOD, I COME, I COME." Today you may come also, just as you are!

Spiritual Death
Ephesians 2:1

The Bible says: "AND YOU HATH HE QUICKENED, WHO WERE DEAD IN TRESPASSES AND SINS;" In the gospels we have recorded the story of the resurrection of three different individuals. Jesus raised a twelve year old girl (Luke 8:49-56); He raised a young man (Luke 7:11-17); and He raised an old man (John 11). You will note that they were all of different ages because Jesus wanted to show us three different kinds of sinners. All three were dead – the child, the young man and the old man. One was not more dead than the other. The only difference lay in the degree of decay. Thus, we learn that children are sinners, though open corruption has not yet set in, young people are sinners and here outward corruption begins to show, and adults are sinners and definite outward corruption is clearly seen. We learn from these illustrations that sin has invaded all walks of life and that, "THE WAGES OF SIN IS DEATH BUT THE GIFT OF GOD IS ETERNAL LIFE."

Abundant Life
John 10:10

The Bible says: "THE THIEF COMETH NOT, BUT FOR TO STEAL, AND TO KILL, AND TO DESTROY: I AM COME THAT THEY MIGHT HAVE LIFE, AND THAT THEY MIGHT HAVE IT MORE ABUNDANTLY." The Amplified Bible describes this offer of Jesus in these words: ". . . I CAME THAT THEY MAY HAVE AND ENJOY LIFE AND HAVE IT IN ABUNDANCE TO THE FULL, TILL IT OVERFLOWS." It is one thing to have life but an entirely different thing to enjoy it in its fullest. Early in my ministry I had this most vividly illustrated. A family in the church I pastored had a son who was a Mongoloid. Now Jay had life. He was much alive, but the tragic thing was, Jay could not speak, eat for himself or do anything one normally does. He had life but not in its fullest. Many people are like that spiritually. They have eternal life and if they died they would not go to hell. However, they have not yet discovered the abundant life that is full and meaningful. A study of God's Word will help one discover this abundant life.

The Winning Choice
Romans 1:20

The Bible says in Romans 1:20: "FOR THE INVISIBLE THINGS OF HIM FROM THE CREATION OF THE WORLD ARE CLEARLY SEEN, BEING UNDERSTOOD BY THE THINGS THAT ARE MADE, EVEN HIS ETERNAL POWER AND GODHEAD; SO THAT THEY ARE WITHOUT EXCUSE!" What a tragedy that so many will miss heaven because of excuses. A man gains everything and loses nothing in becoming a Christian. Suppose for one moment that you trusted Christ and died and there was no heaven or hell. What have you lost? Nothing! Yet you have made this world a better place to live in because of living by the teachings of the Bible. On the other hand, suppose for a moment that you rejected Christ and died and there was a heaven and hell! What have you lost? Everything! Trusting Christ is not only Scripturally right but logically right. This is why God says we will be without excuse if we reject Him

The Blood Of Christ
I Peter 1:18-19

The Bible says in I Peter 1:18-19; "FORASMUCH AS YE KNOW THAT YE WERE NOT REDEEMED WITH CORRUPTIBLE THINGS, AS SILVER AND GOLD, FROM YOUR VAIN CONVERSATION RECEIVED BY TRADITION FROM YOUR FATHERS; BUT WITH THE PRECIOUS BLOOD OF CHRIST, AS OF A LAMB WITHOUT BLEMISH AND WITHOUT SPOT:" Sometime ago I read in the newspaper where several convicts in a penal institution had given 126 pints of blood to a young boy with Leukemia to keep him alive. The young boy had to have two pints a week to stay alive. This was enough to keep him alive for a year and three months. Today I would like to introduce you to Jesus Christ who on the cross of Calvary gave enough blood to keep you alive forever. It is because of this that He invites you to trust Him and says in John 11:26: "WHOSOEVER BELIEVETH IN ME SHALL NEVER DIE." The way to be alive ten million years from now is to believe Him and let His blood cover your sins. Why not do that today?

The Cross Of Christ
Galatians 6:14

The Bible says: "BUT GOD FORBID THAT I SHOULD GLORY, SAVE IN THE CROSS OF OUR LORD JESUS CHRIST, BY WHOM THE WORLD IS CRUCIFIED UNTO ME, AND I UNTO THE WORLD." I knew a football coach once who always carried a small cross in his billfold. One day when he returned from the garbage dump he discovered that he had lost the billfold with a sizable amount of money in it. As he started back to the garbage dump he met his son who stopped him and told him that his billfold had been found and turned in at the school. When he went to pick it up, he was informed that the man who had found it said that when he found the billfold he intended to steal the money out of it. However, when he opened it up and saw the cross, he could not take the money. When a person truly sees and understands the significance of the cross, both their attitudes and actions will be affected. That is why Paul said: "GOD FORBID THAT I SHOULD GLORY SAVE IN THE CROSS OF THE LORD JESUS CHRIST."

I Am Not Ashamed
Romans 1:16

The Bible says in Romans 1:16: "FOR I AM NOT ASHAMED OF THE GOSPEL OF CHRIST: FOR IT IS THE POWER OF GOD UNTO SALVATION TO EVERY ONE THAT BELIEVETH; TO THE JEW FIRST, AND ALSO TO THE GREEK." Jesus made it clear that no one could be saved and be a follower of His who was ashamed of Him, yet what a tragedy that so many refuse to accept Christ because they seemingly are ashamed to identify with Him. Sometimes it is social pride, moral pride or intellectual pride that is responsible for this. This was the case with Aaron Burr who was a traitor of America. On one occasion early in his life, while a student at Yale University, he responded to an invitation that was given during a revival meeting for those who wished to give themselves to Christ. He left his seat and as he walked down the aisle someone said, "Look at Aaron Burr going into the inquiry room." Burr turned and went back to his seat and said, "I was only fooling." Aaron Burr was not fooling, but like many convicted of their sins he rejected Christ because of intellectual pride. Don't let pride rob you of salvation!

Sin's Finished Product
James 1:15

The Bible says: "THEN WHEN LUST HATH CONCEIVED, IT BRINGETH FORTH SIN: AND SIN, WHEN IT IS FINISHED, BRINGETH FORTH DEATH." I heard of a man once who captured a baby python and carried it home as a pet. The man was a snake trainer and he trained the snake to perform with him in a circus act. One night he entered the specially built glass cage to perform his act before a capacity crowd. Slowly the snake began to wind itself around his body until all but his head was enclosed. Suddenly the man began to scream, and the bones in his body began to break and be crushed as the mighty python crushed him to death. The once harmless and powerless pet had become the instrument of his death. Many people find out too late that this is exactly what sin does. They play with it, flirt with it and court it until one day, at an unexpected moment, it destroys them. Multitudes of alcoholics and drug addicts testify to this affect. James the Apostle said this long ago when he said: "... SIN, WHEN IT IS FINISHED BRINGETH FORTH DEATH."

Narrowness
Matthew 7:14

The Bible says: "...STRAIT IS THE GATE, AND NARROW IS THE WAY, WHICH LEADETH UNTO LIFE, AND FEW THERE BE THAT FIND IT." Have you ever noticed that people want to be narrow in every area of their life except in religion. In religion the word "narrow" is often used in a derogatory manner, but Jesus used it to describe the way to heaven. We need to take a new look at narrowness and see that narrowness is necessary for refinement. The higher the life style the more restrictive or narrow it is. Someone has said that it is a long way from cannibalism to culture; narrowness is necessary for *release*. The most successful people are the most restricted; people who live disciplined and narrow lives. The road to a gold medal for the Olympic champion is a narrow road; narrowness is necessary for reliance. I want my banker, doctor and insurance man to be very narrow. I could not trust them if they were not. Neither could I trust a God who was not narrow and exact in what He said. I am glad He has a narrow road. It is easier to trust Him.

God Purchased Possession
I Corinthians 6:20

The Bible says: "FOR YE ARE BOUGHT WITH A PRICE: THEREFORE GLORIFY GOD IN YOUR BODY, AND IN YOUR SPIRIT, WHICH ARE GOD'S." The Bible declares that God's people are a purchased people. The very word redemption means to purchase in a market place. It suggests that you and I, because of our disobedience and rebellion toward God, were slaves to sin and Satan in this wicked and perverse world, but that God came right where we were and purchased us with the blood of His dear Son. A little boy illustrates this most beautifully. One day he made a little boat and as he was playing with it in a stream, it drifted away from him and became lost. Later in a curio shop, he saw it and bought it and as he walked down the street he said, "Once I made you and now I have bought you and you belong to me." The man, redeemed and forgiven of his sins, is a man who has been purchased by God.

How To Take It With You
Luke 12:20

The Bible says: "BUT GOD SAID UNTO HIM, THOU FOOL, THIS NIGHT THY SOUL SHALL BE REQUIRED OF THEE: THEN WHOSE SHALL THOSE THINGS BE, WHICH THOU HAST PROVIDED?" Once at a board of directors meeting in Chicago, a fellow business man reported that one of their fellow directors had died very suddenly. The group replied almost in unison, "How much did he leave?" The reply was, "He left it all." In this materialistic and pleasure maddened world, where man is more concerned about gold than God, riches than redemption, he needs desperately to be reminded of this truth. The Bible calls the man a fool who places so much emphasis on gaining riches that he looses his soul. In the verse that we just read, God seems to say to this rich fool, "What will you do with your wealth when you die?" The answer is, "He will leave it all." Why not, then, labour for that which you can carry with you!

The Greatest Thief Of All
I Peter 4:15

The Bible says: "BUT LET NONE OF YOU SUFFER AS A MURDERER, OR AS A THIEF, . . ." The Bible speaks of many different kinds of thieves, but the greatest thief of all is the man or woman who steals from themselves. During the "Roaring Twenties", Arthur Barry gained an international reputation as probably the outstanding jewel thief of all times, because he robbed only well-known personalities. Finally, he was caught, convicted, and sentenced to prison. In later years, after his release, a young reporter asked him, " . . . Mr. Barry, do you remember the one from whom you stole the most?" Without a moments's hesitation he said, "That's easy. The man from whom I stole the most was Arthur Barry. I could have been a successful businessman, a baron on Wall Street and a contributing member to society, but instead I chose the life of a thief, and spent two-thirds of my adult life behind prison bars." What are you robbing yourself of today? Let Christ give you new meaning to life.

High Cost Of Low Living
Proverbs 26:27

The Bible says: "WHOSO DIGGETH A PIT SHALL FALL THEREIN: AND HE THAT ROLLETH A STONE, IT WILL RETURN UPON HIM." There is much being said these days about the high cost of living. It seems that someone should say something about the HIGH COST OF LOW LIVING. God has a standard for every man to live by, and many pay a high price when they live below that standard. Lawrence Dunbar spoke potent words when he said:

> This is the price I pay,
> Just for one riotous day
> Years of regret and of grief,
> And sorrow without relief.
> Suffer it I will my friend,
> Suffer it until the end,
> Until the grave shall give relief.
> Small was the thing I bought,
> Small was the thing at best,
> Small was the debt, I thought,
> But O God! – the interest.

One pays a high cost to live low. Remember, "WHOSO DIGGETH A PIT SHALL FALL THEREIN."

The True Way Proverbs
Proverbs 14:12

The Bible says: "THERE IS A WAY WHICH SEEMETH RIGHT UNTO A MAN, BUT THE END THEREOF ARE THE WAYS OF DEATH." On January 1, 1929, California Tech was playing Georgia Tech in the Rose Bowl. In the opening minutes of the game, Georgia Tech received. During the run back the ball carrier was hit hard and the football squirted from his hands. The live ball fumbled, fell into the arms of Cal Tech's Roy Riegels. He whirled around, plunged through an opening and ran at his best. The Rose Bowl crowd was wildly alive because Riegels was running in the wrong direction. He finally made sixty-three yards before being tackled by one of his own team mates. However, the blunder set up a score for Georgia Tech that gave them an edge which won the game. That one action gave Roy Riegels a tag which he is known by today, "WRONG WAY" Riegels. Jesus Christ said, "I am the way!" Don't wait until you have crossed the goal line of life to find you went in the wrong direction. Trust Him today!

Jesus Our Mediator
I Timothy 2:5-6

The Bible says: "FOR THERE IS ONE GOD, AND ONE MEDIATOR BETWEEN GOD AND MEN, THE MAN CHRIST JESUS; WHO GAVE HIMSELF A RANSOM FOR ALL,..." Once, in the days of President Lincoln, a father, whose son had been in the army of the Potomac and who was arrested and condemned for desertion, went to plead for his son. The guards had not permitted the old man to get through to the President and with tears streaming down his face, he stood outside the White House. A small boy saw him weeping and asked him what was wrong. He told him and the little boy said, "I can take you to the President." "You?" said the old man. "Yes, he is my father, and he lets me come in any time." Through his son, the old man was able to see the President and gained his own son's pardon. The principle remains true today. The way to get to God the Heavenly Father is through His Son Jesus Christ.

The World's Greatest Banquet
Revelation 19:9

The Bible says: "AND HE SAID UNTO ME, WRITE, BLESSED ARE THEY WHICH ARE CALLED UNTO THE MARRIAGE SUPPER OF THE LAMB..." One of the greatest banquets the world ever had was catered by J.F. Lyons in London in 1925. They had five thousand guests and tables five miles long. There were 1,350 waitresses and seven hundred cooks and porters. Of the 83,000 glasses and plates that were used, 3,500 of them were broken. That without doubt was quite a banquet, but that banquet in no way compares to the one described in Revelation 19 that is set in heaven. All born again believers will be present in honor of Jesus and His Bride. At the banquet in London only selected guests were invited, but at the one in heaven every person is invited from the poorest to the richest. The only qualification is that one be born again from above by trusting Jesus Christ, God's Son. Will you be present at this glorious and Heavenly Banquet?

Knowing God

Isaiah 1:2-3

The Bible says: "HEAR, O HEAVENS, AND GIVE EAR, O EARTH: FOR THE LORD HATH SPOKEN, I HAVE NOURISHED AND BROUGHT UP CHILDREN, AND THEY HAVE REBELLED AGAINST ME. THE OX KNOWETH HIS OWNER, AND THE ASS HIS MASTER'S CRIB: BUT ISRAEL DOTH NOT KNOW, MY PEOPLE DOTH NOT CONSIDER." Boreham tells how that as a child he visited in a friend's house, where there was one room in which he was not permitted to enter. He never understood why, until one day, as he was playing across from the room, the door swung open and inside he saw a body, his own age, in a dreadful state of animal idiocy. He relates how he saw that boy's mother drop to her knees beside his bed and cry out in anguish, "I've fed you and clothed you and loved you – and you've never known me." God must feel the same with multitudes today. This is the intent of the prophet's words: "THE OX KNOWETH HIS OWNER, AND THE ASS HIS MASTER'S CRIB: BUT ISRAEL DOTH NOT KNOW, MY PEOPLE DOTH NOT CONSIDER."

Knowing Christ

Philippians 3:10

The Bible says: "THAT I MAY KNOW HIM, AND THE POWER OF HIS RESURRECTION, . . ." It is a strange paradox that while many know ABOUT Jesus Christ, few KNOW Him personally as Lord and Saviour. Several years ago, I heard Pat Boone give his testimony in Colorado. He related how he had been brought up in the church and how he knew about Christ, but while he knew of Him intellectually, he did not know Him experientially. He related how that many times he had stayed in the Waldorf Astoria Hotels, and that he knew about Mr. Waldorf. He had seen his picture by the elevators and would have recognized him if he would have seen him. However, if someone would have asked him if he knew him personally, he would have had to admit that he did not, for he had never been introduced to him. This is true with many spiritually. Many know about Christ intellectually, but they do not know Him experientially and personally. Today, you can know Him, if by faith you will come to Him and repent of your sins and receive Him as your Saviour!

Lamps Without Light
Matthew 25:8

The Bible says: "AND THE FOOLISH SAID UNTO THE WISE, GIVE US OF YOUR OIL; FOR OUR LAMPS ARE GONE OUT." The story of the ten virgins illustrates for us that morality will not save us. All ten were virgins and morally upright but only five had oil, which is a symbol of the Holy Spirit or the life of God, in them. They were like lamps without light. Before my grandmother died she related, in a dream one night how she heard a voice that said, "Martha, you have been a church member a long time, but you have no oil in your lamp." Immediately she said, "Well, Lord, what must I do?" Then a choir began to sing, "Kneel at the cross, Christ will meet you there, come friend without delay." The next night in a revival meeting, she knelt at an old fashioned altar and asked Jesus to come into her heart and He did. Dear friend, it is not enough to be a church member and live a moral life. We must have oil in our lamps. We must have His life and it comes through faith in Christ.

Salvation
Luke 8:12

The Bible says: "THOSE BY THE WAY SIDE ARE THEY THAT HEAR; THEN COMETH THE DEVIL, AND TAKETH AWAY THE WORD OUT OF THEIR HEARTS, LEST THEY SHOULD BELIEVE AND BE SAVED." If salvation could be bought, most people would go in debt to buy it, but when God's Word says that salvation is a free gift of God that is obtained only by believing and receiving, many miss it because of its simplicity. Too many people feel they must do something, perform some great work to be saved. As a young man, Allen Stewart was like this: he felt that he had to do something and so he joined the church, he sang in the church choir, and he became a busy worker hoping that through these efforts he would gain salvation. Yet, none of them brought inner peace and satisfaction. One day as he read the parable of the sower as told by Jesus in Luke chapter 8, he came to these words: ". . . THEN COMETH THE DEVIL, AND TAKETH AWAY THE WORD OUT OF THEIR HEARTS, LEST THEY SHOULD BELIEVE AND BE SAVED." That day he found peace as he placed his simple faith in God. You, too, can have that peace the same way.

Atheism
Luke 12:20

The Bible says: "BUT GOD SAID UNTO HIM, THOU FOOL, THIS NIGHT THY SOUL SHALL BE REQUIRED OF THEE: THEN WHOSE SHALT THOSE THINGS BE, WHICH THOU HAST PROVIDED?" Here is the familiar story of the rich farmer who had enough time to farm and to make money but not enough time for God, for his soul, or for things of eternal value. The Bible describes him in Luke as a fool, but then what is a fool? Someone said that, "A fool is someone who is unwilling to give up that which he cannot keep for that which he cannot lose." This man was like that! There are too many in the world like him today and whose destiny can best be described by the epitaph on the tombstone of a famous atheist: "HERE I LIE ALL DRESSED UP AND NOWHERE TO GO." Where will you spend eternity? This is a question that demands to be seriously answered. How will you answer that question today?

Locked Out
Luke 13:25

The Bible says: "WHEN ONCE THE MASTER OF THE HOUSE IS RISEN UP, AND HATH SHUT TO THE DOOR, AND YE BEGIN TO STAND WITHOUT, AND TO KNOCK AT THE DOOR, SAYING, LORD, LORD, OPEN UNTO US; AND HE SHALL ANSWER AND SAY UNTO YOU, I KNOW YOU NOT WHENCE YE ARE." Several years ago my family and I lived near the Gulf of Mexico. One afternoon I took the family to the beach for an outing. We had almost a perfect afternoon together. We played, swam and ate a picnic lunch together. We stayed as long as we could, but as dark crept in on us, we all made a run for the car to drive back home. It was then that we sadly discovered the car was locked, and I had accidentally locked the keys in the trunk of the car. I tried everything, but finally realized that there was only one way to get into the trunk of the car and that was with another key. I called a friend to bring it. Jesus is the key to heaven and those who reject Him will one day stand before heaven's locked door with no hope of entrance.

Seriousness Of Hell
Mark 9:43-44

The Bible says: "AND IF THY HAND OFFEND THEE, CUT IT OFF: IT IS BETTER FOR THEE TO ENTER INTO LIFE MAIMED, THAN HAVING TWO HANDS TO GO INTO HELL, INTO THE FIRE THAT NEVER SHALL BE QUENCHED: WHERE THEIR WORM DIETH NOT, AND THE FIRE IS NOT QUENCHED." Several years ago in the course of my duties I was called to the home of a person who had become mentally disturbed. When I arrived at the home I found the lady in bed with a bloody sheet pulled over half her face. I said to her, "Sarah what have you done?" She immediately pulled the sheet back and said as best she could, "Brother Bob, The Bible says it is better to enter into heaven without a member of your body than to go to hell with it, and you know I have had a problem with my tongue, and so I tried to cut it off." Now you understand that no sensible person would do this. The Bible does not say that we could go to heaven by eliminating the member of our body that bothers us, but is only using strong language to reveal the awfulness of hell.

Fools
Luke 12:19-20

The Bible says: "AND I WILL SAY TO MY SOUL, SOUL, THOU HAST MUCH GOODS LAID UP FOR MANY YEARS; TAKE THINE EASE, EAT DRINK, AND BE MERRY. BUT GOD SAID UNTO HIM, THOU FOOL, THIS NIGHT THY SOUL SHALL BE REQUIRED OF THEE: THEN WHOSE SHALL THOSE THINGS BE, WHICH THOU HAS PROVIDED?" Sometimes man gets his values out of place like this rich farmer that God describes as a fool, and they need to be shocked into reality. This is exactly what happened to Lee Trevino, Bobby Nichols, and Jerry Heard sometime ago as these professional golfers were struck by lightning on a golf course. Lee Trevino said later in a news conference, "I found out that a two-foot side hiller is not the most important thing in the world." Bobby Nichols said, "I fell down and got up and started running through the trees and things." These men had a hospital to run to but where will you run at the end of life if you have lived your life with wrong values?

The Great Blackout
Matthew 8:12

The Bible says: "BUT THE CHILDREN OF THE KINGDOM SHALL BE CAST OUT INTO OUTER DARKNESS: THERE SHALL BE WEEPING AND GNASHING OF TEETH." Some time ago, newspapers around the country carried the story of the blackout in New York City that left ten million people in darkness and that literally, shut down the airports, bus terminals, and other means of transportation. Hospitals were forced to use emergency power supplies. Frozen foods spoiled, costing millions. Governor Hugh L. Cary sent state troops into the area, but in spite of all that Mayor Beame described, it was a night of terror for some as the burning and looting continued. Some have called this the "Billion Dollar Blackout," others the "Great Blackout." However, the world's greatest blackout is yet to come. It will be a blackout with no hope of coming light. It will be an eternity of terror for some – for those who have spurned God's grace and rejected Jesus Christ as Saviour. The Bible says these will be cast into outer darkness! Will this be your case?

The Bread Of Life
John 6:35

The Bible says in John 6:35: "AND JESUS SAID UNTO THEM, I AM THE BREAD OF LIFE: HE THAT COMETH TO ME SHALL NEVER HUNGER; . . ." Bread is the staff of life. It is common on every table. Because it is common and essential to life, Jesus used it to illustrate how essential to every man's life He was. Many turn from Christ the true bread to the many kinds of false bread. One of these is ASTROLOGY. Americans spend four million dollars a year on this superstition. Another is HEDONISM, the compulsive pursuit for pleasure. Another is MATERIALISM. Madison Avenue never teaches us to ask if we need something, only if we want it. Today men are searching for bread, but finding only stones. That has led to the pessimism of our day that is exemplified by Earnest Hemingway in his novel *Death In The Afternoon.* There he writes, "There is no remedy for anything in life . . . death is a sovereign remedy for all misfortunes." Later Hemingway followed his own advice by blowing his brains out. Friend, when will you come to Christ and find this true bread that never spoils or fails?

Life's Contrast
Romans 6:23

The Bible says: "FOR THE WAGES OF SIN IS DEATH; BUT THE GIFT OF GOD IS ETERNAL LIFE THROUGH JESUS CHRIST OUR LORD." One day I drove to Dallas to pick up my daughter who was a nursing student at Baylor School of Nursing. As I was waiting for her I walked to a window and looked out. On one side of the street I saw a housing addition that was the very epitome of poverty, while on the other side, I saw some of the most modern buildings in existence. On one side of the street I saw poverty while on the other side signs of affluence. I gazed upon one building that housed all the cancer patients and thought of those dying. I looked at another building where new life was beginning as new babies were being born into the world. As I stood there gazing, I thought of how life surrounds us with its contrasts. It is so spiritual! There is a Satan, but also a Saviour! There is a hell, but also a heaven! There is sin, but also grace and forgiveness. God's Word tells us how to find it.

Hope
Titus 2:11-14

The Bible says: "FOR THE GRACE OF GOD THAT BRINGETH SALVATION HATH APPEARED TO ALL MEN, TEACHING US THAT, DENYING UNGODLINESS AND WORLDLY LUSTS, WE SHOULD LIVE SOBERLY, RIGHTEOUSLY, AND GODLY, IN THIS PRESENT WORLD; LOOKING FOR THAT BLESSED HOPE, AND THE GLORIOUS APPEARING OF THE GREAT GOD AND OUR SAVIOUR JESUS CHRIST." A few years ago a group of sociologists did some case work in New York City to find out why so many people were committing suicide, and they found out that inevitably the people had everything to live with but nothing to live for. They had put their hope in things that would forsake them at death. The person who has trusted Jesus Christ for salvation has a hope that will not only lead to the grave but through the grave and to that day when it finds fulfillment with the second return of Christ.

Empty Hands
Matthew 16:26

The Bible says: "FOR WHAT IS A MAN PROFITED, IF HE SHALL GAIN THE WHOLE WORLD, AND LOSE HIS OWN SOUL? OR WHAT SHALL A MAN GIVE IN EXCHANGE FOR HIS SOUL?" We live in a world with people greedy for gold, making plans for old age with none for the new age. Alexander the Great illustrates the futility of it all. Before he died he instructed his men to cut holes in the side of the casket that was to bear his body and to allow his hands to protrude from them as they bore his body through the streets. Alexander the Great wanted to show everyone that though he had conquered the known world then, that he was leaving it empty-handed. A man's life consisteth not in the abundance of the things he possesseth. The Bible is true, "WHAT IS A MAN PROFITED, IF HE SHALL GAIN THE WHOLE WORLD AND LOSE HIS OWN SOUL?"

The Lamb's Book Of Life
Revelation 20:15

The Bible says in Revelation 20:15: "AND WHOSOEVER WAS NOT FOUND WRITTEN IN THE BOOK OF LIFE WAS CAST INTO THE LAKE OF FIRE." George Whitfield was a great old preacher who would often dramatize his sermons. Once as he stood in Pennsylvania preaching, he looked toward heaven and said, "Father Abraham, whom have you in heaven? Any Methodists? Any Baptists? Any Seceders?" Abraham replied, "No, all who are here are Christians. They are those who have come to Christ and had their sins washed in the blood of the Lamb." When shall this world learn that it is not just "WHAT" you belong to but "WHO" you belong to that shall assure one of entrance into God's Heaven. Vance Havener has said that when we stand before God's Judgment the most important book will not be the "Bank Book of Finance, the Blue Book of Society, or the Church Book of Membership but the Lamb's Book of Life." Only when we come to Christ can our name be recorded in that most important book.

Free Homes
Ephesians 2:8

The Bible says in Ephesians 2:8: "FOR BY GRACE ARE YE SAVED THROUGH FAITH; AND THAT NOT OF YOURSELVES: IT IS THE GIFT OF GOD:..." Have you ever noticed how people are looking for something free? If a store wants to attract a crowd it offers a free bicycle, a free television, or a free car. Recently I heard of an unusual offer, the offer of a free home. It was to be given away in a perfect city with one hundred percent pure water, perpetual lighting, permanent pavement, beautiful music, free transportation, and guaranteed immunity from illness. This home was not offered to just one lucky person, but to everyone who would obtain a contract. The home, of course, was heaven and the contract called for faith in the Lord Jesus Christ who offers salvation as a free gift to all. By the way friend, have you signed your contract yet? If not, do so today for God says: "BEHOLD NOW IS THE ACCEPTED TIME, NOW IS THE DAY OF SALVATION." (II Cor. 6:2)

Eternal Darkness
Joel 2:31-32

The Bible says in Joel 2:31-32: "THE SUN SHALL BE TURNED INTO DARKNESS, AND THE MOON INTO BLOOD, BEFORE THE GREAT AND THE TERRIBLE DAY OF THE LORD COME. AND IT SHALL COME TO PASS, THAT WHOSOEVER SHALL CALL ON THE NAME OF THE LORD SHALL BE DELIVERED:..." A few years ago practically the entire Eastern Coast was plunged into darkness. When the darkness occurred I heard that the New York Hilton Hotel burned thirty thousand candles and a candle on a New York street sold for as much as $7.50. People were stranded on elevators between floors, pilots had no beacons to guide them down, and hospitals had to resort to emergency power units for power to operate. This was called the great blackout, but it wasn't. The Bible speaks of the blackout over Egypt, the blackout at creation, the blackout at Calvary, and the blackout of human sin. But the greatest is the blackout of eternity. Jesus is the light of the world and every man will need this light when he comes to the end of life and the lights go out.

Chapter 3
Moving Toward Maturity

The Christians Benefits
Hebrews 6:9

The Bible says: "BUT, BELOVED, WE ARE PERSUADED BETTER THINGS OF YOU, AND THINGS THAT ACCOMPANY SALVATION, THOUGH WE THUS SPEAK." Recently the newspaper carried the story of an elderly woman who died in West Palm Beach, Florida. During her life, the woman had dressed shabbily and almost in rags. She had begged for food at the doors of her neighbors. Her house was described as filthy and dirty. When the proper authorities went to her house they discovered that she had over one million dollars in cash and securities, yet, she lived like a pauper. That seems strange but not nearly as strange as the way some Christians live. The Apostle Paul says we have been blessed with all spiritual blessings. We have not only been saved but given the blessings and things that accompany salvation. There is more to being a Christian than missing hell when we die. The Christian in salvation is equipped to live a life in the now. A study of God's Word will help us to discover these benefits.

Satan's Lie
Genesis 3:4-5

The Bible says: "AND THE SERPENT SAID UNTO THE WOMAN, YE SHALL NOT SURELY DIE: FOR GOD DOTH KNOW THAT IN THE DAY YE EAT THEREOF, THEN YOUR EYES SHALL BE OPENED, AND YE SHALL BE AS GODS, KNOWING GOOD AND EVIL." Jesus, in the Gospel of John, identifies Satan as a liar and the father of all lies. In the verse we just read we find his first and biggest lie. It is simply that Adam and Eve can be Godly without God. One remembers that God created man in His own image. It was and always has been God's intention to make man like himself, Godly. However, Satan comes and says, "Eat and your eyes will be opened, and you will be like God." People still believe this lie! When will the world learn that a man cannot be Godly without God, spiritual without Spirit, and Christian without Christ. When will we learn that it takes God to be a man!

The Three Men In The Bible
I Corinthians 2:14

The Bible says: "BUT THE NATURAL MAN RECEIVETH NOT THE THINGS OF THE SPIRIT OF GOD: FOR THEY ARE FOOLISHNESS UNTO HIM: NEITHER CAN HE KNOW THEM, BECAUSE THEY ARE SPIRITUALLY DISCERNED." The Bible most emphatically speaks of three men. These three men have always been with us and will be until Jesus returns. Let me briefly identify them today and see which one best describes you. The Bible speaks of the natural man, the carnal man and the spiritual man. The natural man is the unsaved and unregenerate man, the man that God wants to give a new nature to through the new birth. The carnal man is a saved man but who as Paul says seeks the things of the flesh and works for self-satisfaction instead of soul-satisfaction. It is often difficult to distinguish this man from the lost. The spiritual man is the man who has been born again, and who is living the Spirit-controlled life. Which man best identifies you?

Much More
Romans 5:10

The Bible says: "FOR IF, WHEN WE WERE ENEMIES, WE WERE RECONCILED TO GOD BY THE DEATH OF HIS SON, MUCH MORE, BEING RECONCILED, WE SHALL BE SAVED BY HIS LIFE." Many people think that when they are saved and join the church that this is all there is to being a Christian. To those who think that way, they need to read the five "MUCH MORES" that Paul speaks of in Romans 5. These "Much Mores" remind me of the little boy who had never before been to a parade and convinced his father to let him go. The father reached into his pocket and pulled out a dollar and said, "Don't lose it; this is all I have." The little boy headed for town to see his first circus. He arrived in time for the parade. He watched all the parade and then, at the very last, the clown came with the sign which read, "THE END." The little boy rushed up to him and gave him the dollar. What a tragedy that he thought he saw the circus when he only saw the parade. This is true too often with people when they first become Christians. There is much more to come.

Consecration
Romans 12:2

The Bible says: "AND BE NOT CONFORMED TO THIS WORLD: BUT BE YE TRANSFORMED BY THE RENEWING OF YOUR MIND..." When I was a small boy I enjoyed going out and trying to catch lizards. I remember that often I would find a beautiful green lizard on a blade of grass and just about the time I would reach for it, it would jump off onto some piece of wood and turn as brown as the wood itself. I found out that some lizards could take their color from their surroundings and these lizards were called Chameleons. Quite often in life I find Christians like that. Their life styles change from Sunday to Monday. They allow the world to determine their fashions and the kind of life they will live. It was to people like this that Paul said: "DON'T BE CONFORMED TO THIS WORLD," or as Phillips says: "Don't let the world pour you into its mold!" Why not let God mold your life?

Spiritual Handicaps
Romans 8:1

The Bible says: "THERE IS THEREFORE NOW NO CONDEMNATION TO THEM WHICH ARE IN CHRIST JESUS, WHO WALK NOT AFTER THE FLESH, BUT AFTER THE SPIRIT." The phrase "NO CONDEMNATION" simply means "no handicap." What a tragedy it is that many Christians live under self-inflicted and self-imposed handicaps because they walk and live their lives according to the flesh instead of the spirit of God. They remind me of the farmer who planted a pumpkin in a one gallon glass jug. One day, as he walked through his pumpkin field, he found a small pumpkin on a vine and without breaking the vine, placed the pumpkin inside the jug. Finally, when the time came to harvest the pumpkins, he came across the glass jug and found the pumpkin had filled it completely and with no more room to grow, had stopped growing. He broke the jug and found the pumpkin to be the exact size and shape of the jug. Men are often like that pumpkin. They put themselves into jugs which handicap their spiritual growth. Avoid this mistake in your life!

The Indwelling Christ
Ephesians 3:17

The Bible says in Ephesians 3:17: "THAT CHRIST MAY DWELL IN YOUR HEARTS BY FAITH; . . ." This phrase is taken from a prayer that the Apostle Paul prays for believers. He knows that Christ lives in the hearts of those who have believed, but here he is praying that Christ might not only live in us but dwell in us. The word dwell comes from two Greek words meaning; "To live in a home," and "down." The tense speaks of finality and the word for "down" speaks of permanency. Thus, Paul is simply praying that the Christ who lives within us "....MIGHT FINALLY AND PERMANENTLY SETTLE DOWN AND FEEL COMPLETELY AT HOME IN OUR HEARTS." It is not enough for us to have Christ in us; we are to see that He is able to feel at home in us. Paul tells us that the way to do this is through our faith in Christ.

Following Through
Luke 9:23

The Bible says: "AND HE SAID TO THEM ALL, IF ANY MAN WILL COME AFTER ME, LET HIM DENY HIMSELF, AND TAKE UP HIS CROSS DAILY, AND FOLLOW ME," Recently I heard a friend of mine who played tennis in college and who is an avid tennis enthusiast say, "You know, I am having trouble with my tennis. I hit the ball right, but I don't seem to follow through. I had the same problem with golf and the same problem with bowling." Following through is not only a problem a person sometimes has with tennis, golf, or bowling, but a problem one can experience in the Christian life. The Christian life becomes a victorious life only when the Christian follows through. It is not enough simply to be saved and have your sins forgiven. We must follow that up with daily prayer and Bible study. If your Christian life has become static, maybe it is because you are not following through. Jesus said, "take up your cross daily and follow me."

Spirit Controlled Life
Ephesians 5:18

The Bible says: "AND BE NOT DRUNK WITH WINE, WHEREIN IS EXCESS; BUT BE FILLED WITH THE SPIRIT;" A few years ago I heard Richard LeTourneau speak of the giant tree crusher his father's company had built to help clear land in the jungles. It would clear around one hundred acres a day, and was controlled by only four or five buttons, with one operator at the controls. Mr. LeTourneau said if it ever got out of control it could destroy a city block. The one at the controls determined whether it would be an instrument of construction or destruction. A man's life is like that to a certain extent. It can be an instrument of construction or destruction. It is the one who controls it that makes the difference; that is why the Bible says: "BE CONTROLLED BY THE SPIRIT."

Be Filled With The Spirit
Ephesians 5:18

The Bible says: "AND BE NOT DRUNK WITH WINE, WHEREIN IS EXCESS; BUT BE FILLED WITH THE SPIRIT." Normally when we use the word fill we use it in the sense of filling a bottle with water, a balloon with air, or a tank with gas, but that is not the meaning of the word here. Here the word FILLED means to be guided or controlled by the Spirit. Paul makes a contrast here between a person being filled with wine, and a person being filled with the Spirit to emphasize the importance of being filled with the Spirit. When one is filled with wine he is driven and impelled by wine, but when filled with the Spirit he is driven and impelled by the Spirit. As wine brings out everything bad, the Spirit brings out everything good. As wine clouds the mind, the Spirit clears the mind. As wine drives a man to despair, the Spirit drives a man to victory. This is why Paul says: "AND BE NOT DRUNK WITH WINE, BUT BE FILLED WITH THE SPIRIT." Which controls you?

The Strength Of Ignorance
Romans 6:2-3

The Bible says: "GOD FORBID. HOW SHALL WE, THAT ARE DEAD TO SIN, LIVE ANY LONGER THEREIN? KNOW YE NOT, THAT SO MANY OF US AS WERE BAPTIZED INTO JESUS CHRIST WERE BAPTIZED INTO HIS DEATH?" Once I read the story of an immense lion kept securely in a slender cage. A visitor seeing him, asked if the lion could not tear the cage to pieces and get out. The keeper said, "Yes, but he doesn't know it." You see the lion had been put in the cage when very small, at an age when he could not tear the cage apart, and as he grew he was held by a psychological chain. There are so many things that hold people in bondage – things they could overcome and overpower if they only knew the resources available to them. Sin and Satan are among those things. The Bible tells us that when we come to Christ, sin and Satan loose their grip on us and have no power over us. They only dominate us because we let them. That is why the Bible says that we are to know what we have in Christ.

How To Hear God
James 1:21

The Bible says: "WHEREFORE LAY APART ALL FILTHINESS AND SUPERFLUITY OF NAUGHTINESS, AND RECEIVE WITH MEEKNESS THE ENGRAFTED WORD, WHICH IS ABLE TO SAVE YOUR SOULS." Hearing God is important, and James in this verse of scripture tells us that to hear God one must get rid of all defilement as a man strips off soiled garments, or as a snake sloughs off its skin. There are two words that James uses for defilement here. He uses the word filthiness and naughtiness or wickedness. One is used for the filth that soils one's clothing, and the other is used in a medical sense to speak of wax that gets in the ear. James is telling his readers to get rid of everything which would close their ears to the true word of God. When wax gathers in the ear, it can make a man deaf; and a man's own sins can make him deaf to the voice of God. If you are having trouble hearing the voice of God, it may be that you have wax in your ears, and need to get rid of your sins.

Divine Direction
Proverbs 3:5-6

The Bible says: "TRUST IN THE LORD WITH ALL THINE HEART; AND LEAN NOT UNTO THINE OWN UNDERSTANDING. IN ALL THY WAYS ACKNOWLEDGE HIM, AND HE SHALL DIRECT THY PATHS." Once a young couple became lost on a rural road and spotting an old farmer, they stopped their car and asked him a question, "Sir, could you tell us where this road will take us?" Without a moment's hesitation the old farmer said, "Son, this road will take you anywhere in the world you want to go, if you are moving in the right direction." It is not enough to find the right road on which to travel. You must be moving in the right direction. A person can be on the right road and still get run over if they are standing still. One of the wisest men that ever lived tells us how to get the right directions with which to travel through life. He says: "TRUST IN THE LORD . . . IN ALL THY WAYS ACKNOWLEDGE HIM, AND HE SHALL DIRECT THY PATHS." Regular church attendance will help us to know more about trusting him.

Why Have The Showers Been Withheld?
Jeremiah 3:3

The Bible says: "THEREFORE THE SHOWERS HAVE BEEN WITHHOLDEN, AND THERE HATH BEEN NO LATTER RAIN; AND THOU HADST A WHORE'S FOREHEAD, THOU REFUSEDST TO BE ASHAMED." The prophet Jeremiah, here, is explaining why the showers of God's blessings had been withheld from his people. The showers had been withheld because God's people had sinned and they were neither sorry nor ashamed of their wickedness. Their sins had formed a log jam that prevented the flow of God's blessings to them and through them. Years ago, when logs were floated down the river from where they were cut to the saw mills located up and down the rivers, there were log jams that would often occur. When they did, a man called a lumber jack would take a long pole with a hook on the end of it and walk out on the logs until he found the log causing the jam and jerk it loose, enabling the other logs to continue to flow. When God's blessings cease flowing we, too, must find the sin causing the jam and move it so that God's blessings might continue to flow.

God's Cure For Tugging
John 7:37-38

The Bible says: "IN THE LAST DAY, THAT GREAT DAY OF THE FEAST, JESUS STOOD AND CRIED, SAYING, IF ANY MAN THIRST, LET HIM COME UNTO ME, AND DRINK. HE THAT BELIEVETH ON ME, AS THE SCRIPTURE HATH SAID, OUT OF HIS BELLY SHALL FLOW RIVERS OF LIVING WATER." As a small boy, I lived in a saw mill town where the only water system was a well at the intersection of the dirt streets. Therefore, I spent a great deal of my time carrying and tugging water which my mother used for washing the clothes, for cooking, and for bathing. I never shall forget how happy I was when we finally moved to another city and into a house with running water, where all we had to do was to turn the faucet on and run the water into the house. You know many people's religion is like that. They are always toiling and tugging and struggling. Jesus says it will all cease when we discover the rivers of living water that flow from within every believer's life.

Service
Romans 6:16

The Bible says: "KNOW YE NOT, THAT TO WHOM YE YIELD YOURSELVES SERVANTS TO OBEY, HIS SERVANTS YE ARE TO WHOM YE OBEY; WHETHER OF SIN UNTO DEATH, OR OF OBEDIENCE UNTO RIGHTEOUSNESS?" The great preacher R.G. Lee once said, "I know men and women with diamond and ruby abilities who are worth no more to God through the churches than a punctured Japanese nickel in a Chinese bazaar; people who have pipe organ abilities but who make no more music for the cause of Christ than a wheezy saxophone in an idiot's hands; people who have incandescent light power but who make no more light for God than a smoked up lantern with a smoke blackened globe on a stormy night; people who have locomotive powers doing pushcart work for God; people with steam shovel abilities who are doing teaspoon work for God." Paul reminds us that inside the body of every believer there is the flesh and there is the spirit, and both want to use the members of our body. Let me ask you today, "TO WHOM WILL YOU YIELD THE MEMBERS OF YOUR BODY TO SERVE?"

The Risen Life
Colossians 3:1

The Bible says: "IF YE THEN BE RISEN WITH CHRIST, SEEK THOSE THINGS WHICH ARE ABOVE, WHERE CHRIST SITTETH ON THE RIGHT HAND OF GOD." The Apostle Paul says being saved by God's grace is like a dead man being brought back to life. When a person who is dead in trespasses and sin finds new life in Christ he is then to seek those things that are above. No where does God tell us to lay up treasures down here but always in heaven. The real tragedy is that too many prepare for old age and not for the New Age. They have everything to live with but nothing to live for. It is said that after Michelangelo painted the Sistine ceiling he had been in the habit of looking upward so long that he found it impossible to read a book or do a drawing in any position except upward. May God grant that this can become spiritually true in the life of every believer. The risen life is proven by what we seek after. What are your greatest priorities in life?

Living The Risen Life
Galatians 2:20

The Bible says: "I AM CRUCIFIED WITH CHRIST: NEVERTHELESS I LIVE; YET NOT I, BUT CHRIST LIVETH IN ME: AND THE LIFE WHICH I NOW LIVE IN THE FLESH I LIVE BY THE FAITH OF THE SON OF GOD, WHO LOVED ME, AND GAVE HIMSELF FOR ME." A little boy who really enjoyed playing cowboys and Indians spent one entire day riding his stick horse all over the neighborhood. At the end of the day he came home dead tired. He complained to his father that he was so tired he didn't know what to do. The father said, "Well son, why are you so tired?" He said, "Well Daddy, real cowboys have real horses, but I had to do all of my galloping for myself." There is a real message in this modern day parable for Christians, for it is far too often that we do our own galloping instead of letting Christ live in us and empower us to serve Him. In John 8:27 Jesus said. "I do nothing of myself." The Apostle Paul gives us the key to life and service when in Galatians 2:20 he says, ". . . NOT I BUT CHRIST LIVETH IN ME . . ." Why not claim that power for your life?

Sin In The Believer
I John 2:1-2

The Bible says: "MY LITTLE CHILDREN, THESE THINGS WRITE I UNTO YOU, THAT YOU SIN NOT. AND IF ANY MAN SIN, WE HAVE AN ADVOCATE WITH THE FATHER, JESUS CHRIST THE RIGHTEOUS: AND HE IS THE PROPITIATION FOR OUR SINS: AND NOT FOR OURS ONLY, BUT ALSO FOR THE SINS OF THE WHOLE WORLD." The Bible makes it clear that God does not want His children to sin and that the person who habitually and continually does, cannot claim to be saved. However, the fact that verse makes provision for the sinning saint indicates that pollution is possible. While the believer who sins may not lose his relationship with Christ, his fellowship is affected. Union with Christ is so strong that nothing can break it, but our communion is so fragile that the smallest sin can break it. What must the believer do who has sinned? John says if we confess our sins He is faithful to forgive us. This is God's promise to you today.

Possessing The Mind Of Christ
Philippians 2:5

The Bible says: "LET THIS MIND BE IN YOU, WHICH WAS ALSO IN CHRIST JESUS." The real battle that is going on in the world today is the battle for the mind. The one who controls the mind will also control the world. This inspired Paul to write and admonish the Philippians to have the mind of Christ. It is said that when Alexander the Great was twelve years old, his father, King Phillip of Macedonia, arranged for Aristotle to become his companion and tutor. Later, Alexander claimed the great philosopher to be his father. He meant that while he had received his body from Phillip, Aristotle was the father of his mind. Alexander said he was more grateful to Aristotle for knowledge than to Phillip for life. As sons of God we must choose whether we will allow our Heavenly Father or Satan to control our minds and the purpose for our existence. The Bible says: "LET THIS MIND BE IN YOU WHICH WAS IN CHRIST JESUS."

The Power Of The Holy Spirit
Acts 1:8

The Bible says: "BUT YE SHALL RECEIVE POWER, AFTER THAT THE HOLY GHOST IS COME UPON YOU: AND YE SHALL BE WITNESSES UNTO ME BOTH IN JERUSALEM, AND IN ALL JUDEA, AND IN SAMARIA, AND UNTO THE UTTERMOST PART OF THE EARTH." We live in a world in which people are constantly speaking about power. They speak of the power of the atom, the power of the mind, the power of great engines, and the power of money. What is the Christian's power? In Acts 1:8 we are told our power rests in the Holy Spirit of God. The poet put it in these words;

> "A city full of Churches
> Great preachers, lettered men
> Grand music, choirs, and organs
> If these all fail what then?
> Refinement, education, they have the very best
> Their plans and schemes are perfect
> They give themselves no rest
> They have the best of talent, they try their uttermost
> But what they need my Brother, is God the Holy Ghost."

When God saves a person, He empowers that person with the Holy Spirit. Do you know this Power? If not, why not?

Besetting Sins
Hebrews 12:1

The Bible says: "...LET US LAY ASIDE EVERY WEIGHT, AND THE SIN WHICH DOTH SO EASILY BESET US, AND LET US RUN WITH PATIENCE THE RACE THAT IS SET BEFORE US." The Apostle Paul compares the Christian life to a race and here admonishes the believer to put aside besetting sins as a sprinter would put aside weights he had used in training. Often our spiritual progress is hampered because we hang on to sins that impede our progress. We are like the little girl who was going to take part in some sprinting races. To help her, her father tied ankle weights around her legs and she ran the fifty yards in eight seconds. Her father then asked her to go back to the starting line and take the weights off and run it again. To his utter amazement she ran the same distance again in eight seconds. He later discovered she had taken them off her feet and carried them! The believer must not only take sin off but lay it aside.

Steps To Spiritual Power
Psalm 56:12

The Bible says: "THY VOWS ARE UPON ME, O GOD: I WILL RENDER PRAISES UNTO THEE. FOR THOU HAST DELIVERED MY SOUL FROM DEATH: WILT NOT THOU DELIVER MY FEET FROM FAILING, THAT I MAY WALK BEFORE GOD IN THE LIGHT OF THE LIVING?" Many people object to making vows, but in the Bible many of the great men of God were directed by vows. It is a serious thing to make a vow, but the man who refuses is usually one who does not want to make a true commitment. Dr. A.W. Tozer speaks of five things every Christian should commit himself to if he is to have spiritual power. First, he must deal thoroughly with sin; secondly, never own anything; thirdly, never defend yourself; fourthly, never pass anything on about anybody else that will hurt him; and fifthly; never accept any glory. The man who will vow to commit himself to these five principles will know what it is to have spiritual power.

Divine Guidance
Proverbs 3:5

The Bible says in Proverbs 3:5: "TRUST IN THE LORD WITH ALL THINE HEART; AND LEAN NOT UNTO THINE OWN UNDERSTANDING. IN ALL THY WAYS ACKNOWLEDGE HIM, AND HE SHALL DIRECT THY PATHS." I am told by pilots of airplanes that flying on instruments is a serious but interesting part of flying. When one is flying on instruments he is entirely dependent on the instruments to guide him. Many pilots have crashed their planes because they disagreed with the instruments and responded according to reason instead of following the directions given by the instruments. Life is like that. You can't always see what's ahead, but like instruments in the cockpit, Jesus Christ is always willing to guide you through the storms and overcast skies of life. How good to know He's in command at the controls. A study of God's Word will help you to know how to know Him and make Him the pilot of your life.

Pressing Onward
Philippians 3:14

The Bible says: "I PRESS TOWARD THE MARK FOR THE PRIZE OF THE HIGH CALLING OF GOD IN CHRIST JESUS." We remember Peter and Thomas not because of their doubts and failures but because of their great confessions. Theodore Roosevelt once said, "It is not the critic who counts; not the man who points out how the strong man stumbled or where the doer of deeds could have done better. The credit belongs to the man who is actually in the arena; whose face is marred by dust and sweat and blood; who strives valiantly; who errs and comes short again and again; who knows the great enthusiasm, the great devotions, and spends himself in a worthy cause; who at the best knows in the end the triumph of high achievement; and who at the worst, if he fails, at least fails while daring greatly; so that his place shall never be with those cold and timid souls who know neither victory nor defeat." This was the spirit of Paul who said, "I PRESS TOWARD THE MARK FOR THE PRIZE OF THE HIGH CALLING OF GOD IN CHRIST JESUS."

The Christian's Power
Luke 24:49

The Bible says: "AND, BEHOLD, I SEND THE PROMISE OF MY FATHER UPON YOU: BUT TARRY YE IN THE CITY OF JERUSALEM, UNTIL YE BE ENDUED WITH POWER FROM ON HIGH." Christ gave the early believers the commission to evangelize the world, but then commanded them to tarry until they were endued with the power of the Holy Spirit from on high. It is important that we know that the only person who can confront the world with the claims of Christ is the spirit filled believer. Yet it is a sad fact that while many people are on the right side of Calvary they are on the wrong side of Pentecost. They have not paid the price to be filled with His power. The average person in his life time spends twenty-five years sleeping, nineteen years working, six years traveling, nine years watching television, six years dressing, four years sick and six months in devotionals. Is there any wonder that there is a lack of power in the lives of the believers today? Claim God's power today for both your LIFE AND LABOR.

Discipline
I Corinthians 9:24

The Bible says: "KNOW YE NOT THAT THEY WHICH RUN IN A RACE RUN ALL, BUT ONE RECEIVETH THE PRIZE? SO RUN, THAT YE MAY OBTAIN." A famous golfer was once asked, "Isn't golf a lot of luck?" The golfer replied, "It certainly is, but I have noticed the more I practice, the luckier I am." Someone said that the key to living a victorious Christian life is not desire but discipline and dedication. Most people want to live a Christian life, witness and support the church. There is nothing wrong with their desire; they simply lack the discipline and dedication necessary for the achievement of it. Paul, the Apostle, says that living the Christian life is like running a race. One must discipline himself and give the race the very best that he has. Don't blame God for a defeated life until you enter into a disciplined and dedicated life.

Cleaning Out The Well
Genesis 26:18

The Bible says: "AND ISAAC DIGGED AGAIN THE WELLS OF WATER, WHICH THEY HAD DIGGED IN THE DAYS OF ABRAHAM HIS FATHER; FOR THE PHILISTINES HAD STOPPED THEM AFTER THE DEATH OF ABRAHAM: AND HE CALLED THEIR NAMES AFTER THE NAMES BY WHICH HIS FATHER HAD CALLED THEM." Several years ago when my children were all very young, we made a trip one summer down to my parent's farm. We spent several days, and shortly after we returned home I received a letter from my mother. In her letter she told me that after we had left, the water in their well had become polluted. She said that they had discovered that while we were there some of the children had crawled up under the old farm house and had gotten some rotten potatoes and thrown them into the well, polluting the water. Needless to say the well had to be cleaned out. Lives are often like that. They become polluted with sin and get stopped up; then we must come to Christ for cleansing.

Unused Power
Acts 1:8

The Bible says: "BUT YE SHALL RECEIVE POWER, AFTER THAT THE HOLY GHOST IS COME UPON YOU: AND YE SHALL BE WITNESSES UNTO ME..." An American and an English gentleman was viewing the Niagara whirlpool rapids, when he said to his friend, "Come, and I'll show you the greatest unused power in the world." Then he took him to the foot of the Niagara Falls. "There," he said, "is the greatest unused power in the world." "Ah, no, my brother, not so," was the reply. "The greatest unused power in the world is the Holy Spirit of the Living God." It is God's Holy Spirit that convicts men of their sins and convinces them of the love of God and the power of Jesus to save. It is the Holy Spirit that enables the new believer to live the life that they have been given in Jesus. Dear friend, if your life is a struggle, then why not claim this power for your life?

Nothing But Leaves
Mark 11:13

The Bible says: "AND SEEING A FIG TREE AFAR OFF HAVING LEAVES, HE CAME, IF HAPLY HE MIGHT FIND ANYTHING THEREON: AND WHEN HE CAME TO IT, HE FOUND NOTHING BUT LEAVES;..." In Pilgrim's Progress the interpreter took Christiana and her family out into the garden to a tree whose inside was all rotten and gone, and yet it grew and had leaves. Mercy asked, "What means this?" "This tree," said he, "whose outside is fair, and whose inside is all rotten, is that to which many may be compared that are in the garden of God: who with their mouths speak high in behalf of God, but indeed will do nothing for Him; whose leaves are fair, but their heart good for nothing but to be tinder for the devil's tinder box." Jesus in this story is condemning external, hypocritical religion. There is nothing more detesting to a Holy God than people who profess, but do not possess; whose talking is better than their walking and who have a "NOTHING BUT LEAVES" kind of religion.

Being
Ephesians 6:10

The Bible says: "FINALLY, MY BRETHREN, BE STRONG IN THE LORD, AND IN THE POWER OF HIS MIGHT. PUT ON THE WHOLE ARMOUR OF GOD, THAT YE MAY BE ABLE TO STAND AGAINST THE WILES OF THE DEVIL." We, as preachers, so often spend more time telling people how to become Christians than we do telling them how to BE the Christians that they have become. It is not so much what we do but who we are that concerns God, for if our being is not right it is for sure that our doing will amount to little. Therefore God repeatedly uses the imperative form of the word BE. He commands us: To be strong in the Lord (II Tim. 4:1), To be separated (II Cor. 6:17), To be not deceived (Gal. 6:7-9), To be ready (Matt. 10:16), To be filled with the spirit (Eph. 5:18), and to be perfect or mature believers. In light of these commands, what kind of a Christian are you?

Dead Or Alive
Revelation 3:1

The Bible says: "... I KNOW THY WORKS, THAT THOU HAST A NAME THAT THOU LIVEST, AND ART DEAD." What God said to the Church at Sardis He is able to say to any church or individual. You may, through your church attendance, contributions, and public image give the impression of being much alive spiritually, but God knows the real truth about the real you. I read once the story of the captain of a Greenland whaling vessel who one night found himself surrounded by icebergs. The next morning he saw a ship and got as close as he could to it and cried with a loud voice, "SHIP AHOY." There was, however, no response. Looking through the porthole he saw a man sitting at a table as if writing in a log book. However, when he boarded the ship he found the man frozen to death. As he read his log book he discovered the man had been dead and drifting in the Arctic for about thirteen years. I wonder how many listening to my voice today are on board the ship known as the church and to many they appear to be alive, but to God who knows, they are dead. What is your true condition today?

God's Law
Romans 3:19

The Bible says in Romans 3:19: "NOW WE KNOW WHAT THINGS SOEVER THE LAW SAITH, IT SAITH TO THEM WHO ARE UNDER THE LAW: THAT EVERY MOUTH MAY BE STOPPED, AND ALL THE WORLD MAY BECOME GUILTY BEFORE GOD." When I was a small boy I would often visit some of our relatives down on the farm. Inevitably on the back porch there was a broken piece of a mirror nailed on the wall with a basin of water beneath it. The men would come in from the fields and look in the mirror and then wash their face and hands. Now the mirror never washed the dirt from their faces and hands. The mirror only showed them where the dirt was. That is exactly what God's law does for every person. Keeping God's commandments and law cannot save a person. It only shows you the dirt in your life and points you to Jesus who can wash away your sins with His precious blood and take away your guilt. A study of God's Word will help you understand this truth.

Prayer
James 4:3

The Bible says: "YE ASK, AND RECEIVE NOT, BECAUSE YE ASK AMISS, THAT YE MAY CONSUME IT UPON YOUR LUSTS." Recently, while leaving a football game where there had been a considerable amount of questionable activity, I happened to notice one of the teams on their knees praying. I thought how good it is to have such a consciousness of prayer, but several thoughts concerning prayer crossed my mind. I thought of how many rush into God's presence without any preparation. I thought of all those who look upon prayer as a means to get something. As I thought of how both teams had probably prayed to win, a humorous story came to my mind – the story of a bear chasing a rabbit. The rabbit was heard praying, "Lord let me run faster to get away," and the bear was heard praying, "Lord bless this food to the nourishment of my body." Now it is obvious that both prayers could not be answered. The Apostle James says, "YE ASK AND RECEIVE NOT, BECAUSE YE ASK AMISS, THAT YE MAY CONSUME IT UPON YOUR LUSTS." Proper prayer gets proper answers.

Dealing With Our Past
Philippians 3:13-14

The Bible says: "BRETHREN, I COUNT NOT MYSELF TO HAVE APPREHENDED: BUT THIS ONE THING I DO, FORGETTING THOSE THINGS WHICH ARE BEHIND, AND REACHING FORTH UNTO THOSE THINGS WHICH ARE BEFORE, I PRESS TOWARD THE MARK FOR THE PRIZE OF THE HIGH CALLING OF GOD IN CHRIST JESUS." There is nothing perhaps that disturbs more people than their past. Even though many have been saved and had their past sins forgiven, they still live under daily guilt. What does the Bible say about this? The Bible says we must forget the past, follow in the present and face the future. There are two things to do with our past. First, we must not repeat our mistakes; and secondly, we must not become historical. One fellow commented that his wife became "HISTORICAL" during a heated argument. His friend said, "You mean HYSTERICAL." "No," he replied, "I mean HISTORICAL. She brought up everything I had done the last thirty years." If we are to properly deal with our past, we must not become historical.

Saving Faith
James 2:14

The Bible says: "WHAT DOTH IT PROFIT, MY BRETHREN, THOUGH A MAN SAY HE HATH FAITH, AND HAVE NOT WORKS? CAN FAITH SAVE HIM?" Let there be no doubt in anyone's mind. The only way that a man can be saved is through faith in Jesus Christ. However, one needs to make a distinction between SAYING faith and SAVING faith. James here speaks of those who SAY they have faith, yet their faith is never put into practice. It is a kind of faith that only gives mental assent to something. James says even the devils of hell have this kind of faith. The devil believes, and gives assent to the fact of the reality of Jesus. James says the faith that saves is the faith that not only gives mental assent but makes a total commitment to the object trusted. I once read the story of the man who pushed a wheelbarrow over a tight wire stretched over Niagara Falls. He then asked how many believed he could push someone in the wheelbarrow over the falls. The people said they believed he could. However, when he asked for a volunteer there were none. Saving faith not only assents to something but also acts upon it.

When God's Law Is Broken
James 2:10

The Bible says: "FOR WHOSOEVER SHALL KEEP THE WHOLE LAW, AND YET OFFEND IN ONE POINT, HE IS GUILTY OF ALL." There are a multitude of people who believe that if their good outweighs their bad then God will take a dim view toward the bad in their lives. It is obvious that God's Word is not in agreement with such a philosophy. The writer of the book of James looks upon all the laws of God as a whole and to disobey and disregard one of the laws of God is to do so to all of them. D.L. Moody compared God's law to a chain of ten links suspending a man over a precipice. If all ten links break, the man falls to his doom. And if only one link breaks, the man falls to his doom just the same. God's Law is holy and demands both respect and obedience. Remember it was God who said: "THEREFORE SHALL YE OBSERVE ALL MY STATUTES AND ALL MY JUDGMENTS AND DO THEM: I AM THE LORD." (Lev. 19:37).

Excess Baggage
Hebrews 12:1

The Bible says in Hebrews 12:1: "WHEREFORE SEEING WE ALSO ARE COMPASSED ABOUT WITH SO GREAT A CLOUD OF WITNESSES, LET US LAY ASIDE EVERY WEIGHT, AND THE SIN WHICH DOTH SO EASILY BESET US . . ." The Bible compares the Christian life to a race and informs us that it is often lost because of sin. A few years ago a woman walked completely across the United States. When she arrived in Florida she was interviewed by a news correspondent who asked her how she made it. She replied that there were good highways across the mountains, good bridges across the rivers and that she walked the desert at night. He then asked her what she felt had been her greatest problem, and she replied, "THE SAND THAT GOT IN MY SHOES." The Christian's greatest problem is sin, but God's provision for it is found in Jesus Christ. Trusting in Him enables one to lay sin aside.

Walking In The Light
Psalm 119:105

The Bible says: "THY WORD IS A LAMP UNTO MY FEET, AND A LIGHT UNTO MY PATH." The Bible admonishes a person to walk by faith, to walk in good works, to walk in obedience, and also to walk in the light of God's Word. Sometimes we don't like to move out into the unknown unless we can see all the way to the end. However, sometimes we need to recognize that life is much like the lights on an automobile. While the automobile lights may not let us see more than a thousand yards ahead of us, we discover that when we travel that distance the light shines that much further ahead. We need to realize that when we respond to the light, the revelation that God gives us on any particular thing includes more light to follow if we follow the first as far as we can. God never told Abraham where He was going when He called him out of Ur of the Chaldees, He just simply said, "into a land that I will show you." God did not want him or any person to get his eyes so fixed on his destination that he takes his eyes off Him. Walking in the light keeps us trusting Him who is light.

Be Still And Know
Psalm 46:10-11

The Bible says: "BE STILL, AND KNOW THAT I AM GOD: I WILL BE EXALTED AMONG THE HEATHEN, I WILL BE EXALTED IN THE EARTH. THE LORD OF HOSTS IS WITH US; THE GOD OF JACOB IS OUR REFUGE." A man once lost his pocket watch in a haystack. His friends all tried to help him but to no avail. Later to his happy surprise a friend found the watch and brought it to him. When he asked the man how he found it, he replied, "I just laid down on the ground and got real quiet and listened for the tick." Could that be one reason why so many people have such trouble in finding God and discovering His reality? Could they be so busy that they drown His voice out with their many activities? For our troubles, heartaches, despairs, and fears the Bible promises us a place of refuge and safety in God our Heavenly Father. Maybe we need to stop running and get still enough to know Him.

Neglected Vineyards
Song of Solomon 1:6

The Bible says: "...THEY MADE ME THE KEEPER OF THE VINEYARDS; BUT MINE OWN VINEYARD HAVE I NOT KEPT." I think that, perhaps, the greatest tragedy that can happen is for a person to become so concerned in helping other peoples' children, in helping to restore other peoples' marriages, and in helping others to grow spiritually that they neglect their own in the process. This seems to be what Solomon is saying here: "...THEY MADE ME THE KEEPER OF THE VINEYARDS; BUT MINE OWN VINEYARDS HAVE I NOT KEPT." It may be that we need to pull up the weeds and rebuild the wall around our own vineyard. A teacher in a Bible school in Africa assigned each pupil a place in the woods to go and pray each day. Day after day, they would go to that assigned place and after a time, had beaten out a path. When they would cease to pray, weeds would begin to grow in the path and the teacher would slip up to their side and say, "There are weeds growing in your path," and their prayer life would be corrected. Are there any weeds in your vineyard?

Sin And Prayer Or Unanswered Prayers
Isaiah 59:1-2

The Bible says: "BEHOLD, THE LORD'S HAND IS NOT SHORTENED, THAT IT CANNOT SAVE; NEITHER HIS EAR HEAVY, THAT IT CANNOT HEAR: BUT YOUR INIQUITIES HAVE SEPARATED BETWEEN YOU AND YOUR GOD, AND YOUR SINS HAVE HID HIS FACE FROM YOU, THAT HE WILL NOT HEAR." Have you ever wondered why your prayers were not answered? Perhaps you came up with many reasons, but God's Word says one of the main reasons why our prayers are not heard is because of sin that separates us from God. While the sun shines every day, often there are clouds that come between the sun and the earth preventing the sun's rays from reaching the earth. Our sins are like clouds that move in between us and God preventing the blessings of God from reaching us. The prophet Isaiah says concerning prayer that our prayers are not heard not because God's hand is shortened, nor because He cannot hear, but because of sin. You cannot live an UNHOLY LIFE AND COMMUNE WITH A HOLY GOD.

Good For Nothing Christians
Matthew 5:13

The Bible says: "YE ARE THE SALT OF THE EARTH: BUT IF THE SALT HAS LOST HIS SAVOUR...IT IS THENCEFORTH GOOD FOR NOTHING..." Jesus compares the Christian to salt, and suggests that what salt is physically, the believer is spiritually to the world in which he lives. Salt creates thirst, it seasons, it brings pain to infected areas, but above all it checks corruption. Salt never cures corruption, but it does prevent the spread of corruption. It is a sobering thought to realize that as Christians we are either CHECKING or CONTRIBUTING to the corruption of the world. It is said that in the years gone by, when the great preacher D.L. Moody would walk into even a barber shop, men would stop their cursing and telling filthy jokes. It is said that Charles Finney would walk into factories and people would fall under conviction. What does your presence do to those you relate to daily? Jesus said: "IF THE SALT HAS LOST HIS SAVOUR . . . IT IS THEREFORE GOOD FOR NOTHING, . . ."

The Tragedy Of An Incomplete Life
Luke 14:28-30

The Bible says: "FOR WHICH OF YOU, INTENDING TO BUILD A TOWER, SITTETH NOT DOWN FIRST, AND COUNTETH THE COST, WHETHER HE HATH SUFFICIENT TO FINISH IT? LEST HAPLY, AFTER HE HATH LAID THE FOUNDATION, AND IS NOT ABLE TO FINISH IT, ALL THAT BEHOLD IT BEGIN TO MOCK HIM, SAYING, THIS MAN BEGAN TO BUILD, AND WAS NOT ABLE TO FINISH." Several years ago as I drove quite frequently on a particular highway I noticed that someone had begun to build a service station but never completed it. They laid the foundations and even built the walls, but never completed the rest of the building. I often wondered why the owner started the building and didn't finish it. It seemed to be such a waste. Here in Luke, Jesus describes another man who began to build something and didn't finish it; a man who embraced the Christian life but never followed through. The result was that he was mocked. We must remember that nothing is so detrimental to Christianity as this and the faith that fizzles before the finish had a flaw in it at the first.

Life At Its Best
Romans 6:13

The Bible says: "NEITHER YIELD YE YOUR MEMBERS AS INSTRUMENTS OF UNRIGHTEOUSNESS UNTO SIN: BUT YIELD YOURSELVES UNTO GOD, AS THOSE THAT ARE ALIVE FROM THE DEAD, AND YOUR MEMBERS AS INSTRUMENTS OF RIGHTEOUSNESS UNTO GOD." Paul reminds us that our life is an instrument, a tool, a weapon that can be used for good or evil. When it is yielded to God, it becomes a means for working good. Emmanuel Ninger was a great artist and a brilliant man, but he misused his talent as an artist and, along with his pictures, painted phony twenty dollar bills. Finally, he was caught and convicted. After his arrest, his portraits were sold at public auction for over five thousand dollars each. The irony of the story is; it took him almost exactly the same length of time to paint a twenty dollar bill as it took him to paint a five thousand dollar portrait. The Bible says that a man's life can be used to promote either evil or righteousness. It all depends upon the one to whom your life is yielded – Satan or the Saviour.

Motives For Giving
Matthew 6:19-20

The Bible says: "LAY NOT UP FOR YOURSELVES TREASURES UPON EARTH, WHERE MOTH AND RUST DOTH CORRUPT, AND WHERE THIEVES BREAK THROUGH AND STEAL: BUT LAY UP FOR YOURSELVES TREASURES IN HEAVEN, WHERE NEITHER MOTH NOT RUST DOTH CORRUPT, AND WHERE THIEVES DO NOT BREAK THROUGH NOR STEAL:" The one motive that Jesus appealed to in order to lead people to devote their material goods to spiritual needs was not love, not duty, but that of self-interest. He did not appeal to the motive of selfishness, but of self-interest. He taught that the way to permanent gain was through giving. One wealthy business man who gave liberally to the causes of Christ, lost all during the depression. A man asked him one day if he regretted having given so much. He replied, "I wish that I had given more, for that is all that I saved." Someone once said, "You can't take it with you, but you can send it ahead of you." What are you doing with that which God has entrusted to you?

Self Examination
I Corinthians 11:31-32

The Bible says: "FOR IF WE WOULD JUDGE OURSELVES, WE SHOULD NOT BE JUDGED. BUT WHEN WE ARE JUDGED, WE ARE CHASTENED OF THE LORD, THAT WE SHOULD NOT BE CONDEMNED WITH THE WORLD." My father was always a good farmer. His corn, his peas, his potatoes were always just a little better than anyone else's. The reason for that was that my father was constantly inspecting his produce. The moment he found an insect he would kill it. God requires each Christian also to maintain a program of self-examination so that at the first sign of trouble, it can be dealt with. The problem with most Christians, however, is that when things are going well for them they are not easily motivated to this activity. Usually a major conflict has to arise before this takes place. How long has it been since you just sat down and got honest with yourself, admitted your faults, and resolved to find the proper solutions to your problems?

How God Sees Us
I Samuel 16:7

The Bible says: "BUT THE LORD SAID UNTO SAMUEL, LOOK NOT ON HIS COUNTENANCE, OR ON THE HEIGHT OF HIS STATURE; BECAUSE I HAVE REFUSED HIM: FOR THE LORD SEETH NOT AS MAN SEETH; FOR MAN LOOKETH ON THE OUTWARD APPEARANCE, BUT THE LORD LOOKETH ON THE HEART." Recently a friend of mine told of a professional con artist, who had been converted from his ways, who travels over the country talking to banks and businesses about how to protect their businesses against such crooks. He said, "You give me a chauffeur, a Rolls Royce, a five hundred dollar suit and a diamond ring and I can get a hundred dollar check cashed in any city." He had proven it before. He had the chauffeur drive him up in front of the bank where the teller could see him get out. He went in and without difficulty she cashed the check. Later when they asked why she cashed the check for a man who had no account with the bank and that she did not know she simply said, "You could just look at him and tell he had money." We can deceive our fellow man, but not God for He looketh upon the heart.

Fruits Of Repentance
Matthew 3:8

The Bible says: "BRING FORTH THEREFORE FRUITS MEET FOR REPENTANCE." Someone has said that repentance is "being so sorry for your sins that you ain't gonna commit them no more." A humorous story illustrates this point. A mother had carried her son to see the movie, "Snow White and the Seven Dwarfs." They entered during the middle of the picture just before the old witch gave Snow White the poisoned apples. When they came to the same part again, the boy's mother stood up and began to lead him out of the theater. As they were leaving Danny looked back to see the old witch offering Snow White the poisoned apple. He told his mother, "If Snow White eats that apple again, she's crazy." When the Lord forgives a person of their sins following their repentance, in the words of the little boy, "it's crazy to commit them again." The Bible exhorts us to forsake our wicked ways – an exhortation we need to heed daily.

Chapter 4
Thoughts That Triumph

Attitudes
Matthew 5:28

The Bible says: "... BUT I SAY UNTO YOU, THAT WHOSOEVER LOOKETH ON A WOMAN TO LUST AFTER HER HATH COMMITTED ADULTERY WITH HER ALREADY IN HIS HEART." Some men would never think of being unfaithful to their wives by committing the awful sin of adultery, but multitudes of men fail to see that adultery can be committed in the heart. Jesus says if a man looks on a woman to lust after her he hath committed adultery already with her in his heart. Here Jesus teaches a tremendous lesson. He teaches us that sin goes beyond the act to the attitude. In I John 3:15 the Bible says that a man is a murderer if he hates his brother. Sin then is more than an act, it is an attitude of the heart, an attitude that is killing millions. Fulton Ousler says that a noted neurologist said that, "Attitudes are more responsible for disease than germs." When Christ comes into a man's life He controls those attitudes.

Garbage Dump Thinking
Proverbs 23:7

The Bible says: "FOR AS HE THINKETH IN HIS HEART, SO IS HE:..." Recently, I read of a magnificent new shopping center which stands on a former city garbage dump. For over a century, no one saw this location as anything but "THE GARBAGE DUMP." Then some progressive-minded citizens started "seeing" that location as a beautiful new shopping center. Immediately, they stopped dumping garbage and started hauling good clean fill dirt. They did this until a solid foundation was prepared on which the new shopping center was to be built. Many people have allowed their minds to be like a garbage dump cluttered up with that which is useless and good-for-nothing. However, I have told this story today to remind you that it doesn't have to be that way. If you will but give that mind to Christ, He will bring in the fill dirt and make that mind a foundation on which to build a worthy life. This is God's promise in Proverbs: "AS A MAN THINKETH IN HIS HEART, SO IS HE:..." Is your life a garbage dump or a foundation?

Moving Mountains
Matthew 17:20

The Bible says: "... IF YE HAVE FAITH AS A GRAIN OF MUSTARD SEED, YE SHALL SAY UNTO THIS MOUNTAIN, REMOVE HENCE TO YONDER PLACE; AND IT SHALL REMOVE; AND NOTHING SHALL BE IMPOSSIBLE UNTO YOU." All of us have our mountains and we face them in one of two ways, with faith or fear. On the tombstone of Emperor John of Austria are these words: "Here lies a Monarch who had many good desires, but was never able to make up his mind to put any of them into effect." He was in bondage to fear. However, faith accomplishes the impossible. Several years ago the papers gave the account of a high school boy in Philadelphia who performed a mathematical feat which all the great mathematicians of the world said could not be performed. He did it because he had not been made to believe that it could not be done. Jesus says that the way to achieve one's goals is to move the mountains, and the way to move the mountains is by faith.

Vengeance
Romans 12:19

The Bible says: "DEARLY BELOVED, AVENGE NOT YOURSELVES, BUT RATHER GIVE PLACE UNTO WRATH: FOR IT IS WRITTEN, VENGEANCE IS MINE; I WILL REPAY, SAITH THE LORD." I once felt that if someone did me wrong I had to get even with them, but then when I tried, I felt guilty. I discovered one day that it was not the desire for vengeance that caused the guilt, but the way I went about seeking to get vengeance. There is nothing wrong with wanting vengeance, wanting a thing to be made right. Vengeance is a God given drive placed in every man. What God wants us to know is that we are not to seek to settle the score, but leave that to Him who said: "Vengeance is mine, I will repay." When we do this we may learn that the way to get vengeance over hatred is not with more hatred but with love. Vengeance may break a man's spirit, but kindness will break his heart. If we are kind to our enemies, Paul says: "It will heap coals of fire on their heads." That means it will move them to burning shame. If someone has wronged you, why not turn that thing over to God!

Reviling
I Peter 2:21-23

The Bible says: "FOR EVEN HEREUNTO WERE YE CALLED: BECAUSE CHRIST ALSO SUFFERED FOR US, LEAVING US AN EXAMPLE, THAT YE SHOULD FOLLOW HIS STEPS: WHO DID NO SIN, NEITHER WAS GUILE FOUND IN HIS MOUTH: WHO, WHEN HE WAS REVILED, REVILED NOT AGAIN; WHEN HE SUFFERED, HE THREATENED NOT; BUT COMMITTED HIMSELF TO HIM THAT JUDGETH RIGHTEOUSLY." Often when people hurt us, we want to fight back and get revenge, but Christ who is our example never followed this pattern. Peter the Apostle says, "... WHEN HE WAS REVILED HE REVILED NOT AGAIN." We all need the attitude of a prominent woman who was being criticized but who refused to retaliate. When someone asked her why she did not strike back she said, "I read of a queen once that a dog barked at, but the queen did not bark back." Retaliating is about as ridiculous as a queen barking at a dog. When we suffer wrong we must commit ourself to Christ who judges all matters righteously.

Subjects For The Kingdom
Luke 9:62

The Bible says: "AND JESUS SAID UNTO HIM, NO MAN, HAVING PUT HIS HAND TO THE PLOUGH, AND LOOKING BACK, IS FIT FOR THE KINGDOM OF GOD." It is said that during one of the great battles of Alexander the Great that his men were suffering defeat and began to retreat. However Alexander himself was advancing and as he did he came upon a young man among those who were retreating. He stopped and asked him, "What is your name?" The young man replied, "My name is Alexander." It is said that then Alexander the Great said, "Young man change your name or change your directions." To those who claim to be Christian and yet who are found forsaking the faith Jesus simply says, "Change your name or change your directions." Your directions tell an awful lot about you. What direction are you going in today? Jesus said, "He that puts his hands to the plow and looks back is not fit for the Kingdom of God." On the basis of that one statement how would you classify yourself?

What's Right And What's Wrong.
Colossians 3:17

The Bible says: "AND WHATSOEVER YE DO IN WORD OR DEED, DO ALL IN THE NAME OF THE LORD JESUS, GIVING THANKS TO GOD AND THE FATHER BY HIM." Often people will come to me and ask, "Pastor, is this wrong, why is it wrong, or how can we know when something is wrong?" First of all, we need to remember that the Bible is not a rule book with a lot of do's and don'ts, but the Bible does offer us principles that help us to know when something is right or wrong. Here in Colossians 3:17, God gives us a principle to help us know when something is right or wrong. The Bible would tell us that nothing is wrong, first of all, when we can put the name of Jesus upon it. I am sure that you have seen the commercial by Zenith television that says, "The quality goes in before the name goes on." If you think a thing comes up to the standards of Jesus, so that you can stamp the label with His name, then, it is not wrong. Secondly, nothing is wrong when you can praise God for it, through the name of Jesus. Will it glorify God? Apply this principle to every action of your life.

Things To Think On
Philippians 4:8

The Bible says: "FINALLY, BRETHREN, WHATSOEVER THINGS ARE TRUE, WHATSOEVER THINGS ARE HONEST, WHATSOEVER THINGS ARE JUST, WHATSOEVER THINGS ARE PURE, WHATSOEVER THINGS ARE LOVELY, WHATSOEVER THINGS ARE OF GOOD REPORT; IF THERE BE ANY VIRTUE, AND IF THERE BE ANY PRAISE, THINK ON THESE THINGS." If a man thinks right, he will be right. If he thinks wrong, he will be wrong. If he thinks nothing, he will be nothing. I read of a sign in a Y.M.C.A. building that said, "You are not what you think you are, but what you think you are." Emerson stated that, "A man is what he thinks about all day long." But long before Emerson stated that, God said it in His Bible and in Proverbs 23:7, "FOR AS HE THINKETH IN HIS HEART SO IS HE." A man thinks on the wrong things because sin diseased the mind, but when one comes to Christ for salvation, Christ changes, renews and occupies that mind with thoughts that are right.

Sin Of Omission
James 4:17

The Bible says: "THEREFORE TO HIM THAT KNOWETH TO DO GOOD, AND DOETH IT NOT, TO HIM IT IS SIN." They say that if you give a Hindu in India an examination in science or the laws of sanitation he will pass them with flying colors, but if you give him an opportunity to apply them he will inevitably break every law that he has theoretically mastered. However, one does not need to go to India to discover this situation, for there are multitudes of people right here in America who know what God expects of them and many who could quote all ten commandments, but inevitably they break them. They put the god of prosperity or pleasure in the place of God; they take God's name in vain by taking upon themselves the name Christian and then not living for Christ. They kill with their tongue and commit adultery in the heart through lust. God says in His Bible "THEREFORE TO HIM THAT KNOWETH TO DO GOOD AND DOETH IT NOT, TO HIM IT IS SIN."

Thankfulness
I Thessalonians 5:18

The Bible says: "IN EVERY THING GIVE THANKS: FOR THIS IS THE WILL OF GOD IN CHRIST JESUS CONCERNING YOU." The people of America are a blessed people, and yet often their gratitude is best illustrated by the story of a certain man described by the *Christian Herald*. An old farmer was invited to dinner by a man who was well learned and cultured. As was his custom at home, he simply bowed his head and asked God's blessing on the meal and expressed his gratitude for it. When he had finished, his host told him that asking the blessing was old fashioned and that it was not customary any more for well-educated people to pray at the table. The farmer answered that with him it was customary, but that some of his household never prayed over their food. "Ah, then," said the gentleman, "they are sensible and enlightened. Who are they?" The farmer answered, "They are my pigs." The Bible says "IN EVERY THING GIVE THANKS: FOR THIS IS THE WILL OF GOD IN CHRIST JESUS CONCERNING YOU."

Sowing And Reaping
II Corinthians 9:6

The Bible says: ". . . HE WHICH SOWETH SPARINGLY SHALL REAP ALSO SPARINGLY; AND HE WHICH SOWETH BOUNTIFULLY SHALL REAP ALSO BOUNTIFULLY." One of the laws or principles of harvest is simply that a man reaps what he sows. We all know this but too few take the scripture seriously. I remember several years ago hearing the story of a young architect who was in business with his father. The young man was preparing to get married, but his father insisted they finish one more house before he did. In an effort to get through with the house and increase his profit he put in inferior materials, cut back on the amount of lumber to be used, and sought carefully to cover up every mistake. You can imagine his frustration when on the night of his wedding his father handed him the keys to the new house and told him it was his wedding gift. He learned in an unforgettable way that a man reaps what he sows! Have you learned that lesson yet? Why not begin this day taking God and His Word more seriously.

The Eyes Of The Lord
Proverbs 5:21

The Bible says: "FOR THE WAYS OF MAN ARE BEFORE THE EYES OF THE LORD, AND HE PONDERETH ALL HIS GOINGS." On one occasion the police were summoned to a fashionable apartment in New York City that had been burglarized. They searched in vain for a clue that would lead them to the burglar. However, as they were leaving the apartment one of the officers noticed a statue of Christ facing the wall, and thinking that strange, he checked it for fingerprints. He found some that led to the arrest of the burglar. After the burglar was arrested, one of the officers asked him why the statue of Christ was facing the wall. He replied, "As I was going through the apartment I suddenly turned and saw the image of Christ facing me, and I could not stand to see His eyes gazing upon me while I was burglarizing the apartment." What a difference would be made in our lives if we suddenly discovered the true meaning of the words: "THE WAYS OF MAN ARE BEFORE THE EYES OF THE LORD AND HE PONDERETH ALL HIS GOINGS."

Revenge
Romans 12:19

The Bible says: "DEARLY BELOVED, AVENGE NOT YOURSELVES, BUT RATHER GIVE PLACE UNTO WRATH: FOR IT IS WRITTEN, VENGEANCE IS MINE; I WILL REPAY, SAITH THE LORD." An old Saxon warrior united with the church and came forward to be baptized. He told the minister to immerse every part of him except one hand. He was told that the whole body was to be buried with Christ. "No," said the warrior, "I want to keep this hand free to battle my enemies. I do not want it given to Christ." We are often like that. We want to hold back part of our lives from Christ. We are not always willing to trust Him to fight our fights, solve our problems and avenge us of the wrong done to us. I use to think that wanting revenge was wrong, until one day I discovered that it was not revenge that was wrong but the way we went about getting it. If someone does you wrong, the Bible simply exhorts us to trust Him who said: "VENGEANCE IS MINE: I WILL REPAY."

The Umpire Of Peace
Colossians 3:15

The Bible says: "AND LET THE PEACE OF GOD RULE IN YOUR HEARTS, TO THE WHICH ALSO YE ARE CALLED IN ONE BODY; AND BE YE THANKFUL." The word "RULE", here, is an athletic term meaning to be umpire. What Paul is saying is that every man is to permit the umpire, called peace, to rule over his life. Have you ever thought what it would be like to go to a football game, basketball game, or a baseball game where there were no referees or umpires to see that the rules of the game were followed. Well, you may rest assured there would be pandemonium. It is also possible spiritually. The believer is to allow the peace of God to serve as umpire in his life by applying the rules and laws of God to his life. When a man allows peace to apply these rules and law, there is contentment and harmony, but when these rules are disobeyed there is discontentment and unhappiness. One answer for so much unhappiness and discontentment then is to "LET THE PEACE OF GOD RULE IN YOUR HEARTS."

Overcoming Evil
Romans 12:21

The Bible says: "BE NOT OVERCOME OF EVIL, BUT OVERCOME EVIL WITH GOOD." Evil is a force and power that is constantly being exerted upon both the saved and unsaved. The question is, "How are we to deal with evil?" The Bible tells us that the way to conquer evil is through love. Love conquers, and the way it conquers is by overcoming evil with good. The way to overcome an evil thought is to replace it with a good thought. The way to overcome evil things is to replace them with better things. An art dealer once gave a lovely engraving of a Madonna of Raphael to an Oxford undergraduate and told him to hang it on his wall and then all the pictures of jockeys and ballet girls would disappear. One does not need to allow evil to overcome him. He must, however, allow Jesus Christ to move into his life and find a power that overcomes all evil with a love that comes from above.

Fault Finding
Isaiah 58:9

The Bible says: ". . . TAKE AWAY FROM THE MIDST OF THEE . . . THE PUTTING FORTH OF THE FINGER." There is no fault among us any greater than that of fault finding, the pointing of the finger at others. One preacher who was careful about his Christian life found that no matter how hard he tried to do right, a few people always complained. He preached too long or he was "sketchy and incomplete" when he shortened his message. They claimed he had no dignity when he was relaxed and friendly and too aloof and proud when he assumed a more professional air. A lady one day said to him, "Can't you live more carefully so everyone will approve of you?" "Sister," he replied, "If I had a coat of feathers as white as snow and a pair of wings as shining as Gabriel's, somebody would still shoot me down for a black bird." Instead of pointing a critical finger, why not offer someone today a helping hand?

Pretence
Revelation 3:1

The Bible says: "... I KNOW THY WORKS, THAT THOU HAST A NAME THAT THOU LIVEST, AND ART DEAD." One evening in 1808, a sad-faced man entered the offices of Dr. James Hamilton in Manchester, England, and claimed he was sick of life. He said he could find no happiness, that nothing amused him any more, and there seemed to be no alternative but to kill himself. The doctor diagnosed the complaint as severe melancholia and prescribed a little fun and laughter as the remedy. "Go to the circus that's in town," he said, "See Grimaldi the clown. Grimaldi is the funniest man alive. He'll cure you!" "Doctor," said the sad man, "I am Grimaldi." Many like Grimaldi have a name for being alive but are dead, and spend their life pretending. What is the cure? Faith in Christ! We read, "Therefore being justified by faith we have peace with God."

Peace
Isaiah 26:3

The Bible says: "THOU WILT KEEP HIM IN PERFECT PEACE, WHOSE MIND IS STAYED ON THEE:" Recently I read an article on retirement that stated that the average white male dies thirty to forty months after retirement; that men over sixty-five account for one-fourth of the suicides in the United States; that one-third of all marriages decline after retirement and that alcoholism and mental illness plague many retirees. The retiree is not the only one who often has difficulty in the home. Many homes of middle age adults fall apart when the children graduate from school and leave home. Why do these troubles come? What is behind it all? The main problem is that too often the wrong things hold individuals and families together. The center of many people's life is a job, a son, a daughter, a wife or a husband, and when those centers are destroyed, their lives fall apart. The answer is found in Isaiah 26:3, "THOU WILT KEEP HIM IN PERFECT PEACE, WHOSE MIND IS STAYED ON THEE."

How To Have A Good Day
Psalms 118:24

The Bible says: "THIS IS THE DAY WHICH THE LORD HATH MADE; WE WILL REJOICE AND BE GLAD IN IT." Today where you are it may be cloudy or rainy or you may be facing some real problem, but with faith in Christ you can say with David, "THIS IS THE DAY THE LORD HATH MADE; WE WILL REJOICE AND BE GLAD IN IT." Recently a friend sent me an article entitled "Eight Steps to An Enthusiastic Life." It could well be eight steps to having a good day. Here they are: 1) Stop running yourself down, 2) Eliminate self-pity, 3) Quit thinking of yourself and think of others, 4) Remember "he who has a firm will molds the world to himself." (Goethe), 5) Have a goal and put a timetable on it, 6) Stop wasting your mental energy on gripes and post-mortems, 7) Every morning and every evening say with Paul, "I CAN DO ALL THINGS THROUGH CHRIST WHICH STRENGTHENS ME, 8) Three times a day say: "THIS IS THE DAY THE LORD HATH MADE, I WILL REJOICE AND BE GLAD IN IT." You then can be assured of a good day.

Peace At Last
Hosea 2:18

The Bible says: "AND IN THAT DAY WILL I MAKE A COVENANT FOR THEM WITH THE BEASTS OF THE FIELD AND WITH THE FOWLS OF HEAVEN, AND WITH THE CREEPING THINGS OF THE GROUND: AND I WILL BREAK THE BOW AND THE SWORD AND THE BATTLE OUT OF THE EARTH, AND WILL MAKE THEM TO LIE DOWN SAFELY." In Kinsington Garden, London, there is a picture of Waterloo a good while after the battle has passed. The grass and flowers have grown over the field. There is a dismantled cannon, and a lamb has come up from the pasture and lies sleeping at the very mount of the cannon. The picture serves as a perfect illustration of what happens not only to nations but what happens in the lives of individuals when men stop sinning and warring against God. God says there is no peace for the wicked, but when the wicked turn from their sins and trust the living Christ, then God's peace reigns in their hearts and war is known no more.

Living By The Sword
Matthew 26:52

The Bible says in Matthew 26:52: "THEN SAID JESUS UNTO HIM, PUT UP AGAIN THY SWORD INTO HIS PLACE: FOR ALL THEY THAT TAKE THE SWORD SHALL PERISH WITH THE SWORD." One of the great principles of life is that a man usually dies the way he lives. The things you live with are usually the things you die by. A man reaps what he sows is another way to make the point we are seeking to make, and history is full of ironic illustrations to prove that. For example, Maxentine built a false bridge to drown Constantine, but was drowned himself. Maximinus put out the eyes of thousands of Christians and died of an eye disease in agony himself. Alexander VI was poisoned with wine he had prepared for another. And, when Foulon was asked how the starving populace was to live he said, "Let them eat grass." Afterward, the mob, maddened with rage caught him and hanged him, stuck his head upon a spike, and filled his mouth with grass. Jesus said: ". . . THEY THAT TAKE THE SWORD SHALL PERISH WITH THE SWORD." How are you living?

Pride
James 4:6

The Bible says in James 4:6 "BUT HE GIVETH MORE GRACE. WHEREFORE HE SAITH, GOD RESISTETH THE PROUD, BUT GIVETH GRACE UNTO THE HUMBLE." Pride and snobbery are despicapable and detestable anywhere and anytime, but never is it more detestable than when it is found in the religious realm. But what do we mean by pride or snobbery? Someone defined a SNOB as a person who spends all his time licking the feet of those above him and kicking the ones below. What is your attitude? The Pharisee said: ". . . I THANK THEE THAT I AM NOT LIKE OTHER MEN . . ." The Publican said: "GOD BE MERCIFUL TO ME A SINNER . . ." This was the kind of humility that gained him commendation from God and that will do the same for you. James says "GOD RESISTETH THE PROUD BUT GIVETH GRACE UNTO THE HUMBLE." Humility then gains us acceptance before God.

Excuses
Romans 1:20

The Bible says: "FOR THE INVISIBLE THINGS OF HIM FROM THE CREATION OF THE WORLD ARE CLEARLY SEEN, BEING UNDERSTOOD BY THE THINGS THAT ARE MADE, EVEN HIS ETERNAL POWER AND GODHEAD; SO THAT THEY ARE WITHOUT EXCUSE:" There are too many hypocrites in the church; I am as good as the people in the church; I am not sure I can live the Christian life. These are the excuses people often give for not coming to Christ. Often the real reason is pride. When Dr. Harry Ironside's mother tried to win him to the Lord as a boy, he would say, "But Mamma if I go down the boys will laugh at me." She would then say, "Harry they may laugh you into hell, but remember they will never laugh you out of hell." That worked on him until he confessed Christ as his saviour. Remember God says that at the judgment we will be without excuse.

Prosperous But Perishing
Revelation 3:17

The Bible says: "BECAUSE THOU SAYEST, I AM RICH, AND INCREASED WITH GOODS, AND HAVE NEED OF NOTHING; AND KNOWEST NOT THAT THOU ART WRETCHED, AND MISERABLE, AND POOR, AND BLIND, AND NAKED:" Modern man in many ways is to be compared to these people described in Revelation. They are prosperous but perishing. Roger Babson was once asked by the president of Argentina why, with all of its mines of gold, iron, copper and silver that it was so far behind North America. Babson replied, "What do you think?" He replied, "I have come to the conclusion that South America was settled by Spanish, who came to South America in search of gold, but North America was settled by the Pilgrim Fathers who went there in search of God." Multitudes of people today are prosperous but perishing because they have left God out. What place have you made for Him in your life?

The Great Deceiver
Proverbs 20:1

The Bible says: "WINE IS A MOCKER, STRONG DRINK IS RAGING: AND WHOSOEVER IS DECEIVED THEREBY IS NOT WISE." The devil is a deceiver and his main ambition is to deceive others through any means available. Perhaps he has never used anything more effectively than wine and alcohol. Often you hear such comments as these: "Now a person is not a criminal because he drinks;" "A person can take a social drink without becoming a drunkard." Because there is a measure of truth in these statements people are deceived into drinking. However, I agree with Upton Sinclair who said, "I cast my vote against social drinking. I will not keep in my house a dog that bites one out of every five to nine people who stop to pet it, nor will I sanction alcohol because it dooms or harms just one out of every five or sixteen people who drink." Dr. W.R. White said, "Some people may be decent in spite of it, but nobody is made better because of it." The Bible is true. "WINE IS A MOCKER, STRONG DRINK IS A RAGING: AND WHOSOEVER IS DECEIVED THEREBY IS NOT WISE."

Forgive and Forget
Mark 11:25

The Bible says: "AND WHEN YE STAND PRAYING, FORGIVE, IF YE HAVE OUGHT AGAINST ANY: THAT YOUR FATHER ALSO WHICH IS IN HEAVEN MAY FORGIVE YOU YOUR TRESPASSES." The word forgive is one of the most meaningful words in the Bible. It means to send away, to let go or to send off. Its meaning is best seen in the offering of sacrifices in the Old Testament. The priest would take a goat, place his hands upon the head of the goat, confess the sins of the people and then the goat would be carried out into the wilderness where it would be cast over a precipice or sent away never to return. This suggested that God had in forgiving the people sent their sins away never to return. This is the kind of forgiveness we too must have. However, we tie the goat to the back door and say, "Now I'll forgive you, but I won't forget," and then if the one forgiven crosses us we bring in the goat again. Why not send the goat away today and forgive as our Heavenly Father does.

Leftovers
Malachi 1:8

The Bible says: "AND IF YE OFFER THE BLIND FOR SACRIFICE, IS IT NOT EVIL? AND IF YE OFFER THE LAME AND SICK, IS IT NOT EVIL? OFFER IT NOW UNTO THY GOVERNOR; WILL HE BE PLEASED WITH THEE, OR ACCEPT THY PERSON? SAITH THE LORD OF HOSTS." Years ago, Chinese farmers decided they would eat the good potatoes and just use the small ones for seed. The results was that nature reduced all their potatoes to the size of marbles. These farmers learned through bitter experience that they could not keep the best things of life for themselves and use the leftovers for seed. Too many folks today still take all the big things of life for themselves and plant the leftovers. The prophet Malachi was speaking to people like this when he rebuked them for wearying God. They asked him, "Wherein have we wearied God?" He answered, "With your leftover sacrifices and offerings." Malachi said, "You would not give rulers leftovers, and why should you expect God to accept them?" What do you give God? Do you give Him leftovers or the best?

The Correction For Deception
Romans 2:16

The Bible says: ". . . GOD SHALL JUDGE THE SECRETS OF MEN BY JESUS CHRIST ACCORDING TO MY GOSPEL." Several years ago when my nephew was a young boy, he came in from school one day with a note from the teacher stating that he needed to have his eyes examined. My sister immediately carried him to the optometrist for an examination. The doctor sat Don down in the chair and began to ask him to read the chart before him. To the doctor's amazement, Don could not even read the large "E." The doctor said, "Son you really do need glasses, don't you." The doctor then reached over and picked up a pair of frames and put them on Don's eyes. He could then read even the small letters at the bottom. Then came the embarrassing moment. The doctor put his finger through the frames that my nephew thought housed the lenses and said, "Now son, you might fool your mother but you can't fool me." Often people are like that spiritually. They live deceptive lives, deceiving family and friends. They fail to realize that a day of judgment is coming when all secrets shall be judged.

Don't Defile The Temple
I Corinthians 3:16-17

The Bible says: "KNOW YE NOT THAT YE ARE THE TEMPLE OF GOD, AND THAT THE SPIRIT OF GOD DWELLETH IN YOU? IF ANY MAN DEFILE THE TEMPLE OF GOD, HIM SHALL GOD DESTROY; FOR THE TEMPLE OF GOD IS HOLY, WHICH TEMPLE YE ARE." Some time ago, I saw a bumper sticker that stirred my emotions to no end. The message was simple, "Enjoy Smoking." I suppose the reason it stirred me so was that I cannot remember a time in my mother or father's life when they did not smoke. Both of them were chain smokers until one year when they decided to quit. The tragedy was that they quit too late; for you see my mother had an incurable heart condition, and my father had terminal cancer in the lung. It is hard for me to conceive of anyone encouraging someone to enjoy that which in many instances is responsible for untold suffering and even death. The Bible declares that our body was created by God and is the temple of God; that God dwells in it; that it is Holy and the penalty for defiling it is destruction. Take care of it, you will only have one.

Zeal Without Knowledge
Romans 10:2

The Bible says: "FOR I BEAR THEM RECORD THAT THEY HAVE A ZEAL OF GOD, BUT NOT ACCORDING TO KNOWLEDGE." A few years ago my wife planted some peach seeds and to all of our amazement, some peach trees came up. We watched the peach tree grow and finally for the first time one spring we saw the tree blossom, and soon little peaches began to form. I do not believe my wife had ever been so excited about anything. But then one day a very strange thing happened. We went home from Vacation Bible School to find all the peach tree limbs on the ground. My wife had planted the tree so close to the hedge that our boy in his zeal one day as he was trimming the hedge also trimmed the peach tree. I said, "Bob, why did you do it?" He replied, "I thought the first crop was no good and just wanted to help by pruning the tree." He had zeal but not according to knowledge. Many people are like that in the Christian world. They substitute activity for dedication. We must remember that one can have zeal without knowledge.

Laziness
II Thessalonians 3:10

The Bible says: "... IF ANY WOULD NOT WORK, NEITHER SHOULD HE EAT." Recently, I received a call from a person seeking help for another. I asked if the person had a job and the answer was, "...they are trying to get on welfare." I am grateful to live in a country concerned about helping the disabled and unfortunate. However, too many are best described by this rendition: "The Government is my shepherd I need not work! It allows me to lie down on good jobs. It leadeth me in the paths of a parasite for politics sake. Yea, though I walk through the valley of laziness and deficit spending, I will fear no evil, for the government is with me. Its political royalists prepareth an economic utopia for me by appropriating the earnings of my own grandchildren. It filleth my head with false security, my inefficiency runneth over! Surely the government should care for me all the days of my life that I may dwell in a fool's paradise forever." The Bible says: "IF ANY WOULD NOT WORK, NEITHER SHOULD HE EAT."

The Dead Give-Away
Matthew 26:73

The Bible says: "AND AFTER A WHILE CAME UNTO HIM THEY THAT STOOD BY, AND SAID TO PETER, SURELY THOU ALSO ART ONE OF THEM; FOR THY SPEECH BETRAYETH THEE." Sometime ago, I went into a doctor's office and as I conversed with the receptionist, all of a sudden, she asked, "Are you Bob Roberts from the First Baptist Church of Lindale?" I said, "I sure am, how did you know?" She replied, "I listen to you on the radio and I recognized your voice." That day as I left, I sort of breathed a prayer and said, "O Lord, help me to so speak that people can tell from my speech that I am not only pastor of the First Baptist Church of Lindale, but that I am a Christian." I am confident that there is nothing that reveals so much about a person as his speech. When Simon Peter tried to deny the Lord, the little maid said to him, "... THOU ART ONE OF THEM; FOR THY SPEECH BETRAYETH THEE." Does your speech reveal to those about you that you are a born again believer?

Drinking

Proverbs 23:31-32

The Bible says: "LOOK NOT THOU UPON THE WINE WHEN IT IS RED, WHEN IT GIVETH HIS COLOUR IN THE CUP, WHEN IT MOVETH ITSELF ARIGHT. AT THE LAST IT BITETH LIKE A SERPENT, AND STINGETH LIKE AN ADDER." Some people want to justify their drinking habits by saying, "Well the Bible says Jesus turned water to wine and Paul said a little wine was good for the stomach." The thing that many people do not know is that there are two different wines mentioned in the Scripture. The wine that was good for the stomach was nothing more than pure grape juice and used often as a substitute for water since the water in Bible days was often impure. Then there was a fermented wine, a wine that had about twenty-five percent alcohol content. "LOOK NOT UPON WINE WHEN IT IS RED..." refers to fermented wine with alcohol. None of the wine in the Bible compares to modern day wine where large amounts of alcohol have been added. Nothing has drained more blood, hung more crepe, destroyed more homes, snapped more wedding rings, and dug more graves than alcohol. God says shun it like you would a serpent.

A Good Name

Proverbs 22:1

The Bible says: "A GOOD NAME IS RATHER TO BE CHOSEN THAN GREAT RICHES, AND LOVING FAVOUR RATHER THAN SILVER AND GOLD." It is quite common these days for some men who have become well known to allow their names to be used by the merchandising world to sell their goods. Some without compassion or conviction, and often greedy for gold have often allowed their names to be used by the liquor industry to intensify the problem we already have with alcohol. We need more men like the illustrious Robert E. Lee. On one occasion he was approached by the infamous promoters of the Louisiana Lottery. They said to him, "We don't want your money, only your name and for that we will make you rich." General Lee straightened up in his chair, buttoned his old gray tunic, reached for his crutch and thundered, "Gentlemen, I lost my fortune in the war. I lost my home in the war. I lost everything in the war but my name. My name is not for sale. . . ." The Bible says, "A GOOD NAME IS RATHER TO BE CHOSEN THAN RICHES." What value is there attached to yours?

Selling Out
Matthew 26:22

The Bible says: "AND THEY WERE EXCEEDING SORROWFUL, AND BEGAN EVERY ONE OF THEM TO SAY UNTO HIM, LORD, IS IT I?" Judas sold the Lord for thirty pieces of silver, but that each of the disciples recognized that they were capable of doing the same thing is a truth often overlooked. Every man needs to realize that in every soul there lies coiled and dormant like hibernating snakes, evils that a very slight rise in temperature will wake up into poisonous activity. An old river boat captain illustrates this. A man boarded his ship one day and offered him an enormous amount of money to carry on some illegal traffic. The captain informed the man that he was honest and would not think of doing anything illegal. The man doubled and trippled his offer, but the answer was still no. When the man offered the captain four times the original offer the captain drew his gun and ordered the man off his boat. The man asked why? The captain replied, "YOU'RE GETTING TOO CLOSE TO MY PRICE!" How much would you sell Christ out for?

God's Standard For Judgement
Romans 2:2

The Bible says in Romans 2:2: ". . .WE ARE SURE THAT THE JUDGMENT OF GOD IS ACCORDING TO TRUTH. . ." One of the great discoveries that we will make at the judgment will be that it will be based on what we really are instead of what we think we are. So often man gets a distorted view of himself. As a child I always liked to go to the house of mirrors when the county fair would come to town. The way you looked depended upon the mirror. People use a variety of mirrors today in searching for their identity. They often try to see themselves in others through comparison; and when they do this they often pick the most "backslidden" person in the church in order to make themselves look pretty good. God says that at the judgment the "REAL YOU" will stand up and that we will be judged according to TRUTH, the real truth about the man on the inside. Be careful that you don't deceive yourself.

The Way To Happiness
Psalms 144:15

The Bible says: "HAPPY IS THAT PEOPLE, THAT IS IN SUCH A CASE: YEA, HAPPY IS THAT PEOPLE, WHOSE GOD IS THE LORD." A very precious lady once asked me, "Brother Bob, why am I so unhappy?" I responded to her question by saying that if most people had the kind of car that she had, lived in the kind of home she lived in and had the money she had, they would think they would be happy. She said, "But Brother Bob, my husband and I were happier when we made only forty or sixty dollars a week." Where is true abiding happiness found? Voltaire found that it was not in unbelief for he wrote later, "I wish that I had never been born." Lord Byron found that it was not in pleasure for he lived a life of pleasure and later wrote, "The worm, the canker the grief are mine alone." Jay Gould did not find it in money for he said, "I suppose I am the most miserable man on earth." The Bible says that true happiness is found in God and the Psalmist wrote: ". . .HAPPY IS THAT PEOPLE WHOSE GOD IS THE LORD."

Alcohol
Proverbs 23:29-30

The Bible says: "WHO HATH WOE? WHO HATH SORROW? WHO HATH CONTENTIONS? WHO HATH BABBLING? WHO HATH WOUNDS WITHOUT CAUSE? WHO HATH REDNESS OF EYES? THEY THAT TARRY LONG AT THE WINE; THEY THAT GO TO SEEK MIXED WINE." Upton Sinclair in his book, *Cup Of Fury*, describes what alcohol did to some seventy-five of his friends and relatives, among which were Jack London, Sinclair Lewis, Scott Fitzgerald, Edward A. Robinson and others. He states, " . . .I put before the public this tragic record of a half-century of genius twisted and tortured by alcohol, and I ask that it be read with one fact, that three out of four of today's college students are drinking. I want them to know the story. I want them to see that the chains of despot are easy to assume when young but of unimaginable hardness to break in later years. I ask if this is what they want out of life?" The Bible says it is the source of woe, contentions, and babblings, and when we make it easily accessible, then we become guilty of contributing to a man's woe.

Denying The Flesh
Romans 13:14

The Bible says in Romans 13:14: "BUT PUT YE ON THE LORD JESUS CHRIST, AND MAKE NOT PROVISION FOR THE FLESH, TO FULFILL THE LUSTS THEREOF." In the life of every believer there is a tug of war going on between the flesh and the spirit. The believer is directed to yield to the spirit and make no provision for the flesh. Too many are like the little boy I heard of who was forbidden by his father to go swimming one day. However, later in the day as the father was returning home he passed by the swimming hole to find the boy in swimming. When he asked why he had disobeyed the order, the boy related that he had just come to watch the other boys, but got so close to the water that they got him wet and so he just decided to go on in swimming. The father said, "But why do you have your swimsuit on?" The little fellow said, "Well, I just wore it so that if I got tempted I could go on in." The Bible says: "MAKE NO PROVISION FOR THE FLESH."

God's Plan For Happiness
Psalm 1:1-2

The Bible says: "BLESSED IS THE MAN THAT WALKETH NOT IN THE COUNSEL OF THE UNGODLY, NOR STANDETH IN THE WAY OF SINNERS, NOR SITTETH IN THE SEAT OF THE SCORNFUL. BUT HIS DELIGHT IS IN THE LAW OF THE LORD; AND IN HIS LAW DOTH HE MEDITATE DAY AND NIGHT." A lady once said to me, "Brother Bob, why am I so unhappy?" I said, "If most people had what you have they would think themselves to be very happy." She replied, "You know, I was happier when my husband and I made forty dollars per week than I am now." One writer said that many people are unhappy because they interpret the future in light of the present and since they are presently unhappy they feel they always will be. In Psalm 1 God tells us how to be happy. The happy person is one who does not walk in the counsel of the ungodly, he does not stand in the way of sinners and he does not sit in the seat of the scornful, but his delight is in the Law of the Lord. If you are unhappy why not try God's plan for happiness.

Danger Of Delay
Ephesians 4:26

The Bible says: "BE YE ANGRY, AND SIN NOT: LET NOT THE SUN GO DOWN UPON YOUR WRATH:" Often one realizes too late the things we should have done or said. Thomas Carlyle loved Jane Welsh Carlyle, but he was a cross-grained, irritable creature and he never made life happy for her. Unexpectedly she died. Later as he went through her papers and notebooks a mournful memory came back to him. He spent sleepless nights realizing too late what she had felt and suffered under his childish irritabilities. He cried over and over again, "If I could see her but once more, were it but for five minutes, to let her know that I always loved her through all that. She never did know it, never." There is a time for saying and doing things and when that time is past, they can never be said, and they can never be done. All of this and more is meant in those words, "LET NOT THE SUN GO DOWN UPON YOUR WRATH." Tell someone you love them today.

Checkpoints For Christians
II Corinthians 13:5

The Bible says; "EXAMINE YOURSELVES, WHETHER YE BE IN THE FAITH; PROVE YOUR OWN SELVES. KNOW YE NOT YOUR OWN SELVES, HOW THAT JESUS CHRIST IS IN YOU, EXCEPT YE BE REPROBATES." Some time ago I was flying across country with a pilot who attended the church I pastored. Suddenly he made a sharp turn to the right. I said, "Bill, why did you do that. I thought one of the advantages of flying was going in a straight path." He replied, "That's right, but we just reached a checkpoint." I found out that all over the country there are VOR stations for pilots to use as checkpoints to make sure that they are on the right course. God has some VOR stations or checkpoints for believers. Paul says we should check with them and examine ourselves to make sure we are saved and on course. Our attitude toward others, toward prayer, toward God's will for our life, toward the word of God, toward the Holy Spirit are but a few things that help us determine if we are saved and on course. Examine yourselves today.

Living Dangerously
I Thessalonians 5:22

The Bible says: "ABSTAIN FROM ALL APPEARANCE OF EVIL." I heard of a queen who was seeking to employ someone to drive her carriage. She had several to apply, and to each of the applicants she asked this question, "How close to the cliff can you drive the carriage without falling off?" Each of the applicants tried to give an answer that would be better than the other. However, when she asked the last applicant that question, he replied, "If you are in there as far away as I can," and she hired him. Maybe the question that many need to be asking themselves is this, "How close can I come to danger without being hurt?" Too many flirt with sin, with Satan and with the world. They, seemingly, try to see how close they can come without being overcome by its allurements. The real question is not how close we can come, but rather how far we can stay away. The Bible says that we are to "ABSTAIN FROM ALL APPEARANCE OF EVIL."

Criticism
Romans 2:1

The Bible says in Romans 2:1: "THEREFORE THOU ART INEXCUSABLE, O MAN, WHOSOEVER THOU ART THAT JUDGEST: FOR WHEREIN THOU JUDGEST ANOTHER, THOU CONDEMNEST THYSELF; FOR THOU THAT JUDGEST DOEST THE SAME THINGS." It is not the recognition of sin in others that is forbidden here but the condemnation of the person who sins that Paul speaks of. What should one do when he is criticized and condemned by others? The first thing to do is to be sure you are right where being right counts – before God. If you are right in God's eyes, you can afford to be wrong in man's eyes. The next thing to do is to forget your critics. H.W. Beecher said, "Life would be a perpetual flea hunt if a man were obliged to run down all the innuendoes, inveracities, insinuations, and misrepresentations which are uttered against him." Thirdly, if a person is honest with himself and God, he has no business worrying about malicious criticism. If you worry about what people think of you, it means you have more confidence in their opinions than in your own.

How To Live And Be Loved
Romans 15:2

The Bible says: "LET EVERY ONE OF US PLEASE HIS NEIGHBOR FOR HIS GOOD TO EDIFICATION." One of the problems that modern man has is that of relating to his fellow man. Some time ago I heard my good friend Tilson Maynard give ten ways to get along with others. He suggested that 1) you love people and not use them, 2) that you develop an understanding look at life through the other man's eyes, 3) that you compliment more than you criticize, 4) that you be fair and honest, 5) that you not be angry, 6) that you be kind, 7) that you have a sense of humor, 8) that you smile, 9) that you cooperate more than you oppose and 10) that you go to school to Jesus Christ the supreme headmaster and live by the Golden Rule. The man that puts these simple rules into practice will do what the Bible commands and that is to "...PLEASE HIS NEIGHBOR FOR HIS GOOD TO EDIFICATION."

Forgiveness
Ephesians 4:32

The Bible says: "AND BE YE KIND ONE TO ANOTHER, TENDERHEARTED, FORGIVING ONE ANOTHER, EVEN AS GOD FOR CHRIST'S SAKE HATH FORGIVEN YOU." The Bible teaches that regardless of the offence that we are to be forgiving. There is nothing more detrimental to one's spiritual, emotional, mental, and physical being as an unforgiving spirit. Dr. S.I. McMillen in his book *None Of These Diseases*, says that ulcerative colitis, toxic goiters, and high blood pressure are only a few of the scores of diseases caused by bitterness and unforgiveness. He says, "The moment I start hating a man, I become his slave. I can't enjoy my work any more because he controls my thoughts. . .even vacations cease to give me pleasure. . .I can't escape his tyrannical grasp on my mind. When the waiter serves me porterhouse steak, it might as well be stale bread and water...." It is for this reason that Solomon wrote: "BETTER A DISH OF VEGETABLES WITH LOVE THAN THE BEST BEEF SERVED WITH HATRED." (Proverbs 15:17)

Pursuing Peace
Romans 14:19

The Bible says: "LET US THEREFORE FOLLOW AFTER THE THINGS WHICH MAKE FOR PEACE, AND THINGS WHEREWITH ONE MAY EDIFY ANOTHER." As believers we are not to be critical but complimentary of one another and constantly look for things that will make for peace. Charles Simeon of Cambridge laid down three rules for his own practice in pursuing peace and harmony: 1) To hear as little as possible whatever is to the prejudice of others; 2) To believe nothing of the kind until absolutely forced to; 3) To always believe that if the other side were heard a very different version would be given of the matter. "I consider love as wealth," added the saintly scholar, "and as I should resist a man who should come and rob my house so would I resist a man who would weaken my regard for any human being." Think of the problems in homes, churches and businesses that would be resolved if this same principle was followed.

Heaven
Colossians 3:1-2

The Bible says: "IF YE THEN BE RISEN WITH CHRIST, SEEK THOSE THINGS WHICH ARE ABOVE, WHERE CHRIST SITTETH ON THE RIGHT HAND OF GOD. SET YOUR AFFECTION ON THINGS ABOVE, NOT ON THINGS ON THE EARTH." A man was passing along the street when he saw a blind boy seated on his father's knee. The boy was holding in his hand a kite string, and the kite flying away up in the air. The man asked, "Is it any satisfaction to you to fly that kite when you can't see it?" "O yes, sir," he replied, "I cannot see it, but I can feel it pull." And so it is that while we as believers cannot see the thrones and all that God has prepared for us, out here in this world filled with the blindness of sin, we can feel the tug of heaven as it pulls at our heart. A study of God's Word will tell us more about that eternal city.

Heavenly Aspirations
Romans 8:5-6

The Bible says: "FOR THEY THAT ARE AFTER THE FLESH DO MIND THE THINGS OF THE FLESH; BUT THEY THAT ARE AFTER THE SPIRIT THE THINGS OF THE SPIRIT. FOR TO BE CARNALLY MINDED IS DEATH; BUT TO BE SPIRITUALLY MINDED IS LIFE AND PEACE." Here the believer is challenged to think on and seek after the things that are spiritual and heavenly. One criticism often raised against Christians is that they are so heavenly minded that they are no earthly good. Well, maybe we need to remember the words of C.S. Lewis who said that, "The early patriarchs and apostles and evangelists left their mark ON EARTH because their minds were PREOCCUPIED WITH HEAVEN. It is since the Christians have ceased to think of the other world that they have become so ineffective in this one. Aim at heaven and you will get earth thrown in – aim at earth and you will get neither." God says He will keep him in perfect peace whose mind is stayed on Him. What is your mind stayed on? Think heavenly things.

Learning To Love Oneself
Matthew 22:39

The Bible says: ". . . THOU SHALT LOVE THY NEIGHBOUR AS THYSELF." We are often told that what the world needs is to learn to live by the great commandment: "THOU SHALT LOVE THY NEIGHBOUR AS THYSELF." However, I am not sure that I would want some neighbors, I have known through the years, to love me as they love themselves. Quite frankly, I don't think that some of them even liked themselves, much less love themselves. This commandment will work only when man has the right attitude toward himself that God would have him to have. He must accept himself, with all his seemingly defects, as a person made by God in God's image. Mildred Newman and Dr. Bernard Berkowitz in their book *How To Be Your Own Best Friend*, ask a penetrating question that will help us understand what I am trying to say. They ask, "If we cannot love ourselves, where will we draw our love for anyone else?" You can't give away something you don't have. The Bible says: "LOVE THY NEIGHBOR AS THYSELF."

Covering Sin
Proverbs 28:13

The Bible says: "HE THAT COVERETH HIS SINS SHALL NOT PROSPER: BUT WHOSO CONFESSETH AND FORSAKETH THEM SHALL HAVE MERCY." The National Alliance-Concerned with School-age parents reported some time ago, that more girls fourteen and younger received abortions in 1975 than delivered children, and that teenagers account for one in five births in the United States. (They stated that for each 3,193 pregnancies among girls fourteen and younger, about 1,193 or more than fifty percent resulted in abortions.) At least 15,000 abortions were recorded in that age group in 1975. The report further states that this group made up only 1.5 percent of the estimated one million legal abortions that year. Now I ask you how can any nation expect God to bless them with such mass murder going on all around them. While it may be true that abortion could be necessary to save life, it should never be such a horrible way to cover and conceal one's sin. God says "HE THAT COVERETH HIS SINS SHALL NOT PROSPER, BUT WHOSO CONFESSETH AND FORSAKETH THEM SHALL HAVE MERCY."

Revival
Psalms 85:6-7

The Bible says: "WILT THOU NOT REVIVE US AGAIN: THAT THY PEOPLE MAY REJOICE IN THEE? SHEW US THY MERCY, O LORD, AND GRANT US THY SALVATION." Today, one would think that the way we promote revivals, and talk about them, that revival is something that takes place at the church house. Some people seemingly believe that it is something that takes place at some particular Bible Center. Where does real revival take place? Let a man who lived through the Welsh Revival answer that question. A young man, who had heard of the great revival, traveled to Wales to attend the services. When he got out at a country station, he asked a policeman standing in the village square, "Where is the Welsh Revival?" The man in blue drew himself up to his full height, patted his chest, and said, "The Welsh Revival, sir, is under these buttons!" That's the thrust of the entire matter. Revival is something that happens in the heart of man that shapes and reshapes his life. This is the revival that is needed today.

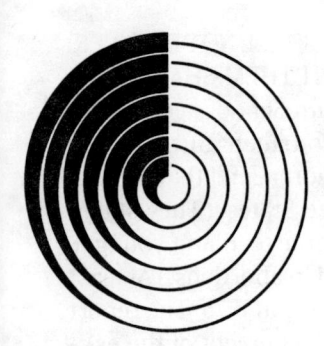

Chapter 5

Death and Dying

Crossing The Branch
Philippians 1:21-23

The Bible says: "FOR TO ME TO LIVE IS CHRIST, AND TO DIE IS GAIN ... I AM IN A STRAIT BETWIXT TWO, HAVING A DESIRE TO DEPART, AND TO BE WITH CHRIST; WHICH IS FAR BETTER." The word "DEPART" here, suggests the dissolution of a chemical, the lifting of an anchor or the striking of a tent. The verse of scripture suggests that, in death, one is not destroyed, but simply changes one shore for another. I heard this illustrated most beautifully a few years back when I attended the funeral service of the great black preacher, Moses P. Timms of Tyler, Texas. As a boy his mother had sent him to the field with some water for his father and the workers. When he returned with the water, his mother asked why, to which he replied, "I couldn't find them." Then his mother said, "Oh, son, I forgot to tell you but they have crossed over the branch." Death is sort of like that – when Christ comes for us in death we just simply cross over the branch. Therefore we need not fear it.

Death, Preparing To Meet God
Amos 4:12

The Bible says: "THEREFORE THUS WILL I DO UNTO THEE, O ISRAEL: AND BECAUSE I WILL DO THIS UNTO THEE, PREPARE TO MEET THY GOD, O ISRAEL." Recently I had an occasion to visit with a man who had just found out that he had a cancerous condition that was inoperable. He said, "I asked the doctor how long I had, and he said a year and a half or so." I said to the man, "You know, it is wonderful that you have the privilege of knowing this so that you can prepare accordingly. Too often we take life and death too lightly. We live as though we will always live, and make no preparation for death. Billy Sunday once said a person heard a knock at the door and went to the door and asked who was there. The reply came back, "I am death." "But who called you?" the person replied. "No one called me, for if I waited until I was called for, I would never come." The certainty and unexpectedness of death demands that man "PREPARE TO MEET GOD."

Fear Of Death
Hebrews 2:14-15

The Bible says: "FORASMUCH THEN AS THE CHILDREN ARE PARTAKERS OF FLESH AND BLOOD, HE ALSO HIMSELF LIKEWISE TOOK PART OF THE SAME; THAT THROUGH DEATH HE MIGHT DESTROY HIM THAT HAD THE POWER OF DEATH, THAT IS, THE DEVIL; AND DELIVER THEM WHO THROUGH FEAR OF DEATH WERE ALL THEIR LIFETIME SUBJECT TO BONDAGE." There are far more people in prison and bondage than just those behind iron and steel bars. Many people who walk up and down the streets of a free world are in a prison called fear. They, more than anything, fear death. Why could a believer, whose hope is in a living Saviour, fear death? Once, a little girl, who lived near a cemetery, had to pass through it to get home. Even though, often, the sun had already set, she never seemed to be apprehensive. Someone asked her one day, "Aren't you afraid to go through the cemetery?" "Ah, no," she replied, "I am not afraid, for my home is just beyond!" Remember, when the fear of death comes, that now, in Christ, our home is just beyond.

The Sting Of Death
I Corinthians 15:55-56

The Bible says: "O DEATH, WHERE IS THY STING? O GRAVE, WHERE IS THY VICTORY? THE STING OF DEATH IS SIN; AND THE STRENGTH OF SIN IS THE LAW. BUT THANKS BE TO GOD, WHICH GIVETH US THE VICTORY THROUGH OUR LORD JESUS CHRIST." Recently I heard of a young boy that was once allergic to bees; and one day while he was in the car with his father, a bee got inside. He became frantic for fear the bee would sting him. Finally, the father caught the bee in his hand and held it until it stung him. Then the father said, "Son you don't have to fear the bee any longer for a bee can sting only once and I have taken his sting." When Jesus died for our sins, He did for us what the father did for the son; He took the sting out of death. Now we need not fear death. Now we can say with the Apostle Paul, "THANKS BE TO GOD, WHICH GIVETH US THE VICTORY THROUGH OUR LORD JESUS CHRIST."

Immortality
I Corinthians 15:51-52

The Bible says: "BEHOLD, I SHEW YOU A MYSTERY; WE SHALL NOT ALL SLEEP, BUT WE SHALL ALL BE CHANGED, IN A MOMENT IN THE TWINKLING OF AN EYE, AT THE LAST TRUMP: FOR THE TRUMPET SHALL SOUND, AND THE DEAD SHALL BE RAISED INCORRUPTIBLE, AND WE SHALL BE CHANGED." One day as two scientists, one a Christian and the other an atheist, worked, a silver cup fell into a vat filled with acid. It dissolved immediately. The Christian scientist thought it would be a good opportunity to prove a spiritual point to his atheistic friend. Thus, he added a catalytic agent to the acid solution and precipitated the silver that had been dissolved out of the acid. He then carried it to a master craftsman where it was remolded into a new cup. In death, the believer is not destroyed, only changed. A study of God's word will help us understand death much better.

The Way Of The Cross Leads Home
I Corinthians 1:18

The Bible says: "FOR THE PREACHING OF THE CROSS IS TO THEM THAT PERISH FOOLISHNESS; BUT UNTO US WHICH ARE SAVED IT IS THE POWER OF GOD." For many the cross is a trinket you put on a bracelet or something you hang around your neck, but to the child of God it is the way to God. A small boy who became lost from his home demonstrates this so beautifully. When the local officers picked him up, he could only tell them he lived near the big cross. The officers decided that he must be speaking of a cross on a church steeple, and so they began to drive him past all of the churches. Finally as they neared another church with a cross on the steeple he began to shout, "There it is, there it is, I can find my way home now. You turn the corner, cut through the graveyard and I live just beyond." Unless Christ returns before death, we must all go through the graveyard, but for the person who is following the cross, Home is just beyond.

When Death Becomes Invisible
John 8:51

The Bible says: "VERILY, VERILY, I SAY UNTO YOU, IF A MAN KEEP MY SAYING, HE SHALL NEVER SEE DEATH." It is amazing to find how many people live with a horrible fear of death. However, the Lord Jesus promises that those that believe in Him "shall absolutely not see death." There are many meanings to this word "see." The word suggests physical sight, mental discernment, to view something attentively, to scrutinize, to fix one's eyes upon, or to look at a thing with interest and for a purpose. This is the meaning of John 8:51. What our Lord is saying is that when a Christian is being put to sleep in Jesus (I Thess. 4:14) as he is dying, he will not look at death with interest or for a purpose, but as an indifferent spectator, for he will have his eyes fixed on Jesus and, in dying, he does not see death, but Jesus. The terrors of death are only experienced by those who reject Christ as their Saviour. Could it be that the reason you fear death is that you have not trusted Jesus, the Victor over death?

God's Unchanging Hand
Psalms 23:4

The Bible says: "YEA, THOUGH I WALK THROUGH THE VALLEY OF THE SHADOW OF DEATH, I WILL FEAR NO EVIL: FOR THOU ART WITH ME; THY ROD AND THY STAFF THEY COMFORT ME." As a little boy lay dying, a Salvation Army girl interested in his salvation stood outside his room and heard the following conversation: A father said, "Hold on son, hold on, soon it will be all over with." A mother said, "Hold on son, hold on, remember long ago we decided there was nothing after death." A sister said, "Hold on brother, hold on, remember after death there is nothing." The little boy said, "Mother, Daddy, and Sister, I know we decided long ago there was nothing after death but I am going out into eternity and there is nothing to hold on to." When death comes to carry you into eternity, what will you hold to? A study of God's word will prepare one for this inevitable hour.

The Benefits Of Dying
Philippians 1:21

The Bible says: "FOR TO ME TO LIVE IS CHRIST, AND TO DIE IS GAIN." Have you ever noticed that people don't like to talk about dying! To many, death is a horrible monster to be feared, but to the believer death is but a friend that helps us to understand our riches in Christ. This is why Paul said, "to die is gain." Now, perhaps, you are asking, but what can one gain through death? Let me briefly illustrate. Recently, a young man of thirty-two years had cancer and was going to die. He related to a nursing student that through this discovery he also discovered his family. Realizing that he was going do die he began to work only half a day and would come home and spend the other half with his family. He said, "I only have one regret and that is that I did not discover them earlier." If we would consider death more seriously, perhaps, we would live our lives with more meaning. A study of God's word will aid us in understanding death.

Life's Great Change
I Corinthians 15:51-52

The Bible says: "BEHOLD, I SHEW YOU A MYSTERY; WE SHALL NOT ALL SLEEP, BUT WE SHALL ALL BE CHANGED, IN A MOMENT, IN THE TWINKLING OF AN EYE,. . ." Often when we lose a loved one in death we feel that a life has been wasted or even destroyed. However, for the believer whose faith is in Jesus Christ, we know that death is not the end but only the beginning of a greater life. A story I once heard illustrates this beautifully. A little boy while playing one day found a bird nest on the ground full of beautiful eggs. He told his mother about it and a few days later returned with her to the nest to find nothing but egg shells. He felt the eggs had been destroyed, but the mother, realizing what he was thinking said, "The eggs have not been destroyed, but inside those eggs were other birds that have come out and been given life and now sing in the trees." Thus, death only enables the believer to find a new way of expressing life.

God's Judgement
Hebrews 9:27

The Bible says: "AND AS IT IS APPOINTED UNTO MEN ONCE TO DIE, BUT AFTER THIS THE JUDGMENT." Govett in his book, THE RIGHTEOUSNESS OF GOD, points out that there are four chances of escape for the man who transgresses a human law: if a man commits a crime, it is possible the offence shall remain undiscovered; it is possible for him to escape beyond the bounds of the jurisdiction which could punish him; it is possible that even though detected and captured and brought to trial there may be a breakdown in the legal procedure and that he may go free; it is possible that the criminal may escape from prison. However, none of these possibilities are available for the man who transgresses the laws of God. Preparation for God's judgment is imperative: "IT IS APPOINTED UNTO MEN ONCE TO DIE, BUT AFTER THIS THE JUDGMENT." A study of God's word will help one prepare for this inevitable appointment.

How To Face Death
Psalms 116:15

The Bible says: "PRECIOUS IN THE SIGHT OF THE LORD IS THE DEATH OF HIS SAINTS." To many death is a horrible monster to be feared and a dreaded sight to behold. However, the Psalmist David said from God's point of view it is a precious sight; precious because a child of God is coming home. Recently I had this illustrated to me in such a beautiful way. During a Sunday morning service as I was presenting the message an elderly man, who loves the Lord and is faithful to our church, was seemingly suffering a heart attack. As the men gathered around him to carry him out he made the statement to his wife, "I don't believe I am going to make it." Immediately she replied, with the faith that both of them had lived by, "Well, Honey, I don't know of a better time to die than when worshipping the Lord." How precious it is to see people who have such a simple and yet profound faith in God that the possibility of death does not frighten them nor cause them to panic. This same faith is available to all.

Danger Of Boasting
Proverbs 27:1

The Bible says: "BOAST NOT THYSELF OF TOMORROW; FOR THOU KNOWEST NOT WHAT A DAY MAY BRING FORTH." Several years ago, a man trusted the Lord and joined the church of which I was the pastor. His brother operated one of the largest package stores and night clubs in Texas. He sought to win that brother to faith in Christ, but repeatedly failed. He said to him once almost in desperation, "Frank, when you die, we won't even be able to get a preacher to conduct your funeral." The man replied, "Well just stuff me in a stump somewhere." A short time later I was summoned to that man's death bed at his request. No longer was he brazen and boastful, but in those sober moments with death staring him in the face he gave his all to Christ. As I left, and later as I conducted his funeral, the words of Proverbs 27:1 took on a new meaning. "BOAST NOT THYSELF OF TOMORROW; FOR THOU KNOWEST NOT WHAT A DAY MAY BRING FORTH."

Deadly Defiance
I Corinthians 10:12

The Bible says: "WHEREFORE LET HIM THAT THINKETH HE STANDETH TAKE HEED LEST HE FALL." A friend of mine I was once witnessing to said to me, "Bob, if I have as much fun in hell as I have in going, it is going to be a great place." Perhaps you too have heard people scoff at hell and death and openly defy it. As one who has stood by many dying people, I want you to know that when death begins to close in, their attitude is altogether different. Sir Thomas Scott, on his deathbed, said, "Until this moment I thought there was neither a God nor a hell. Now I know and feel that there are both, and I am doomed to perdition by the just judgment of the Almighty." M.F. Rich, an atheist cried, "I would rather be on a stove and broil for a million years than to go into Eternity with the eternal horrors that hang over my soul! I have given my immortality for gold, and its weight sinks me into an endless, hopeless, helpless hell." "LET HIM THAT THINKETH HE STANDETH TAKE HEED LEST HE FALL."

Let Me Die
I Kings 19:4

The Bible says: "BUT HE HIMSELF WENT A DAY'S JOURNEY INTO THE WILDERNESS, AND CAME AND SAT DOWN UNDER A JUNIPER TREE: AND HE REQUESTED FOR HIMSELF THAT HE MIGHT DIE; AND SAID, IT IS ENOUGH; NOW, O LORD, TAKE AWAY MY LIFE;...." How sad that some people become so weary with life that they want to die – some even to the point they attempt suicide. There were at least five people in the Bible who prayed that they might die: Sampson, Elijah, Rachael, Balaam, and Simeon. Others like Rebekah, Moses, Job and Jonah complained of being weary with life. How foolish that a person would think suicide could solve anything. There are many reasons why one should never resort to this measure. First, man is created by God and to destroy that creation is to destroy what belongs to God. Second, God has a purpose for every life and to destroy that life is to cut off forever any possibility of fulfilling that purpose. Thirdly, taking one's life does not solve problems but creates problems other's can never solve. Fourthly, God is bigger than your problem. Why not trust Him.

Roll Call In Heaven
Revelation 20:15

The Bible says: "AND WHOSOEVER WAS NOT FOUND WRITTEN IN THE BOOK OF LIFE WAS CAST INTO THE LAKE OF FIRE." It is said that during the First World War a Red Cross attendant found a dying soldier on the battlefield. He was beyond all human aid yet his lips were moving as though in speech. The attendant carefully held the dying man's head on his arm and spoke in his ear, "What is it? What are you trying to say?" the dying man, with a peaceful smile on his face whispered, "The roll-call of heaven is being called and I am waiting to hear my name." Then in a few moments with a radiant smile on his face he was heard to explain, "They are calling my name. Here! I am here!" Dear friend is your name written in the Lamb's Book of Life? When the roll is called in heaven will you be there? Acceptance of Jesus Christ as Saviour gives to us this blessed assurance. Why not invite Him into your heart today?

Hope Of Life After Death
John 14:19

The Bible says in John 14:19: "YET A LITTLE WHILE, AND THE WORLD SEETH ME NO MORE: BUT YE SEE ME: BECAUSE I LIVE, YE SHALL LIVE ALSO." Jesus proved through His own resurrection from the dead that we too shall live after death. William Jennings Bryan in his book *The Prince Of Peace* exemplifies what we are saying. He told of bringing three grains of wheat back from Egypt which had slumbered for thirty centuries in an Egyptian tomb. After he planted the grains on his Nebraska farm where they germinated and produced their kind, he asked himself this question, "If God will give a grain of wheat the power to live after it has slept in the grave for three thousand years, will he deny to man, his masterpiece, the capacity also to rise from the grave after his body has reposed there through the centuries?" The main reason the believer need not fear death is because he has the hope of life after death. Jesus said, "BECAUSE I LIVE YE SHALL LIVE ALSO."

Telling Someone How To Die
Hebrews 2:14-15

The Bible says: "FORASMUCH THEN AS THE CHILDREN ARE PARTAKERS OF FLESH AND BLOOD, HE ALSO HIMSELF LIKEWISE TOOK PART OF THE SAME; THAT THROUGH DEATH HE MIGHT DESTROY HIM THAT HAD THE POWER OF DEATH, THAT IS, THE DEVIL; AND DELIVER THEM WHO THROUGH FEAR OF DEATH WERE ALL THEIR LIFETIME SUBJECT TO BONDAGE." There is no fear that holds more people in bondage any more than the fear of death. A dying young boy asked his mother what dying was like. At first she did not know how to answer, and so she asked God to help her and He did. The mother reminded the son that as a little boy she would tell him to go to bed and he would beg her to let him get in her bed. She would agree but always the little boy would wake up in his own bed. The mother reminded the child that during the night, after he had gone to sleep, the father would ease in the room, pick him up, and carry him to his own bed. This, she said, is what the Lord does for us in death. He puts us to sleep and then picks us up and puts us in our own bed. The little boy feared death no more – neither should you.

Life After Death
I Corinthians 15:19

The Bible says: "IF IN THIS LIFE ONLY WE HAVE HOPE IN CHRIST, WE ARE OF ALL MEN MOST MISERABLE." There is a lot being said and written these days about life after death. Some of the great psychiatrists and psychologists of our time have interviewed people who were dying, and who were brought back to life after their body seemingly died, and through these interviews, we have become confident that there is a consciousness after death. It seems rather strange that what God's Word has said all along, some are finally believing because of the testimony of these psychologists. Sure, there is a life after death – a life spent in hell or in heaven. In hell, the rich man who had rejected the Lord lifted his eyes in torment. In heaven, Lazarus was seen in Abraham's bosom. In heaven, we shall have a body, we shall be recognizable, we shall fellowship with one another and serve the Lord. This is why Paul says: "IF IN THIS LIFE ONLY WE HAVE HOPE IN CHRIST, WE ARE OF ALL MEN MOST MISERABLE."

Dead Men Talk
Hebrews 11:4

The Bible says: "BY FAITH ABEL OFFERED UNTO GOD A MORE EXCELLENT SACRIFICE THAN CAIN, BY WHICH HE OBTAINED WITNESS THAT HE WAS RIGHTEOUS, GOD TESTIFYING OF HIS GIFTS: AND BY IT HE BEING DEAD YET SPEAKETH." Have you ever heard someone say dead men don't talk? That is an old adage that is not true, because dead men do talk. In this modern world in which we live men continue to talk long after they have died. They continue to speak through books they have written, through tape recordings, through films made of them, through the news media, but above all they continue to speak through the lives of others they influenced while passing through this world. Abel had such a profound faith in God, that it influenced others and so long after he was dead the Bible said: "HE BEING DEAD YET SPEAKETH." Your relationship to Christ will surely determine what you will say to others long after you are dead. Make sure it is right.

Chapter 6
Caring and Sharing

How To Hang On To Life
Matthew 10:39

The Bible says: "HE THAT FINDETH HIS LIFE SHALL LOSE IT: AND HE THAT LOSETH HIS LIFE FOR MY SAKE SHALL FIND IT." Millions of people are trying to discover how to hang on to life, and to live a little longer and a little better without ever realizing that the principle behind hanging on to life is losing it. A story I heard recently illustrates this beautifully. Several years ago, two men, trying to find purpose in life, had gone on a retreat in the Himalayan Mountains. Suddenly a storm came upon them, and they began to rush toward the lodge. In their haste, they stumbled over a man nearly frozen to death. One of the men said, "We must help him." The other said, "He is too far gone, and we will lose our life also if we tarry." He went on, but the first man tarried behind. As the first man neared the mission with his friend, he stumbled over something in the way. He looked down and to his amazement it was the frozen body of the man who was afraid to tarry. The way to hang on to life is to lose it in Christ and the lives of others.

Soul Winning
Jude 22-23

The Bible says in Jude 22-23: "AND OF SOME HAVE COMPASSION, MAKING A DIFFERENCE: AND OTHERS SAVE WITH FEAR, PULLING THEM OUT OF THE FIRE; HATING EVEN THE GARMENT SPOTTED BY THE FLESH." There is nothing any closer to the heart of God, and nothing more expected and demanded by God than soul winning. God expects every saved person to tell every lost person about the saving grace of God. Jude tells us that we are to be bold with some, careful with others, but concerned about all. Never are soul winners as negligent as the woman whom Rudyard Kipling describes in "The Convert." He tells of Lisbeth, a native Indian girl, disappointed in love who seeks help from an unsympathetic and cold chaplain's wife, Lisbeth turned her back on Abutrarty saying with a heavy heart, "To my own gods I go. It may be they shall give me greater ease than your cold Christ and tangled trinities." The believer's attitude drives people further from Christ or to Him. What do unsaved people think when they see you?

Motives For Service
II Corinthians 5:14

The Bible says: "FOR THE LOVE OF CHRIST CONSTRAINTETH US..." Several years ago, in a previous pastorate, we had given an old church building to a man to tear it down for us. When he had almost completed the demolition of the building he came to me and said, "Reverend, where is the cornerstone?" I replied, "Jesus is the cornerstone!" He replied, "I know that, but when we build a church we put a big piece of marble in one of the corners at the front and put the names of the deacons and pastor on it. When I do something around my church I like for them to recognize me for it." While there is basically nothing wrong with a cornerstone, our service to Jesus should never be motivated by anything save love. This is why the Apostle Paul who conducted more mission tours, and built more churches than any man who ever lived said: "THE LOVE OF CHRIST CONSTRAINETH US."

Helping The Weak
Romans 14:1

The Bible says: "HIM THAT IS WEAK IN THE FAITH RECEIVE YE, BUT NOT TO DOUBTFUL DISPUTATIONS." I visited a man once who had been an alcoholic, and through the Alcoholic Anonymous Association had found help. He had not had a drink for over a half year. He attended the AA meetings two to three times a week, but I could not get him to come to church. Finally, I asked him why it was that he would go to the AA meetings and yet not come to church. He would keep saying he had to make sure he had overcome his problem. When I asked him why he replied, "Well Brother Bob I know that if I got drunk again that my AA friends would understand and try to help me, but I am not sure the people in the church would understand." Now of course the church is not to encourage or even condone drunkenness, but if men in their sins can't find help and compassion there, then how can they know of the love and power of God that can change their lives? God's Word commands us to help the weak and be careful about criticizing them.

Showing Our Gratitude
Mark 5:20

The Bible says: "AND HE DEPARTED, AND BEGAN TO PUBLISH IN DECAPOLIS HOW GREAT THINGS JESUS HAD DONE FOR HIM: AND ALL MEN DID MARVEL." Here is the marvelous story of the demoniac, who having been set free from the power of Satan, is seen demonstrating his gratitude to the Saviour by sharing with his friends what the Lord had done for him. Gratitude is a real mark of any believer, especially the kind that is demonstrated through sharing the faith. Stanly Jones tells of a physician who found a stray dog with a broken bone. He took him home, put the leg in splints and kept him until he was able to walk. Then one day, the seemingly ungrateful dog disappeared. The doctor was surprised that after so much kindness, the dog should leave him. However, the next morning there was a scratching at the door and when the doctor opened the door, there was the dog, but with him another dog, lame as he had been. In dog language, he had told what his healer had done for him and invited his friend to be healed. This is the kind of gratitude that should characterize every Christian.

The Sting Of Sin
I Corinthians 15:55-56

The Bible says: "O DEATH, WHERE IS THY STING?...THE STING OF DEATH IS SIN..." I read the story of a soldier who was dying on the battlefield. The chaplain bent over him and asked, "Sir is there anything that I can do for you?" The soldier wept and sobbed as he said, "Oh, Chaplain, Chaplain! I don't need someone to DO something for me. I need someone who can UNDO SOME THINGS!" Death stings because of sin and one never faces sin like he does when he comes to die. In 1778 when Voltaire the atheist lay down to die he cried out, "I'm abandoned by God and man!" He said to Dr. Throchin, his physician, "I'll give you half of what I'm worth if you will give me six months more of life." When the doctor said, "That cannot be," Voltaire answered: "Then I shall go to hell and you will go with me." When actor Charles Churchill died in 1764 he said. "What a fool I have been." When Thomas Paine was dying he said, "O Lord, help me, for I cannot bear to be left alone." The Bible says sin stings, but faith in Christ takes the sting out.

Redeeming The Time
Ephesians 5:15-16

The Bible says: "SEE THEN THAT YE WALK CIRCUMSPECTLY, NOT AS FOOLS, BUT AS WISE, REDEEMING THE TIME, BECAUSE THE DAYS ARE EVIL." The phrase "redeeming the time," suggests that man is to buy every opportunity to serve Christ. Today we suffer because of missed opportunities. Let me illustrate. In 1915 Leon Trotsky, noted leader of the 1917 Bolshevik Revolution in Russia, attended Sunday School in Chicago with a friend. The teacher did not show up and Trotsky walked away from that Sunday School class never to attend another one. Joseph Stalin, who caused many millions of people to die, was sent to study to be a priest in the Russian Church, but it had become so worldly and corrupt that he rebelled and turned to communism as a way of life. Mahatma Gandhi, leader of millions in India, studied Christianity in England, but rejected it because Christians didn't live up to the teachings of Christ. Someone's tomorrow depends upon your response to today's opportunities.

Missions
Acts 16:9

The Bible says: "AND A VISION APPEARED TO PAUL IN THE NIGHT; THERE STOOD A MAN OF MACEDONIA, AND PRAYED HIM, SAYING, COME OVER INTO MACEDONIA, AND HELP US." One night while spending the night with my sick father in the hospital he became delirious and demanded things of me that I couldn't do. I called the nurse who made sure nothing was wrong and then gave him a shot. He went back to sleep, but the next morning he said, "I had a terrible dream about you last night. I dreamed I asked you to help me and you wouldn't." As I talked with him that morning I thought of the masses of people around the world, lost without Christ, crying out as did this Macedonian, "COME OVER . . . AND HELP US." I thought of how little we are doing by way of missions to win our world to faith in Christ. I thought of the Judgment Day when I would stand to give an account of how I had answered the cries for help from the lost. I prayed, "Oh, God don't let one person say to me that day, 'I asked you to help me, but you wouldn't'."

The Salt Of The Earth
Matthew 5:13

The Bible says: "YE ARE THE SALT OF THE EARTH; BUT IF THE SALT HAS LOST HIS SAVOUR, WHEREWITH SHALL IT BE SALTED? IT IS THENCEFORTH GOOD FOR NOTHING, BUT TO BE CAST OUT, AND TO BE TRODDEN UNDER THE FOOT OF MEN." Jesus so often used physical truth to illustrate a spiritual truth. Here He is wanting the believer to understand the spiritual role of the believer through a comparison to the physical element salt. Salt is used to preserve, to purify and to save. Salt is not an antiseptic but an ascetic. Salt never cures corruption. It only prevents the spread of corruption. Any farmer knows that you can put salt on meat that is already contaminated, and it will not remove the contamination. However, it will prevent the contamination from spreading. This same principle is true spiritually. The Christian cannot cure the world of all of its corruption; but when Christ is living in the Christian, he can check corruption and prevent it from spreading. This is why Jesus said: "YOU ARE THE SALT OF THE EARTH..."

Conviction
John 16:7-8

The Bible says: "...IT IS EXPEDIENT FOR YOU THAT I GO AWAY: FOR IF I GO NOT AWAY, THE COMFORTER WILL NOT COME UNTO YOU; BUT IF I DEPART, I WILL SEND HIM UNTO YOU. AND WHEN HE IS COME, HE WILL REPROVE THE WORLD OF SIN, AND OF RIGHTEOUSNESS, AND OF JUDGMENT." To many the Holy Spirit is but an experience that brings joy to the believer. However, in the Bible we see His chief function as that of convicting men of sin and drawing them to Jesus Christ the Saviour. He is able to perform this function through born again believers. Jesus said to the believers, "... WHEN HE IS COME TO YOU: HE WILL CONVICT THE WORLD OF SIN." The real evidence of being filled with the spirit is that the Holy Spirit convicts others through your life. Lord Peterborough, a skeptic, said after being compelled to spend a night with Fenelon, the great French preacher, "If I spend another night, I will become a Christian in spite of myself." When your life becomes a disturbing factor to others then you will truly know that the Holy Spirit has come to you.

Ye Are The Light Of The World
Matthew 5:16

The Bible says: "LET YOUR LIGHT SO SHINE BEFORE MEN, THAT THEY MAY SEE YOUR GOOD WORKS, AND GLORIFY YOUR FATHER WHICH IS IN HEAVEN." When I was about ten years of age, I spent a week with an aunt who lived in the country on a farm. During the week that I was there, a revival meeting was in progress, and so we attended each night. Everything went fine, until we would start home each night and, then, we would have trouble. You see, the old "Model A" Ford didn't have any headlights and my cousin and I would sit on the front fenders and hold a flashlight for my aunt to see to drive down the old country road, hoping to stay out of the ditches. I think of that often. For you see, Jesus says that, as Christians, we are the light of the world. Could it be that one reason why so many people end up in the ditches with wrecked lives is that we've let our lights grow dim.

Enemies Of The Cross
Philippians 3:18

The Bible says: "FOR MANY WALK, OF WHOM I HAVE TOLD YOU OFTEN, AND NOW TELL YOU EVEN WEEPING, THAT THEY ARE THE ENEMIES OF THE CROSS OF CHRIST." Dr. Alexander Whyte tells the story of a man who dreamed that he saw Jesus tied to a whipping post and a soldier was scourging him. He saw the whip in the soldier's hand with its thick lashes, studded here and there with bits of lead which were intended to cut into the flesh. As the soldier brought the whip down on the bare shoulders of Jesus, the dreamer shuddered as he saw the marks and bloodstains it left behind. When the soldier raised his hand to strike again, the dreamer rushed forward, intending to stop him. As he did so, the soldier turned around and the dreamer recognized himself. We often think that the men who crucified Jesus must have been cruel, and yet we fail to see that whenever we do wrong, we, too cause the heart of Jesus to bleed with sorrow, and pain and in this sense become enemies of the cross. What does your life tell others about the cross?

The Greatest Desire Of Men
John 8:29

The Bible says: "AND HE THAT SENT ME IS WITH ME: AND THE FATHER HATH NOT LEFT ME ALONE; FOR I DO ALWAYS THOSE THINGS THAT PLEASE HIM." The greatest desire of Jesus was to please God the Father. This desire should be present in every Christian. Dr. Tom Malone illustrates this in a significant way. He relates that on one occasion while traveling across the country he was seeking to purchase a ticket at an unusually busy terminal. People were pushing and shoving and complaining to the clerk. Finally, when his turn came to purchase the ticket he asked the clerk if all the confusion did not make him nervous. The clerk replied, "No sir, you see," and pointing to a glass window, "I have but one desire and that is to please the man behind that window." What a tragedy that far too often we try to please everyone, but the one who made us and the one that ultimately we must all stand before for judgment.

Carriers
Acts 9:15

The Bible says: "BUT THE LORD SAID UNTO HIM, GO THY WAY: FOR HE IS A CHOSEN VESSEL UNTO ME, TO BEAR MY NAME BEFORE THE GENTILES, AND KINGS, AND THE CHILDREN OF ISRAEL." Recently I had a fever blister on my lip and went to the pharmacist for some medicine. When I received the small container of ointment, I asked what was in it. The pharmacist said, "Well, it has a little of this and a little of that, but the liquid is but a **carrier for the** medicine." I thought, "You know, that is exactly what every **Christian** is." A Christian is a carrier of the message of the Lord **Jesus Christ**. This is our main purpose and reason for existence: that **we might bear** and carry the good news of Jesus Christ and His salvation to those who know Him not. Dear friend, when you stand before the judgment **seat of Christ,** will you be able to say that you have truly been a **bearer of the** life and message of Jesus.

The Secret Of Obedience
II Corinthians 5:14

The Bible says: "FOR THE LOVE OF CHRIST CONSTRAINETH US;..." or as the Amplified Bible says: "FOR THE LOVE OF CHRIST CONTROLS AND URGES AND IMPELS US . . ." The Bible repeatedly demands obedience from those who follow Christ, but what is it that inspires man to this obedience? Someone has suggested that there are three levels to obedience. First, there is the level of fear. This is the level on which children live. The child obeys because he is afraid of punishment. Many Christians live on this level. Secondly, there is the level of bargaining. This is seen in adolescence. The youth obeys to get something. The boy mows the lawn and the father gives him the car keys. Thirdly, there is the level of love. This is the highest level of all. The mother prepares the meals, washes the clothes and keeps the house, not because of fear or what she can get, but because of love for the family. Paul says that the thing that inspires the believer to obedience is love. Is this true in your life.

Church Attendance
Hebrews 10:24-25

The Bible says in Hebrews 10:24-25: "AND LET US CONSIDER ONE ANOTHER TO PROVOKE UNTO LOVE AND TO GOOD WORKS: NOT FORSAKING THE ASSEMBLING OF OURSELVES TOGETHER,..." I often hear someone say, "Well I can live as good out of the church as in the church." I always want to ask, "But do you?" It seems to me that if Jesus loved the church and gave Himself for it and while on this earth attended His synagogue regularly that we can not go wrong by following His example. The word religion comes from the Latin word "RE" and "LIGO" meaning to bind together. This is one of the chief purposes of the church – binding people together in fellowship and service. An old chieftain once handed several men a stick and instructed them to break it, which they did. Then he tied several together in a bundle and gave the same command, but not even the strongest man could break the bundle. "That," he said, "is the difference between working separately and working together." Every man needs the strength the church offers.

Saints
Romans 16:1-2

The Bible says: "I COMMEND UNTO YOU PHOEBE OUR SISTER, WHICH IS A SERVANT OF THE CHURCH WHICH IS AT CENCHREA: THAT YE RECEIVE HER IN THE LORD AS BECOMETH SAINTS . . ." Someone said that a saint is someone who makes it easier for someone else to believe in God. Surely no one illustrates this better than Stanley who went to Africa to find Livingstone. Stanley testified that when he arrived he was as "prejudiced as the biggest atheist in London." However, later he became so impressed by Livingstone's life of dedication and gentleness that he said, "I was converted by him although he had not tried to do it." Phoebe in the New Testament was this kind of a saint. What kind of a saint are you? Does your life convince others of the reality of Jesus Christ? If not, why not?

Laborers Together
I Corinthians 3:9

The Bible says: "FOR WE ARE LABOURERS TOGETHER WITH GOD: YE ARE GOD'S HUSBANDRY, YE ARE GOD'S BUILDING." Sometimes, the secular world views churches in various denominations as businesses in competition with one another. Nothing could be further from the truth. In all actuality, each local church assembly serves only as a branch office for the one body of Christ. Paul put it this way: "WE ARE LABOURERS TOGETHER WITH GOD: . . ." Several years ago while pastoring in Silsbee, Texas, a little girl was lost in the woods one Sunday afternoon. The search party went out and men went in all directions, but the search that went on through the night and next day, yielded nothing. Finally, the men agreed that they were to be divided, with darkness coming, they joined hands and together made one big sweep in the Neches River Bottom, and in only hours, the girl was found. This principle of cooperation needs to work not only in the church, but also in the home, and every facet of life.

Wells Without Water
II Peter 2:17

The Bible says: "THESE ARE WELLS WITHOUT WATER, CLOUDS THAT ARE CARRIED WITH A TEMPEST; TO WHOM THE MIST OF DARKNESS IS RESERVED FOR EVER." When I was a small boy I lived in a logging town where there were none of the conveniences of city living. Since we did not have running water in our house we had to go to a well that was located in the intersection of two dirt streets to secure water for our home. Sometimes the well would run out of water, and men would have to go down into the well and clean it out. When the well was cleaned out the water would begin to flow freely again, and soon the well was full of water. Lives are like that. Sometimes we as Christians allow various things to enter our lives and clog up the well, thus preventing the flow of the water of God's Holy Spirit through us. When this happens – when our lives become wells without water, they must be cleaned out. The real proof of a well rests in the water it produces. If the well produces no water, it is clogged up or simply a fake. Does your life quench the thirst of a thirsty world?

A Sinning Brother
Galatians 6:1

The Bible says: "BRETHREN, IF A MAN BE OVERTAKEN IN A FAULT, YE WHICH ARE SPIRITUAL, RESTORE SUCH AN ONE IN THE SPIRIT OF MEEKNESS; CONSIDERING THYSELF, LEST THOU ALSO BE TEMPTED." When a fellow believer sins what must one do? Should one talk about him, criticize him, condemn him? The Bible says we are to restore him. The word RESTORE means to reconcile factions, to set broken bones. The word restore suggests that a believer who sins is not DETACHED BUT DISLOCATED. He is to the body of Christ what a broken bone would be to our physical body. A dislocated arm is useless, a source of pain, and a handicap to the rest of the body, and so is a believer whose fellowship with Christ has been broken. A doctor who would refuse to help a person with a broken limb would be considered less than humane, and a Christian who would refuse to restore a fellow believer in the spirit of Christ would be considered less than Christian. This is what we must do when a believer sins and suffers from a broken fellowship.

Let Your Light Shine
Matthew 5:16

The Bible says: "LET YOUR LIGHT SO SHINE BEFORE MEN, THAT THEY MAY SEE YOUR GOOD WORKS, AND GLORIFY YOUR FATHER WHICH IS IN HEAVEN." In a dark world the child of God is to offer light to struggling souls seeking to find their way back to God. He must never allow the wick to burn down so low as to blacken the globe and prevent the light from getting out. When the light of heaven is extinguished, men plunge into despair. I heard the story once of an old flagman on a railroad who became careless about his job and seeing a train approaching the crossing, jumped out too late and began to wave his lantern in a desperate attempt to stop the oncoming car. The car failed to see him and hit the train, thus taking the lives of several. The flagman was brought to trial and asked hundreds of questions. He was finally acquitted and released. As he was leaving the courthouse someone overheard him say, "I am glad that they did not ask me one question. I am glad they did not ask me if the lantern was burning." Jesus said, "YE ARE THE LIGHT OF THE WORLD." Let me ask you, "Is your lantern burning?"

The Power Of Influence
Acts 4:13

The Bible says: "NOW WHEN THEY SAW THE BOLDNESS OF PETER AND JOHN, AND PERCEIVED THAT THEY WERE UNLEARNED AND IGNORANT MEN, THEY MARVELLED; AND THEY TOOK KNOWLEDGE OF THEM, THAT THEY HAD BEEN WITH JESUS." Soren Kierkegaard tells of a circus tent that caught on fire only forty-five minutes before the scheduled performance. The only fully dressed member of the group was a clown and he was sent to town for help. With an air of emergency, he sought aid from every-one he encountered. The clown pleaded for assistance, but no one took him seriously. People heard what he had to say according to their expectations of a clown's performance. His talk on fire was HEARD in light of how people saw him! Only when the people saw the smoke did they take him seriously. Our verse of scripture tells of Peter and John who were uneducated but there was no doubt in the people's minds about their commitment to Jesus Christ. They truly possessed all they professed – a most urgent need in the church today.

The Great Exposure
Numbers 32:23

The Bible says: "... BE SURE YOUR SIN WILL FIND YOU OUT." We live in a world in which people don't like for you to be too frank about sin, and because of that it has been so minimized that sinners are referred to as psychological and sociological misfits and drunkards are referred to as alcoholics. We need to get back to the Bible and let it call sin by its proper name. One prominent preacher did exactly that and was called in by the leaders of his church. They said, "We don't want you to talk as plainly as you do about sin because if our boys and girls hear you talking so much about sin, they will more easily become sinners. Call it a mistake if you will, but do not speak so plainly about it." The minister took down a small bottle of strychnine that had a label marked poison on it. He said, "I see what you want me to do. You want me to change the label. Suppose I take off this label and put on some mild label such as essence of peppermint. Don't you see that the milder you make the label the more dangerous you make the poison." The Bible says, "Be sure your sins will find you out."

God's Response To His Enemies
Romans 5:10

The Bible says: "FOR IF, WHEN WE WERE ENEMIES, WE WERE RECONCILED TO GOD BY THE DEATH OF HIS SON, MUCH MORE, BEING RECONCILED, WE SHALL BE SAVED BY HIS LIFE." During the Revolutionary War there lived in Epharata, Pennsylvania a Baptist preacher by the name of Peter Miller who enjoyed the friendship of General Washington. There also lived a wicked man by the name of Michael Whitman who did all in his power to abuse this pastor. One day this wicked man was accused of treason and sentenced to death. Peter Miller walked seventy miles to see General Washington and plead for his life. Washington said, "No Peter, I cannot grant you life for your friend." "My friend?" replied Peter Miller, "this man is my bitterest enemy." "What!" cried Washington. "You have walked seventy miles to save the life of an enemy? That puts the matter in a different light. I will grant the pardon." Christ came more than seventy miles for man, his enemy. He came all the way from heaven. What will you do with Him today?

God's Principle For Receiving
Luke 6:38

The Bible says: "GIVE, AND IT SHALL BE GIVEN UNTO YOU; GOOD MEASURE, PRESSED DOWN, AND SHAKEN TOGETHER, AND RUNNING OVER, SHALL MEN GIVE INTO YOUR BOSOM. FOR WITH THE SAME MEASURE THAT YE METE WITHAL IT SHALL BE MEASURED TO YOU AGAIN." In the Bible the principle behind all receiving rests in our giving. If we want love, then we must give love. If we want mercy, we must give mercy. If we want more material things, we must be willing to give more materially to those in need. This is what Jesus is saying in this passage, "Give and it shall be given to you." Recently I had this truth driven home to my heart in a real way. An electrician was speaking with his minister, and the minister asked him, "Is it true that electricity cannot get into you unless it can get out of you?" The electrician said that was absolutely so and related how on one occasion his life was spared. He was brought into contact with a high voltage cable but because he was not grounded the electricity could not get out of him. Dear friend, remember God's love cannot get into you unless first of all it can get out of you.

Living By Love
John 13:35

The Bible says: "BY THIS SHALL ALL MEN KNOW THAT YE ARE MY DISCIPLES, IF YE HAVE LOVE ONE TO ANOTHER." The one principle that is to govern our relationship to our fellow man is the principle of love. Love thinks of others as well as self. A man once dreamed that he died and went to hell and there was a huge banquet table with all kinds of delicious food. However, the frustrating thing about it all was that everyone seated at the table had arms like forks that were in a fixed position preventing them from eating the food. He then dreamed that he went to heaven and in heaven he saw the same table surrounded by people with arms like forks in a fixed position. The only difference was that in heaven each person was feeding the person across the table from him. They had learned that if they were to be partakers of the delicious food they must help one another. We need to learn that lesson in the world we live in. We need to rediscover the principle of love that thinks of others as well as self. A study of God's Word helps us to understand this principle of love.

The Power Of Living With Others
Romans 14:7

The Bible says: "FOR NONE OF US LIVETH TO HIMSELF, AND NO MAN DIETH TO HIMSELF." During the days of the great depression a man, homeless and penniless, told how he was wandering through the country looking for a job. He came to a railroad yard in a cold, midwestern town and shivering from the cold he crawled up into a box car to find four or five other men of similar circumstances there. Suddenly the train began to move and the cracks in the box car allowed the wind to blow through with greater force than it had been on the outside. They all sat shivering and freezing until one of the men suggested that they all get back to back and cover themselves with a large piece of paper they had found in the box car. Soon the heat from their bodies began to warm them. That night they discovered what all men need to discover: that in this world we need one another. The church is a good place to discover how we can help one another to stay warm.

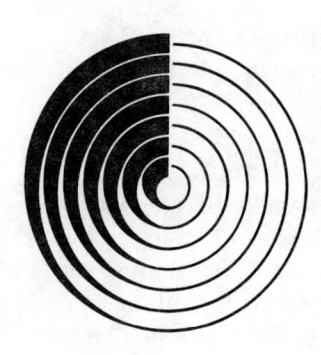

Chapter 7

Hope For The Home

A Christian Home
Joshua 24:15

The Bible says: "... CHOOSE YOU THIS DAY WHOM YE WILL SERVE... BUT AS FOR ME AND MY HOUSE, WE WILL SERVE THE LORD." There was an artist once who wanted to paint a beautiful picture and so he went to three people, a preacher, a wife and a soldier and asked them what, to them, was the most beautiful thing in the world. The preacher said faith; the wife said love; and the soldier said peace. The artist then went home and as he walked into his home he saw in his children faith. He saw in his wife love, and peace he saw everywhere. So he painted the picture and named it "Home," and what a home it was with Faith, Peace, and Love. Someone has said that home is the father's kingdom, the mother's world and the children's paradise. Yet it is a sobering fact that nearly three out of every four homes end in divorce. Perhaps there are many reasons, but one big reason is that God is left out. This is why Joshua, the man of God said: "BUT AS FOR ME AND MY HOUSE WE WILL SERVE THE LORD."

Letting Your Influence Count
Matthew 5:16

The Bible says: "LET YOUR LIGHT SO SHINE BEFORE MEN, THAT THEY MAY SEE YOUR GOOD WORKS, AND GLORIFY YOUR FATHER WHICH IS IN HEAVEN." Charles Francis Adams was an ambassador to Great Britain during Abraham Lincoln's Presidency. He was a busy man, but not too busy to stop and carry his eight year old son fishing one day when he stopped him and begged him to. He wrote in his diary concerning that day, "Went fishing with my son; a day wasted." Later after the son died, someone read in the son's diary this account of that day, "Went fishing with my father; the most glorious day of my life." Little did the father realize how much influence he had upon his son's life that day. Without doubt this is what Jesus had in mind when He said, "LET YOUR LIGHT SO SHINE BEFORE MEN, THAT THEY MAY SEE YOUR GOOD WORKS, AND GLORIFY YOUR FATHER WHICH IS IN HEAVEN." We are not compelled to know all that the light of our influence touches, but we are compelled to make sure that the light of our Christian influence for Christ does shine.

Eternal Separation
Luke 17:36

The Bible says in Luke 17:36: "TWO MEN SHALL BE IN THE FIELD; THE ONE SHALL BE TAKEN, AND THE OTHER LEFT." Jesus is illustrating how that when He returns everyone will not be ready to go with Him. He says some will be taken, and some left, or the lost will be left and the saved will be taken. So often people do all within their power to live together as families on this earth, but make absolutely no provision to spend eternity together. One saintly woman had led all her children but one to the Lord, and as she lay dying she called each of the saved by and said, "GOOD NIGHT, I WILL SEE YOU IN THE MORNING WHEN JESUS COMES." However, to the one who had rejected Christ, with tears in her eyes she said, "GOOD-BYE SON, GOOD-BYE." He said, "But mother to the others you said good night but to me you said good-bye. Why?" She related how she knew this would be the last time she would see him since he had refused to be saved. That thought so gripped his heart that he fell to his knees and cried for forgiveness. Where will your family spend eternity?

Home
I Samuel 2:20

The Bible says in I Samuel 2:20: "AND ELI BLESSED ELKANAH AND HIS WIFE, AND SAID, THE LORD GIVE THEE SEED OF THIS WOMAN FOR THE LOAN WHICH IS LENT TO THE LORD. AND THEY WENT UNTO THEIR OWN HOME." Today the home, God's first institution, is being sorely attacked by Satan. Perhaps we need more homes like that which Arthur W. Hewitt speaks about. After choir practice one day he carried a young girl down a road that skirted a beautiful lake. Suddenly they came upon a shack on the side of the mountain overlooking the lake, and the girl asked him to stop. She saw the look of amazement upon his face and said, "I know it's not much to look at, but it's a wonderful place to see from." The home is the window through which our children get their first glimpse of life. A study of God's word will keep the window clean.

Marriage
Genesis 2:23-24

The Bible says: "AND ADAM SAID, THIS IS NOW BONE OF MY BONES, AND FLESH OF MY FLESH; THEREFORE SHALL A MAN LEAVE HIS FATHER AND HIS MOTHER, AND SHALL CLEAVE UNTO HIS WIFE: AND THEY SHALL BE ONE FLESH." It is a sad fact that now there are almost as many divorces each year as there are marriages. One big reason is that men and women are rejecting one another because of differences instead of receiving one another as a gift from God as did Adam. When Adam saw Eve he said, "THIS IS BONE OF MY BONES AND FLESH OF MY FLESH . . .", or as Jack Taylor says, "This is the rest of me." Before he was incomplete, but now with her he is completed. Because of that he will leave father and mother and cleave unto her. Every wife is a gift from God. Since God gives no bad gifts, then whatever there is about her man does not like, it is but an effort on God's part to meet some deficiency in his life and make him complete. When some men see this, God will then turn some houses into homes.

Following A Father's Footprints
Philippians 3:17

The Bible says: "BRETHREN, BE FOLLOWERS TOGETHER OF ME, AND MARK THEM WHICH WALK SO AS YE HAVE US FOR AN ENSAMPLE." It is extremely important for the Christian to realize that his life is to be an example to someone else for good or bad. I read of one father who had this truth driven home to his heart in an unforgettable way. One winter morning he related that as he walked through the snow to work that he looked behind him to see his small son stretching his legs out so as to follow in his steps. He turned and commanded him to go back, but the little fellow said, "No Daddy. I am coming right in your footprints." The father suddenly realized that it was his custom to stop each day at the local bar and that the foot prints he was leaving were leading in the wrong direction. The Apostle Paul said, "BE FOLLOWERS...OF ME...YE HAVE US FOR AN EXAMPLE." Can you say that today?

A Mother's Influence
Romans 14:7

The Bible says: "FOR NONE OF US LIVETH TO HIMSELF, AND NO MAN DIETH TO HIMSELF." It is a simple fact that every person is influencing someone else for good or for bad. Early in my life I lived next door to a woman who was a drunkard. One day this woman, in a drunken stupor, drove the car she and her daughter were riding in off a bridge into a large body of water. Later, the car was finally discovered and a rescue unit sought to retrieve their bodies. They found during the rescue process that the daughter had crawled through a window and was free except for her legs. You see, the mother in desperation and fear had grabbed hold of the daughter's legs hoping to be helped, but instead they both were drowned. We see this far too often in life. You are either HELPING SOMEONE or HOLDING THEM BACK. Every person is either carrying someone to heaven with them, or dragging them down into hell. The Bible tells us how to live and help others. Study it today, and follow its teachings.

The Peril Of Working Mothers
Titus 2:4-5

The Bible says that young women are ". . .TO BE SOBER, TO LOVE THEIR HUSBANDS, TO LOVE THEIR CHILDREN, TO BE DISCREET, CHASTE, KEEPERS AT HOME. . ." An American judge said sometime ago that if ". . . Mothers would spend more time at home with their children that there would not be as many young girls on their way to prostitution before they reach thirteen years of age." How sad it is that so many mothers yield to the appeal to leave the home needlessly. One woman summarized many women's attitudes toward the home when she said to a real estate man, "Why should I need a home? I was born in a hospital, educated in a college, courted in an automobile, married in a church, I take my meals in a cafe, spend my afternoons playing bridge, and my evenings at the movies, and when I die I will be buried by the undertaker and placed in a cemetery. No thanks, I don't need a home, only a garage." the greatest need in America today is for HOMES WITH MOTHERS IN THEM.

The Right Way To Give
II Corinthians 8:5

The Bible says: "AND THIS THEY DID, NOT AS WE HOPED, BUT FIRST GAVE THEIR OWN SELVES TO THE LORD, AND UNTO US BY THE WILL OF GOD." Giving is a wonderful way to express our love and appreciation to family and friends. However, it can be a cheap inexpensive substitute for what we should do. I read, once, of a young sixteen year old girl who was a chronic invalid and whose mother was a pleasure loving woman and who could not endure the idea of being shut in with her daughter. Therefore, she travelled a lot, and yet she was so mindful to send gifts to the daughter back home. One birthday, the girl received a beautiful Italian vase, but to her nurse's utter amazement she said, "Take it away, take it away," and in utter despair cried out, "Oh, Mother, Mother, do not send me any more books, flowers, vases or pictures. I want you." Don't let your giving be a cheap substitute for yourself. True giving always involves the giving of oneself first.

The Man Who Might Have Been
I Corinthians 9:26-27

The Bible says: "I THEREFORE SO RUN, NOT AS UNCERTAINLY; SO FIGHT I, NOT AS ONE THAT BEATETH THE AIR: BUT I KEEP UNDER MY BODY, AND BRING IT INTO SUBJECTION: LEST THAT BY ANY MEANS, WHEN I HAVE PREACHED TO OTHERS, I MYSELF SHOULD BE A CASTAWAY." History is filled with illustrations of men and women who had the potential of making invaluable contributions to their world but who failed because of a lack of initiative, a wasteful life, or immoral conduct. Somewhere I came across these words that express what I am thinking today:

> ACROSS THE FIELDS OF YESTERDAY,
> THERE OFT TIMES COMES TO ME
> A LITTLE BOY JUST BACK FROM PLAY,
> THE BOY I USE TO BE
> AND OH HE SMILED SO WISTFULLY,
> ONCE HE WAS CREPT WITHIN,
> I WONDER IF HE FINDS IN ME
> THE MAN I MIGHT HAVE BEEN.

Don't let history remember you as a castaway. Study God's Word and let it guide you to be the man God made you to be.

The Power Of A Changed Life
II Corinthians 5:17

The Bible says: "THEREFORE IF ANY MAN BE IN CHRIST, HE IS A NEW CREATURE: OLD THINGS ARE PASSED AWAY; BEHOLD, ALL THINGS ARE BECOME NEW." Many skeptics and modern philosophers often find it amusing to attack the church and the Gospel message the church proclaims to man in need of a word of hope. However, the most convincing evidence of the validity of the church and the power of the Gospel is seen in the lives that are changed by Jesus Christ who is presented in the Gospel. Dr. Hershel Hobbs in his book, *An Exposition Of The Gospel Of John*, tells of a former drunkard who had been born from above. In his presence someone questioned whether or not Jesus changed the water into wine. He replied, "I don't know whether He turned water into wine when He was in Palestine, but I do know that in my own house He has turned beer into furniture."

Adultery
Exodus 20:14

The Bible says: "THOU SHALT NOT COMMIT ADULTERY." There is a lot being said about sex these days, but what does God have to say about sex? God's Word would teach us that sex is good, sex is right, sex is Holy, provided it is enjoyed in the realm that God intended, which is inside the bonds of matrimony. Sex becomes wrong any other place. The fact that sex is a privilege that is being abused today was indicated early this year by a report given by the National Center for Health Statistics. They reported that in 1974 there were 418,000 illegitimate births recorded for a three percent increase over the previous year. That means that if 418,000 young women gave birth to illegitimate babies that 418,000 young men were responsible for it. We have then, violated the seventh commandment of our God. How can any nation claim to be great with such blatant disobedience? We in America need an old fashioned revival of holiness and repentance, and it must begin in regard to marriage and the home.

The Fruit Of A Father's Sin
Galatians 6:7

The Bible says in Galatians 6:7: "BE NOT DECEIVED; GOD IS NOT MOCKED: FOR WHATSOEVER A MAN SOWETH, THAT SHALL HE ALSO REAP." Too often we forget that along with sowing the seeds of sin there comes the reaping. A father in a certain city had this driven home to his heart in an unforgettable way. One night he was called to the local emergency room of the hospital to find his only daughter to be one of eight that was killed in an automobile accident. When he found that all eight, who were recent high school graduates, were drunk he said, "I wish I could find the man who sold my girl that liquor; I would kill him." That night he went home and opened the bar as usual and there found a note that said, "Dear Daddy, we tried all over town tonight to get something to drink and couldn't. I came home and got one of your bottles. I know you won't care." The man later had a nervous break down. When will man learn that "... WHATSOEVER HE SOWS HE MUST ALSO REAP."

No Double Standards Please
James 1:8

The Bible says: "A DOUBLE MINDED MAN IS UNSTABLE IN ALL HIS WAYS." There is nothing more devastating to the minds of the youth than the double standard that too many of them see. Many parents do not want their children to get on drugs, yet they drink alcohol; they don't want their kids to smoke pot, yet they smoke tobacco; they don't want them to be immoral, yet often they are unfaithful before them and so often divorce. Years ago Dr. Perry Webb related how one day a young man came to his office for counseling. He was a very rebellious person. Dr. Webb sensed he was rebellious to his parents and reminded him that one of the Ten Commandments stated, "THOU SHALT HONOUR THY FATHER AND THY MOTHER." The young man turned to Dr. Webb and said, "But tell me sir, how can you honour and respect a father who is a drunkard and a mother who is a prostitute?" The Apostle James would tell us to be living examples; to be stable; be consistent for "A DOUBLE MINDED MAN IS UNSTABLE IN ALL HIS WAYS."

Dealing With Delinquency
Joshua 24:15

The Bible says: "...CHOOSE YOU THIS DAY WHOM YE WILL SERVE; WHETHER THE GODS WHICH YOUR FATHERS SERVED THAT WERE ON THE OTHER SIDE OF THE FLOOD, OR THE GODS OF THE AMORITES, IN WHOSE LAND YE DWELL: BUT AS FOR ME AND MY HOUSE, WE WILL SERVE THE LORD." So often a parent will say to me, "Pastor shall I force my child to go to Sunday School and church?" The answer to that question is almost always "YES." They often then ask, "But why?" J. Edgar Hoover once gave a good answer to that question. He said, "How do you answer junior when he comes to the breakfast table on Monday morning and announces rebelliously, 'I'm not going to school today,' or later when he says, 'I'm not going to take a bath,' or 'I'm not going to take medicine?' Well, you know the answer! Junior goes to school, and he takes the medicine, and he goes to the doctor." The same should be true with regard to spiritual things. When we do this, juvenile delinquency is dealt a powerful and effective blow in the most important place – the home.

A Son's World In His Father's Hand
Joshua 24:15

The Bible says in Joshua 24:15: "...CHOOSE YOU THIS DAY WHOM YE WILL SERVE ... BUT AS FOR ME AND MY HOUSE, WE WILL SERVE THE LORD." It was a great father that made this declaration when he was about to die. We need more fathers like this today. One father had this most vividly illustrated to him one night as he watched the news. The father, having heard the news commentator speak about some troubled spots in the world, went into his son's bedroom to get a globular map of the world that sat on his desk. The father had picked the map up and was about to leave the room when his son, who was supposed to be asleep on the bed said, "DADDY, WHERE ARE YOU GOING WITH MY WORLD?" This is a question that every father must answer. What better way can we answer than to say with Joshua, "...AS FOR ME AND MY HOUSE, WE WILL SERVE THE LORD."

Neglect
Song of Solomon 1:6

The Bible says: "...THEY MADE ME THE KEEPER OF THE VINEYARDS; BUT MINE OWN VINEYARD HAVE I NOT KEPT." Theodore W. Brennan wrote:

"I looked upon a farm one day that once I used to own.
The barn had fallen to the ground; the fields were overgrown.
The house in which my children grew, where we had lived for years,
I turned to see it broken down, and brushed aside the tears.
I looked upon my soul, one day, to find it, too,
had grown with thorns and nettles everywhere; the seeds of neglect had sown.
The years had passed while I cared for things of lesser worth;
the things of heaven I let go, while minding things of earth.
To Christ, with bigger tears, I cried, 'O Lord, forgive.'"

What a tragedy that any of us could become so involved in helping others, in serving mankind, in strengthening the family ties of others that we neglect our very own family and soul. It was this awesome truth that gripped the heart of Solomon and caused him to write: "...THEY MADE ME THE KEEPER OF THE VINEYARDS; BUT MINE OWN VINEYARDS HAVE I NOT KEPT."

What's Wrong With The World
Jeremiah 18:4

The Bible says: "AND THE VESSEL THAT HE MADE OF CLAY WAS MARRED IN THE HAND OF THE POTTER: SO HE MADE IT AGAIN ANOTHER VESSEL, AS SEEMED GOOD TO THE POTTER TO MAKE IT." Many people are asking the question, "What's wrong with the world?" There is nothing wrong with the world; it is the people in the world whose lives have been marred by sin and who need to be put back together by God, the potter. Harmon Killebrew tells the story of a young boy who tried to get his father to help him put a puzzle of the world together, but the father was tired and refused to help. The little fellow tried repeatedly. After some time, he rushed into the room with the puzzle complete. The father asked him how he did it. He answered, "I turned the puzzle over, and there was a picture of a boy on the back. I discovered that if I put the boy together all right, the world came out okay." Why not let the great potter put your life back together today. When men's lives are put back together, we will find that the world will be okay.

When Love Grows Cold
Matthew 24:12

The Bible says: "AND BECAUSE INIQUITY SHALL ABOUND, THE LOVE OF MANY SHALL WAX COLD." Jesus declared before He went back to heaven that one of the marks of the age just before He would return would be a decline in love. He declared that because of iniquity or sin that fathers and mothers; husbands and wives would lose love, a natural affection for one another. Without a doubt this is a characteristic of this present age. On November 18, 1977 I read the tragic story of a mother who was taken into custody and held on $100,000 bail. The newspaper stated that she was arrested for the murder of her nine year old daughter whom she murdered because her boy friend told her to choose between him and the daughter. We read stories like that, and people ask what's wrong? Jesus says that because iniquity shall abound the love of many shall wax cold. The solution to such problems as this is faith in Jesus Christ. The Bible declares that one of the marks of a truly saved person is that he loves others.

Christian Commitment
Luke 9:23

The Bible says: "AND HE SAID TO THEM ALL, IF ANY MAN WILL COME AFTER ME, LET HIM DENY HIMSELF, AND TAKE UP HIS CROSS DAILY, AND FOLLOW ME." A man who had been married to a woman for twenty-five years related how she had grown cold toward him, and so, on their twenty-fifth anniversary, he decided to take advantage of the opportunity to ask her why. He said, "I have given you furs, cars, homes, diamonds and all you have wanted and yet, you have grown cold toward me and I ask you why?" She replied, "I am glad you had the courage to ask. It is true that you have given me all these things, but never have you given me yourself!" This happens all too often in the Christian world. People are willing to give Christ their souls, so when they die they won't go to hell, but they want to hold back with their lives. Jesus says, "If a man becomes a true believer and disciple he must make a complete commitment of himself to Christ."

Chapter 8
Comfort and Cheer

God Cares
I Peter 5:7

The Bible says: "CASTING ALL YOUR CARE UPON HIM; FOR HE CARETH FOR YOU." Sometimes we get to feeling that no one cares for us. We feel our family doesn't care, our friends don't care and sometimes we even feel God doesn't care. Recently God's care for us was brought home to my heart in a real way. A dear friend of mine was to undergo surgery and it was apparent that there was a malignancy. Early in the morning the doctor came into her room and sat down on the bed and said, "Virginia, God gave me a song for you today and I want to sing it." The doctor then sang all the verses of the song I would like to leave with you today.

> BE NOT DISMAYED WHATEVER BE TIDE,
> GOD WILL TAKE CARE OF YOU.
> BENEATH HIS WINGS OF LOVE ABIDE,
> GOD WILL TAKE CARE OF YOU.
> GOD WILL TAKE CARE OF YOU,
> THRO' EVERY DAY, O'ER ALL THE WAY
> HE WILL TAKE CARE OF YOU,
> GOD WILL TAKE CARE OF YOU.

This is why Peter said, "Cast all your care upon Him; for He careth for you."

God's Promise Of The Rainbow
Genesis 9:13,15

The Bible says: "I DO SET MY BOW IN THE CLOUD, AND IT SHALL BE FOR A TOKEN OF A COVENANT BETWEEN ME AND THE EARTH...AND I WILL REMEMBER MY COVENANT, WHICH IS BETWEEN ME AND YOU AND EVERY LIVING CREATURE OF ALL FLESH; AND THE WATERS SHALL NO MORE BECOME A FLOOD TO DESTROY ALL FLESH." When God destroyed the earth with a flood because of man's wickedness, he put a rainbow in the sky as a promise He would never do it again. I want you to note that this rainbow is in heaven and visible to all; it is directed toward heaven and aimed from man as if the arrow has already been discharged. The bow has no string which shows that the Master will not shoot, and thus becomes a symbol of peace and friendship. The bow is God's promise that the hope of the world is in Jesus – a promise that becomes valid when we put our faith in Christ.

The Second Coming Of Christ
Hebrews 9:28

The Bible says: "SO CHRIST WAS ONCE OFFERED TO BEAR THE SINS OF MANY; AND UNTO THEM THAT LOOK FOR HIM SHALL HE APPEAR THE SECOND TIME WITHOUT SIN UNTO SALVATION." So often in this life people grow weary with the conflicts and pressures of life and even feel that God has forsaken them, but in the Bible we have the perfect assurance that one day He shall return for us and deliver us from this present evil world. A story I heard recently illustrates this beautifully. Two young men grew up together, went to school together, graduated together and entered the armed services together. One day in a heated conflict one was wounded on the battlefield, but the other had to go on. Later, when the fighting receded, the friend, against orders, went back for his friend. When he drew near his side his dying friend said, "I knew that you would come back." Dear friend, when the troubles and trials of life seem to be too much for us, just remember our Lord Jesus Christ will come back for us.

The Power Of The Spoken Word
Matthew 17:20

The Bible says: "... IF YE HAVE FAITH AS A GRAIN OF MUSTARD SEED, YE SHALL SAY UNTO THIS MOUNTAIN, REMOVE HENCE TO YONDER PLACE; AND IT SHALL REMOVE; AND NOTHING SHALL BE IMPOSSIBLE UNTO YOU." I am constantly amazed at the power of the spoken word. A judge speaks and a man is sentenced to death; a man and woman speak and a marriage is conceived; a sinner speaks words of repentance and a soul is redeemed; an individual speaks words of courage and people are inspired. There is power in the spoken word. Several years ago, the actor that was playing the part of Peter in the movie, "A MAN CALLED PETER," did such an excellent job that following the scene he received congratulations from all the members of the cast, but especially from one actress whose name was Majorie Rambeau. As she walked up to congratulate him, the audience was awe stricken. You see, Marjorie Rambeau had been involved in an accident and left paralyzed. However, she was so encouraged by his words of faith and encouragement that she literally got up and walked and kept on walking. Remember, there is power in the spoken word – power to speak mountains out of the way.

The Face Of The Lord
Revelation 22:4

The Bible says: "AND THEY SHALL SEE HIS FACE; AND HIS NAME SHALL BE IN THEIR FOREHEADS." There are many who constantly are seeking the "favor" of God but few who truly seek the "face of God." The heart of God must be grieved by those who constantly come seeking his blessings but not a closer walk with Him where His presence is felt. I am reminded of the little girl whose mother was putting her to bed. The child realized that she was in darkness and was afraid. She asked, "Mother, am I to be left alone in the dark?" The mother replied, "Yes, but you have God with you all the time." "Yes, I know that God is with me all the time," exclaimed the little girl, "but I want somebody who has a face." How God yearns for His children to know Him in such a real and personal way. While we must now trust Him by faith as we look through the glass darkly, how warmly comforting it is to know that in heaven the Bible says, "THEY SHALL SEE HIS FACE..." God's face shall be seen by those who sincerely seek Him.

The Blessing Of Believing
John 20:29

The Bible says: "JESUS SAITH UNTO HIM, THOMAS, BECAUSE THOU HAST SEEN ME, THOU HAST BELIEVED: BLESSED ARE THEY THAT HAVE NOT SEEN, AND YET HAVE BELIEVED." A man once dreamed that he saw three nuns praying, and the Lord Jesus entered the room. Jesus went to the first nun and put His hands upon her head and spoke a few words to her; He went to the second and just put His hands upon her head; and He just simply walked by the third. The man surmised that the first nun must have loved and trusted the Lord more than the other two, but Jesus informed him that it was quite the contrary. The Lord said, "the first nun on which I placed my hands is very weak and constantly needs to feel my touch and hear my voice. The last one is very strong. She has a deep love and trust for me and her love and trust is not dependent upon the touch of my hand or the word of my mouth, for she knows I am faithful and will keep every word I have promised." To me this constitutes the blessing of believing, and explains what Jesus meant when He said, "BLESSED ARE THEY THAT HAVE NOT SEEN AND YET HAVE BELIEVED."

The Power Of God's Word

James 1:21

The Bible says: "WHEREFORE LAY APART ALL FILTHINESS AND SUPERFLUITY OF NAUGHTINESS AND RECEIVE WITH MEEKNESS THE ENGRAFTED WORD, WHICH IS ABLE TO SAVE YOUR SOULS." The person who desires to live a holy life must realize that this is possible only through the Word of God that is engrafted or implanted into our heart. James uses the figure of grafting here to illustrate this principle. A favorite preacher of mine tells of how on a trip down to Florida he had this truth driven home to his heart. He said that a resident of Florida showed him a beautiful lemon tree in his back yard that bore sweet and delicious oranges. He had grafted a bud from a cultivated orange tree into the lower trunk of the lemon tree. As soon as the bud started to grow, showing that it was receiving nourishment from the roots, he cut off the trunk just above the engrafted bud, which continued to grow and eventually bore sweet fruit. This is what God does with a life committed to Him. He turns bitter lives into sweet lives when He implants and infuses His word into us.

Joy In The Lord

Philippians 4:4

The Bible says: "REJOICE IN THE LORD ALWAY: AND AGAIN I SAY, REJOICE." Anthisthenes made the queer statement that he would "rather be mad than pleased." The cynic philosophers argued that "pleasure was only the pause between two pains." You have a longing for something – that is the pain; you get it; the longing is satisfied and there is a pause in the pain; you enjoy it and the moment is gone; and the pain comes back again. And, in truth, that is the way that pleasure works. But the Christian joy is not dependent on things outside a man; its source is in the man, not in the circumstances. It comes from the consciousness of the living presence of the living Lord, the certainty that nothing separates us from the love of God in Him. The true believer's happiness is, then, not dependent upon happenings, but upon the Lord Himself. This is why Paul says: "REJOICE IN THE LORD ALWAY."

The Security Of The Saved
Ephesians 1:13-14

The Bible says: "IN WHOM YE ALSO TRUSTED, AFTER THAT YE HEARD THE WORD OF TRUTH, THE GOSPEL OF YOUR SALVATION: IN WHOM ALSO AFTER THAT YE BELIEVED, YE WERE SEALED WITH THAT HOLY SPIRIT OF PROMISE, WHICH IS THE EARNEST OF OUR INHERITANCE . . ." Often times, until financial arrangements can be made to close out a business transaction, one is asked to put up some "EARNEST" money. The purchaser, by giving the seller part of the purchase price, simply pledges to complete the transaction and if he does not, then simply loses what is called "the earnest money." In Ephesians, Paul says when a man hears the gospel, believes the gospel and trusts the gospel for salvation that God the Father seals the transaction by giving the new believer the Holy Spirit, which is His promise that He will complete the redemptive work that He has started. This constitutes the believer's security. Do you have this eternal security.

Counseling
Psalm 1:1

The Bible says: "BLESSED IS THE MAN THAT WALKETH NOT IN THE COUNSEL OF THE UNGODLY,..." Recently a noted lady columnist who had offered advice and counsel to marriages in difficulty for the last twenty years announced her own marriage was ending in divorce and stated, "The lady with all the answers does not know the answer to this one." This sad but shocking story serves to remind us that thousands of dollars are spent each year by distressed persons seeking counsel from various people who have not yet learned to solve their own problems. People often need counseling and should seek it. God says in Proverbs 12:15, "THE WAY OF THE FOOL IS RIGHT IN HIS OWN EYES: BUT HE THAT HEARKENETH TO COUNSEL IS WISE." It is imperative that we not forget the one that God describes as "THE WONDERFUL COUNSELOR," and the one that has never lost a case. Blessed and happy indeed is the man who finds counsel in Jesus Christ.

Pleasing God
Hebrews 11:6

The Bible says: "BUT WITHOUT FAITH IT IS IMPOSSIBLE TO PLEASE HIM: FOR HE THAT COMETH TO GOD MUST BELIEVE THAT HE IS, AND THAT HE IS A REWARDER OF THEM THAT DILIGENTLY SEEK HIM." The greatest desire of every believer should be to please God. I am confident that we will seek to please Him by faith when we realize that He sees everything we do and hears everything we say. A young college football player was not very good and saw little action until something happened in his life; his father died. The next game after the funeral he persuaded the coach to let him be on the kick-off team. He did so well that the coach let him play the entire game. Later the coach asked him what had happened to inspire him so. He replied, "Coach, my father who recently died was blind. He never saw me play a ball game, but today as I went out on that field I knew he was watching me for the first time, and I did my best." When God becomes real in our lives, we seek to please Him by doing our best for Him.

Repentance
Luke 13:3

The Bible says: "I TELL YOU, NAY: BUT, EXCEPT YE REPENT, YE SHALL ALL LIKEWISE PERISH." The Bible commands man that is unsaved and unregenerated and unforgiven to repent of his sins. Repentance is a mark of a man forgiven and on the way to heaven, but what is repentance? The word repentance means, among many things, "to change." When one repents of his sins he changes some things. He changes his mind about himself, about others, about his own behavior, and above all he changes his mind about God. He finds at long last that God is not against him, but He is for him. A father illustrates this beautifully. He was trying to get his son who was sleeping with him one night to go to sleep. He had tried everything but nothing seemed to work. Finally he threatened to whip him. The little boy grew silent. The father thought surely he was asleep when all of a sudden, out of the darkness, the little fellow said, "Daddy, are you looking in my direction?" The father said, "Yes son, I am looking in your direction." When we repent we find God has been looking in our direction all the time.

The Robe Of Righteousness
Revelation 19:7-8

The Bible says: "LET US BE GLAD AND REJOICE, AND GIVE HONOUR TO HIM: FOR THE MARRIAGE OF THE LAMB IS COME, AND HIS WIFE HATH MADE HERSELF READY. AND TO HER WAS GRANTED THAT SHE SHOULD BE ARRAYED IN FINE LINEN, CLEAN AND WHITE: FOR THE FINE LINEN IS THE RIGHTEOUSNESS OF SAINTS." Here is a beautiful picture of the church, the bride of Christ, as it is being presented to Him. John here and in 6:11 describes her wedding garment as a Robe of Righteousness. In Jesus' day He wore two robes, an inner and outer robe. The inner robe speaks of justification that comes by faith. The outer robe speaks of sanctification that comes by works. It is the outer robe of righteousness that John describes in Revelation. Bernard Newman tells of a peasant girl once who sewed constantly. He asked her if she never tired. "Oh no," she replied. "You see, I am making my wedding dress." In light of your life and works, what kind of robe will you wear?

Subjects Of The Kingdom
I Corinthians 6:9-11

The Bible says: "KNOW YE NOT THAT THE UNRIGHTEOUS SHALL NOT INHERIT THE KINGDOM OF GOD? BE NOT DECEIVED: NEITHER FORNICATORS, NOR IDOLATERS, NOR ADULTERERS, NOR EFFEMINATE, NOR ABUSERS OF THEMSELVES WITH MANKIND, NOR THIEVES, NOR COVETOUS, NOR DRUNKARDS, NOR REVILERS, NOR EXTORTIONERS, SHALL INHERIT THE KINGDOM OF GOD. AND SUCH WERE SOME OF YOU: BUT YE ARE WASHED, BUT YE ARE SANCTIFIED, BUT YE ARE JUSTIFIED IN THE NAME OF THE LORD JESUS, AND BY THE SPIRIT OF OUR GOD." Some people think that the only people who go to church and who can be saved are those who have never sinned. Here Paul gives us a vivid description of the subjects of the Kingdom. Many in the church today who are Christians formerly were drunkards, thieves and covetous, but they met Christ and He changed them. This is what Henry Ward Beecher meant when he said, "The church is not a gallery for the exhibition of eminent Christians but a school for the education of the imperfect ones, a nursery for the care of the weak ones and a hospital for the healing of those who need assiduous care."

Reaping Where We Have Not Sown
John 4:37-38

The Bible says: "AND HEREIN IS THAT SAYING TRUE, ONE SOWETH, AND ANOTHER REAPETH. I SENT YOU TO REAP THAT WHEREON YE BESTOWED NO LABOUR: OTHER MEN LABOURED, AND YE ARE ENTERED INTO THEIR LABOURS." Recently I had this truth pressed home to my heart in a real way. A very precious lady in our church died, who among many things left behind a very productive garden. The family invited us out to gather some vegetables and as we were gathering the vegetables I said to my son, "This is what the Bible means when it says, '. . . I SENT YOU TO REAP THAT WHEREON YE BESTOWED NO LABOUR . . .'" Suddenly I realized anew and afresh all of life is like that. I enjoy freedom and liberty in a country fought for and paid for with the blood of others. I pastor a church built and maintained through the years by the prayers and concern of others, and above all, I enjoy a life that is eternal because of Jesus Christ who purchased and provided it for me. Don't take life lightly.

Brokenness
Psalm 34:18

The Bible says: "THE LORD IS NIGH UNTO THEM THAT ARE OF A BROKEN HEART; AND SAVETH SUCH AS BE OF A CONTRITE SPIRIT." Today we live in a broken world; laws are broken, lives are broken, homes are broken, minds are broken. Today if you suffer from brokenness, do not despair, for there is hope. The Bible says, "THE LORD IS NIGH UNTO THEM THAT ARE OF A BROKEN HEART." We often cast aside the broken things and call them "JUNK" and useless, but God does the opposite. He casts aside the unbroken as useless. Before God can make us, He has to break us. Consider the great men of the Bible and you will discover them to be broken men. Earlier, Jacob, whose name meant supplanter, lived a life of deception. However, after he wrestled with the angel and was broken, his name was changed to Israel or Prince with God. Now Jacob was useful. Jacob discovered what we need to discover and that is "THAT OUR MAKING IS OUR BREAKING."

Those Whom God Uses
I Corinthians 1:27-29

The Bible says: "BUT GOD HATH CHOSEN THE FOOLISH THINGS OF THE WORLD TO CONFOUND THE WISE; AND GOD HATH CHOSEN THE WEAK THINGS OF THE WORLD TO CONFOUND THE THINGS WHICH ARE MIGHTY; AND BASE THINGS OF THE WORLD, AND THINGS WHICH ARE DESPISED, HATH GOD CHOSEN, YEA, AND THINGS WHICH ARE NOT, TO BRING TO NOUGHT THINGS THAT ARE: THAT NO FLESH SHOULD GLORY IN HIS PRESENCE." I heard of a woman once who lived most of her life thinking of herself as a weed. She could never picture herself as a flower making up a beautiful bouquet. She thought of herself as useless, and without value to herself or others, and only in the way. However, one day a friend shared with her the love of God, and suddenly she realized that God loved her and had accepted her and had a purpose for her life. She further realized that she was made in the very image of God, by God Himself and to reject herself was to look with criticism and skepticism upon what God had made. Her life took on a new purpose with a new found joy – a joy that can come to you when you are willing to accept yourself as God does.

Overcoming Fear
Isaiah 41:10

The Bible says: "FEAR THOU NOT; FOR I AM WITH THEE: BE NOT DISMAYED; FOR I AM THY GOD: I WILL STRENGTHEN THEE; YEA, I WILL HELP THEE; YEA, I WILL UPHOLD THEE WITH THE RIGHT HAND OF MY RIGHTEOUSNESS." I don't know why but as a young boy I was afraid of the dark, and living in an area where there was little electricity didn't help matters. Since we heated our house with wood and cooked on a wood stove, you can understand that the path to the wood pile was pretty well beaten out. Sometimes I got a little negligent with some of my chores and didn't get enough wood in for the night and Daddy would have to say, "Son, go to the woodpile and get some more wood." Being afraid of the dark, I would say, "Daddy, will you stand on the porch and wait for me." For some reason, I just didn't seem to be afraid when I knew that Daddy was near. Many times our Heavenly Father calls upon us to perform duties that demand courage. In times like this it is always comforting to know that He is always near.

God's Answer For Hopeless Situations
Zechariah 4:6

The Bible says: "... THIS IS THE WORD OF THE LORD UNTO ZERUBBABEL, SAYING, NOT BY MIGHT, NOR BY POWER, BUT BY MY SPIRIT, SAITH THE LORD OF HOSTS." Man often finds himself in situations that appear to be hopeless and without solution. Such was the case of Zerubabel. Yet right in the midst of that seemingly hopeless situation God reminded him that while man did not have the strength or power to overcome the overwhelming odds, His spirit would be the sustaining power and force to overcome the enemy. In other words, "... NOT BY MIGHT, NOR BY POWER, BUT BY MY SPIRIT SAITH THE LORD ..." It has long been said, and rightly so, that there are no hopeless situations; there are only men who have grown hopeless about them. There is something in the Christian hope that nothing can kill. It is a conviction that God is still alive. However hopeless your situation, just remember God said, "... NOT BY MIGHT, NOR BY POWER, BUT BY MY SPIRIT."

The Joy Of Thankfulness
Psalm 95:1-2

The Bible says: "O COME, LET US SING UNTO THE LORD: LET US MAKE A JOYFUL NOISE TO THE ROCK OF OUR SALVATION. LET US COME BEFORE HIS PRESENCE WITH THANKSGIVING, AND MAKE A JOYFUL NOISE UNTO HIM WITH PSALMS." A few years ago I was visiting a friend of mine in the Methodist Hospital in Houston, Texas. He had lost practically all use of his muscles. I shall never forget that as I visited with him, his wife turned to me and said, "Brother Bobby, have you thanked God for your muscles today?" I had to admit that I had not, and in so doing, realized that there were far too many things in my life that I daily took for granted. We need to be as grateful for the little things as the big. I think it was Thomas Secker who said, "He enjoys much who is thankful for little, a grateful mind is both a great and happy mind." If gratitude on the part of our children brings joy to our heart, how happy the heart of God must be when we, His children, express gratitude to Him.

Assurance Of Salvation
Romans 8:16

The Bible says: "THE SPIRIT ITSELF BEARETH WITNESS WITH OUR SPIRIT, THAT WE ARE THE CHILDREN OF GOD." God desires that His children know that they are saved. Someone once said, "if you could be saved and not know it, you could lose it and not miss it." I John 5:13 says the Epistle of John was written that new converts could know that they were saved! In Romans 8:16, Paul tells us that we can know that we are saved when our human spirit agrees with God's Holy Spirit. That means there is inward peace when the human and the divine element in us come into agreement. Let me use an experience to illustrate this. I was born in a farm house near San Augustine, Texas in 1935. The doctor did not register my birth and consequently, when I began to try to get a birth certificate, I had trouble. The county clerk said, "But, Mr. Roberts, we don't have a record of your birth." I said, "but man, look at me, you know I have been born. My mother and father told me where and when it happened." Just as my spirit bore witness with my parents that I was their son, so my spirit bears witness with God's Holy Spirit that I am His son. Are you sure that you are saved?

Assurance
I John 5:13

The Bible says: "THESE THINGS HAVE I WRITTEN UNTO YOU THAT BELIEVE ON THE NAME OF THE SON OF GOD; THAT YE MAY KNOW THAT YE HAVE ETERNAL LIFE, AND THAT YE MAY BELIEVE ON THE NAME OF THE SON OF GOD." Often people ask, "Can a person really know that they are saved?" The answer is most emphatically, yes! The Apostle Paul testifies of this truth in all of his writings and says, "I KNOW IN WHOM I HAVE BELIEVED." The Apostle Peter commands us to make our calling and election sure. The entire Epistle of I John is written to give assurance of salvation. The word KNOW is used in excess of thirty times. Our experience with Christ, our obedience to His word, our love of righteousness, our love of the brethren, our response to the word of God, our separation from the world, and the witness of the spirit all give the believer assurance that he has been saved. Remember that if you could be saved and not know it, you could lose it and never miss it. Yes the Bible says we can know that we are saved.

Heritage
Hebrews 12:1-2

The Bible says: "WHEREFORE SEEING WE ALSO ARE COMPASSED ABOUT WITH SO GREAT A CLOUD OF WITNESSES, LET US LAY ASIDE EVERY WEIGHT, AND THE SIN WHICH DOTH SO EASILY BESET US, AND LET US RUN WITH PATIENCE THE RACE THAT IS SET BEFORE US, LOOKING UNTO JESUS THE AUTHOR AND FINISHER OF OUR FAITH..." During our bicentennial, we took time to remember our great heritage and the price our founding fathers paid for the freedom we now enjoy. Truly, as the Scripture has said, "OTHER MEN HAVE LABORED AND WE HAVE ENTERED INTO THEIR LABOURS." Napoleon of old helps us realize this even more. On July 1, 1798 he landed in Alexandria, Egypt and proceeded to conquer the entire nation in about three weeks. At the conclusion of the campaign, he marshalled his armies in the shadows of the pyramids of Egypt and said, "SOLDIERS, FORTY CENTURIES LOOK DOWN ON US TODAY." Not only do the centuries look down but the saints who have preceded us look down to encourage us on in life's great race. May God help us to not fail them.

Safe And Secure In Christ
Psalm 32:6-7

The Bible says: "FOR THIS SHALL EVERY ONE THAT IS GODLY PRAY UNTO THEE IN A TIME WHEN THOU MAYEST BE FOUND: SURELY IN THE FLOODS OF GREAT WATERS THEY SHALL NOT COME NIGH UNTO HIM. THOU ART MY HIDING PLACE; THOU SHALT PRESERVE ME FROM TROUBLE; THOU SHALT COMPASS ME ABOUT WITH SONGS OF DELIVERANCE." Men seek safety in prosperity, prominence, and many earthly things, but man's greatest safety is in Christ during the storms and floods of life. A man once dreamed of seeing two sets of foot prints walking along the seaside in the sand. One was his and the other was Christ's. However, every so often he saw something strange. He would see only one set of footprints and he could not understand it. In the dream he was brought face to face with Christ and he asked the Lord about it. He commented to the Lord that it looked as though there were times that the Lord had forsaken him for there was only one set of footprints in the sand. "No," said the Lord, "when you saw only one set, those were mine, for I had to reach down and pick you up and carry you for you had grown weak." It is true, our greatest safety is in Christ during the storms and floods of life.

God's Grace Is Sufficient
II Corinthians 12:9

The Bible says: "AND HE SAID UNTO ME, MY GRACE IS SUFFICIENT FOR THEE: FOR MY STRENGTH IS MADE PERFECT IN WEAKNESS. MOST GLADLY THEREFORE WILL I RATHER GLORY IN MY INFIRMITIES, THAT THE POWER OF CHRIST MAY REST UPON ME." Irish Evangelist W.P. Nicholson of old tells how he went to Edinburg for some special electrical treatments in years gone by. He was asked to sit in a chair while the doctor sat down and began to read the daily paper. After waiting some time Mr. Nicholson asked that the treatment might begin. "You are being treated now," was the answer. Mr. Nicholson said, "But I do not feel anything." The doctor then picked up a board with lights on it and pressed it to his chest and they all lit up. Then the doctor said, "The reason you don't feel anything is that you are insulated." Every child of God has the power and grace of God flowing through him and even though he does not always feel it, he finds it there when needed.

The Anchor Of Hope
I Corinthians 15:19

The Bible says: "IF IN THIS LIFE ONLY WE HAVE HOPE IN CHRIST, WE ARE OF ALL MEN MOST MISERABLE." The news media all over the world is saying that there is no hope for the world. Philosophers are saying that we are doomed. Winston Churchill said in his day that our problems are beyond us. One Portland, Oregon newspaper said some time ago that a famine was to soon sweep our land. One Stanford University sociologist has said that nothing can prevent millions from starving to death. This is what great men are saying, but what does God say? Is there any hope? God says that we are to put our hope in Christ, an anchor that is sure and steadfast. It is a hope that will lead us not only to the grave but through the grave. It is hope that is based on anything less than Christ that leaves a man as Paul says, "miserable." What are you hoping in?

The Peculiar People Of God
Titus 2:14

The Bible says: Jesus ". . . GAVE HIMSELF FOR US, THAT HE MIGHT REDEEM US FROM ALL INIQUITY, AND PURIFY UNTO HIMSELF A PECULIAR PEOPLE, ZEALOUS OF GOOD WORKS." A Christian is not peculiar because of the way he dresses or the way he necessarily acts, but because of a possession. The word peculiar means actually a private, unique possession. The word comes from two words one meaning "around" and the other "to be." To understand that, draw a circle and put a dot in the middle of the circle. As the circle is around the dot, so God is around each one of His saints. The circle monopolizes the dot, and has the dot all to itself. So God has His own all to Himself and in this sense Christians are said to be peculiar inasmuch as they are God's own private possession. In this position the believer is not only God's possession but under God's protection. No temptation or trial can penetrate that circle to get to us without God's permissive will. This is the privilege of being God's peculiar people.

Holders On
Hebrews 10:38-39

The Bible says: "NOW THE JUST SHALL LIVE BY FAITH: BUT IF ANY MAN DRAW BACK, MY SOUL SHALL HAVE NO PLEASURE IN HIM. BUT WE ARE NOT OF THEM WHO DRAW BACK . . . ." A British book on labor referred to two kinds of workmen among steel workers. There were the "riviters" and the "holders-on." The riviters with their pneumatic hammers make a lot of noise and almost give the impression they are the only ones doing anything. The holders-on simply take their pincers and grip the red-hot iron without much noise while the riviters do their work. These two crafts must work together to complete any job. These two smiths stand for two classes of people we meet everywhere – those who are active and noisy, and others who simply do their work without making much fuss, but who are always at their place of responsibility and can be trusted. The church needs more holders-on. How would you classify yourself?

The Forgiving Father
Luke 15:18-20

The Bible says: "I WILL ARISE AND GO TO MY FATHER, AND WILL SAY UNTO HIM, FATHER, I HAVE SINNED AGAINST HEAVEN, AND BEFORE THEE, AND AM NO MORE WORTHY TO BE CALLED THY SON: MAKE ME AS ONE OF THY HIRED SERVANTS. AND HE AROSE, AND CAME TO HIS FATHER. BUT WHEN HE WAS YET A GREAT WAY OFF, HIS FATHER SAW HIM, AND HAD COMPASSION, AND RAN, AND FELL ON HIS NECK AND KISSED HIM." Once Abraham Lincoln was asked how he was going to treat the rebellious southerners when they had been defeated and returned to the union of the United States. The questioner expected that Lincoln would take vengeance, but he answered, "I WILL TREAT THEM AS IF THEY HAD NEVER BEEN AWAY." It is this kind of love that God the Father has and that causes Him to forgive the vilest sinner who comes back to Him. A study of God's word will help one to know God's forgiveness.

Sincerity
Philippians 1:9-10

The Bible says: "...I PRAY ... THAT YE MAY APPROVE THINGS THAT ARE EXCELLENT; THAT YE MAY BE SINCERE AND WITHOUT OFFENCE TILL THE DAY OF CHRIST." Paul here prays that the Philippian believers might live a life of sincerity. The word sincere is derived from a Latin expression meaning "without wax." This word is used to translate a Greek word meaning "suntested." We are told that the ancients had a very fine porcelain which was greatly valued. Often when it was being fired it would crack, and dishonest dealers would fill in the cracks with a pearly white wax which concealed the crack. However, if it was held to the sunlight the wax would melt and the crack would be revealed. Thus, the apostle would have the saints tested by the sunlight of God's truth and holiness and found to be SINCERE AND WITHOUT WAX.

Living Letters
II Corinthians 3:2

The Bible says: "YE ARE OUR EPISTLE WRITTEN IN OUR HEARTS, KNOWN AND READ OF ALL MEN." A few years ago I had the privilege of meeting an elderly Presbyterian preacher who was a graphologist, or one who studied peoples' handwriting for the purpose of character analysis. He could tell by the way one would slant their letters, cross their "t's" or dot their "i's" whether they were extroverts, introverts, withdrawn or outgoing. Now while some of us might question the practice, it does suggest a spiritual truth. Paul says in II Corinthians 3:2 that Christians are epistles, "KNOWN AND READ OF ALL MEN." Some preachers in Paul's day felt they needed letters of recommendation to introduce them to new groups, but Paul felt his best letter of recommendation was that written in the lives of those to whom he had ministered. What kind of letter of recommendation is your life writing for your pastor and your Lord.

Let's Go Back
Luke 5:5

The Bible says: "AND SIMON ANSWERING SAID UNTO HIM, MASTER, WE HAVE TOILED ALL THE NIGHT, AND HAVE TAKEN NOTHING: NEVERTHELESS AT THY WORD I WILL LET DOWN THE NET." The Bible reminds us that human deficiency is no alibi for not obeying Christ's command, and that Christ will never do FOR US what He wants to do through us. We must remember that the evil forces that bombard us are but attempts of Satan to cause us to feel incapable. Evil forces will make you miscalculate your potential and lose the blessings of God. Dr. S.W. Wright tells the story of a man who sought to raise the meanest dog in town. He fed him gun powder and everything to make him mean. Finally he thought he succeeded and carried him for a walk upon which they met a yellow looking animal that appeared also to be mean. He took his muzzle off and the dog charged the yellow animal that swallowed him whole. He asked the owner of the yellow animal what kind of a dog that was, upon which he replied, "Before I cut his tail off and painted him yellow, it was an alligator." Don't let Satan cause you to miscalculate your deficiencies.

Walking By Faith
II Corinthians 5:7

The Bible says: "FOR WE WALK BY FAITH, NOT BY SIGHT." One of the greatest sermons ever preached on faith was preached by Rev. Andrew Fuller to the North-Hamptonshire Association. The sermon was born out of a real life situation. There had been heavy rains. The rivers were flooded and at one crossing, Fuller, who was riding on horseback, hesitated. A farmer watching him shouted, "Go on sir, you are quite safe." Fuller urged his horse into the water, but when it rose to the saddle he stopped again. "Go on sir; all is right!" came the voice of the farmer again, and Fuller found out that in a few paces the water shallowed. That day he learned the meaning of the scripture that says, "WE WALK BY FAITH, NOT BY SIGHT." However, the child of God must remember that our walk is always on solid ground, though it might be hidden or concealed from us. Remember this when the waters of trouble rise up against you.

Hand-Me-Down Religion
John 18:34

The Bible says: "JESUS ANSWERED HIM, SAYEST THOU THIS THING OF THYSELF, OR DID OTHERS TELL IT THEE OF ME?" When Pilate asked Jesus if He was the King of the Jews, Jesus responded by saying, "SAYEST THOU THIS THING OF THYSELF, OR DID OTHERS TELL IT THEE OF ME?" It is not enough to believe in Christ because mother, father or friend does. We must believe because we have had an encounter with Him. When we stand before God at the Judgment, we will discover that a "Hand-me-down religion" won't work. Multitudes need to discover this before it is too late. John Wesley did. He had always thought he was a true Christian, until one day his ship was caught in a storm on the Atlantic Ocean and fear got hold of him. During the storm, he noticed the only people not afraid were some Moravian missionaries. When the storm was over, John Wesley asked one of them, "Were you not afraid?" "Afraid," said the Moravian, "why could I be afraid? I know Christ." And looking into John Wesley's face he said, "Do you know Christ?" And for the first time he realized he did not. What about you? Do you know Christ?

The Price Of Following Christ
Matthew 5:11-12

The Bible says: "BLESSED ARE YE, WHEN MEN SHALL REVILE YOU, AND PERSECUTE YOU, AND SHALL SAY ALL MANNER OF EVIL AGAINST YOU FALSELY, FOR MY SAKE. REJOICE, AND BE EXCEEDING GLAD: FOR GREAT IS YOUR REWARD IN HEAVEN..." There are many reasons perhaps why people do not become followers of Jesus Christ. However, one of the more prominent reasons is that many cannot cope with the pressure the world puts upon that person who makes Jesus not only their Saviour but also their Lord. In the olden days a certain Christian was called upon by his emperor to denounce his faith in the deity of Christ. He refused to do so. The emperor then said, "The whole world is against you." Then the Christian said, "I am against the whole world." Sometimes when we stand up for Jesus it seems like the whole world is against us, but we must remember that Christ is with us and that gives us a majority position.

The Greater One
I John 4:4

The Bible says: "YE ARE OF GOD, LITTLE CHILDREN, AND HAVE OVERCOME THEM: BECAUSE GREATER IS HE THAT IS IN YOU, THAN HE THAT IS IN THE WORLD." As a young boy I grew up with a friend who was much larger and seemingly stronger than myself in every way. He was a bully by nature and so you can understand that for several years I lived with a fear that one day I would displease him to the extent that he would jump on me and whip me. I was not a fighter as a youth, but after a few years of this fear, Billy did something to me that caused me to stand up against him. I was amazed to find out that when he really realized that I was going to fight him that I nearly scared him to death. After that confrontation, I never feared him again for I discovered that I was able to properly defend myself. Many of God's children are like I was with Billy. They live in fear of what Satan might do to them. How encouraging it is to know that God's Word says, "GREATER IS HE THAT IS IN YOU THAN HE THAT IS IN THE WORLD." No wonder Paul said. "I CAN DO ALL THINGS THROUGH CHRIST WHICH STRENGTHENETH ME."

God's Ability
I Thessalonians 5:24

The Bible says: "FAITHFUL IS HE THAT CALLETH YOU, WHO ALSO WILL DO IT." I knew a man, once, who was a tremendous man. He was a good moral man who had been reared in a Christian home, and yet this man was not a Christian. I asked him one day why he was not a Christian and he replied, "I am afraid that I can't live it." I said, "You are exactly right. You can't and God never said you could, but Christ can live it through you." The Christian life is not only a hard life; it is an impossible life. The only man who ever lived the life that God demands without failure was Jesus, and that is why, by faith, we must trust Him to do for us what we cannot do ourselves. This is the meaning of the words of the poet who said: "I CAN'T, HE NEVER SAID I COULD. HE CAN, HE ALWAYS SAID HE WOULD." This is what the Bible means when it says: "FAITHFUL IS HE THAT CALLETH YOU, WHO ALSO WILL DO IT."

Divine Confidence
II Timothy 2:1-2

The Bible says: "THOU THEREFORE, MY SON, BE STRONG IN THE GRACE THAT IS IN CHRIST JESUS. AND THE THINGS THAT THOU HAST HEARD OF ME AMONG MANY WITNESSES, THE SAME COMMIT THOU TO FAITHFUL MEN, WHO SHALL BE ABLE TO TEACH OTHERS ALSO." One of the biggest problems with which most of us have to contend is the problem of discouragement or the fear of failure. I remember, one time, I got really discouraged in a church where I was serving as pastor, and I went to one of my deacons who was manager of a large tire store. I shared my burden with him and Andy Kohn looked at me and said, "Pastor, sometimes my superior gives me my quota or the number of tires to sell for the month, and I think, man that's impossible. Then, however I think, you know, my boss must have a lot of confidence in me or he would not set my quota so high, and I get to work and sell more than my quota." When the task that God gives us seems impossible, let us remember, He must have a lot of confidence in us, so let's do our best.

Discouragement
Numbers 21:4

The Bible says in Numbers 21:4: "AND THEY JOURNEYED FROM MOUNT HOR BY THE WAY OF THE RED SEA, TO COMPASS THE LAND OF EDOM: AND THE SOUL OF THE PEOPLE WAS MUCH DISCOURAGED BECAUSE OF THE WAY." There is no sin the Christian has to cope with more than the sin of discouragement. Discouragement constantly knocks at all of our hearts' doors. Dr. Moses P. Timms illustrates this as only he could. He said the devil once had an auction sale to sell everything he had. He sold everything but one thing hanging in the corner of the ceiling. Someone asked, "How much will you take for that?" The devil said, "That's not for sale. You see that is discouragement and when all else fails, discouragement works." To those like the Israelites, who became discouraged along the way, God says: "... BE STRONG AND COURAGEOUS... FOR WITH US IS THE LORD OUR GOD TO HELP US AND FIGHT OUR BATTLES."

Failure Is Not Final
Luke 22:31-32

The Bible says: "AND THE LORD SAID, SIMON, SIMON, BEHOLD, SATAN HATH DESIRED TO HAVE YOU, THAT HE MAY SIFT YOU AS WHEAT: BUT I HAVE PRAYED FOR THEE, THAT THY FAITH FAIL NOT: AND WHEN THOU ART CONVERTED, STRENGTHEN THY BRETHREN." So often one is tempted to single out all the failures of Simon Peter, or the so called "doubting Thomas" and others who sought to serve the Lord. These men serve to remind us that failure is not final, and that the man who never fails is also the man who never attempts anything. We remember Babe Ruth as the Home Run King. Babe Ruth knocked 714 home runs during his career. What many people do not know is that he also was the "Strike Out King," for he struck out 1,330 times. History records that he struck out two times for every one home run he hit. Babe Ruth reminds us that failure is not final. Don't let your failures keep you from pressing on. Remember Jesus said to Peter: "...I HAVE PRAYED FOR THEE THAT THY FAITH FAIL NOT AND WHEN THOU ART CONVERTED, STRENGTHEN THE BRETHREN." Your failures can only qualify you for tomorrow's successes.

False Prophets
I John 4:1

The Bible says: "BELOVED, BELIEVE NOT EVERY SPIRIT, BUT TRY THE SPIRITS WHETHER THEY ARE OF GOD: BECAUSE MANY FALSE PROPHETS ARE GONE OUT INTO THE WORLD." Once while driving to Dallas, I happened to look in my rear view mirror to discover a car making every move that I made. I soon discovered I was being followed. I wondered why, but all of a sudden I realized why. A few weeks back I had borrowed a friend's C.B. radio for a trip to a convention and had put a small antenna on my car. When I returned home, I returned the radio but kept the antenna on the car. That day I suddenly realized that the car following me thought I had a C. B. radio and was following me for direction and protection, when really I had no radio. I wonder how many people today are looking to some man who appears to be a spiritual leader for help when the one they are looking to has no contact with God himself. This is why God's Word says, "TRY THE SPIRITS WHETHER THEY BE OF GOD . . ."

Fools For Christ's Sake
I Corinthians 4:10

The Bible says: "WE ARE FOOLS FOR CHRIST'S SAKE, BUT YE ARE WISE IN CHRIST; WE ARE WEAK, BUT YE ARE STRONG; YE ARE HONOURABLE, BUT WE ARE DESPISED." Webster defines a fool as one who acts absurdly or stupidly, or pursues a course contrary to wisdom. The truly born again believer, however, often acts contrary to the wisdom of man. Now let me illustrate what I mean. Several years ago a Brinks armored truck lost something like $250,000 in cash out in California. A man found the money and returned it. He was rewarded $10,000 in cash. However, later he testified that he wished he had never found the money because people were calling him a fool for returning it. They called him a fool for doing the only right and Christian thing to do. The Christian is ever to do the right thing even if it means being called a fool. It is better to be a fool for Christ than to be a thief for the devil.

Worldly Affection
Colossians 3:2

The Bible says: "SET YOUR AFFECTION ON THINGS ABOVE, NOT ON THINGS ON THE EARTH." The Bible repeatedly warns the believer against loving the world or getting too close to the world. The world He speaks of is of course not the world He made but the sinful world that man has made. The result of getting too close to the world is exemplified in the story of Sinbad the Sailor who sailed into the Indian Sea. Out of the sea there arose a Magnetic Rock that slowly and silently attracted Sinbad's ship until finally it got so close that the bolts began to be drawn out of the ship. Finally the ship fell apart as the sailors awoke. The world is like this magnetic rock that slowly pulls us so close until our very lives are destroyed by it before we wake up to what is taking place. This is why the Bible says: "Set your affection on things above, not on things on the earth."

Impossibilities
Luke 18:27

The Bible says in Luke 18:27: "AND HE SAID, THE THINGS WHICH ARE IMPOSSIBLE WITH MEN ARE POSSIBLE WITH GOD." Sometimes we as individuals face some seemingly impossibilities as Israel did when she faced the Red Sea with the Egyptian Army behind her. When we do we need to remember the words of the poet who said:

> Have you come to the Red Sea place in your life
> Where in spite of all you can do,
> There is no way out, there is no way back,
> There is no other way but through?
> Then wait on the Lord with a trust serene
> Till the night of your fear is gone,
> He will send the wind, he will heap the floods,
> When He says to your soul, Go on!
> And His hand will lead you through – clear through
> Ere the watery walls roll down,
> No foe can reach you, no wave can touch,
> No mightiest sea can drown.
> The tossing billows may rear their crests,
> Their foam at your feet may break,
> But over the bed you will walk dry shod
> IN THE PATH THAT YOUR LORD WILL MAKE.

(Annie Johnson Flint)

It Starts In The Heart
Matthew 23:25-26

The Bible says: "WOE UNTO YOU, SCRIBES AND PHARISEES, HYPOCRITES! FOR YE MAKE CLEAN THE OUTSIDE OF THE CUP AND OF THE PLATTER, BUT WITHIN THEY ARE FULL OF EXTORTION AND EXCESS . . . CLEANSE FIRST THAT WHICH IS WITHIN THE CUP AND PLATTER, THAT THE OUTSIDE OF THEM MAY BE CLEAN ALSO." Several years ago as a young minister I had lunch one day in one of the member's homes. I sat down and was served a large, luscious baked potato wrapped in foil. As I began to unwrap it, I noticed a large nail placed right in the middle of it. Having never seen that before, I laid aside my pride and exposed my ignorance by asking why the nail was in the potato. The host graciously explained that the nail was an aluminum nail put in the potato to make it bake from the inside out. That day I learned a great spiritual principle. People often try to get right with God by acting like the Pharisees. They clean up on the outside, but real Christianity begins inside. It begins in the heart. Man's greatest need then is not a new start but a new heart! It is not reformation but regeneration.

Beautiful Feet
Romans 10:15

The Bible says: ". . . AS IT IS WRITTEN, HOW BEAUTIFUL ARE THE FEET OF THEM THAT PREACH THE GOSPEL OF PEACE, AND BRING GLAD TIDINGS OF GOOD THINGS!" How strange that God would make such a statement. Now one could understand it if He had said how beautiful are the lips of them that preach the gospel, but He says how beautiful are the feet. This verse reminds us that our walking is more important than our talking. It is not enough to profess with our lips that we are Christians, we must possess with our lives those traits that reveal to others that we are. Someone has said, "You are writing a Gospel, a chapter each day, by deeds that you do, by words that you say. Men read what you write whether faithless or true, say, what is the Gospel according to you?" One infidel when saved said, "I trusted Christ because of a man who walked Christ before me for twenty-eight years." Can someone say that about you? Live in such a way that someday he can.

Seizing Our Opportunities
Ephesians 5:15-16

The Bible says: "SEE THEN THAT YE WALK CIRCUMSPECTLY, NOT AS FOOLS, BUT AS WISE, REDEEMING THE TIME, BECAUSE THE DAYS ARE EVIL." A business man, harassed and discouraged from overwork, took his problem to a psychiatrist who promptly told him to do less work. "Furthermore," prescribed the doctor, "I want you to spend an hour each week in the cemetery." "Why do you want me to do that and what should I do in the cemetery?" "Not much. Take it easy, look around. Get acquainted with some of the men already in there and remember that they didn't finish their work either. Nobody does, you know." Since it is true that, at death, many of us will leave unfinished tasks behind; we should heed the challenge of the Apostle Paul when he said, ". . . Redeeming the time, . . ." or literally take advantage of every opportunity. This may necessitate establishing some proper priorities and of trusting God more.

Steadfastness
Luke 19:13

The Bible says: "AND HE CALLED HIS TEN SERVANTS, AND DELIVERED THEM TEN POUNDS, AND SAID UNTO THEM, OCCUPY TILL I COME." A young convert told of how he was in the "Lost Battalion" during World War I and was cut off from food and water by the Germans. They had only one shell left and finally decided to use it as a signal. They waited until night and turned the cannon straight up and shot the last shell, hoping the Americans would see it. The next morning an airplane dropped canteens of water and bread with a note saying, "Hold on. We are coming!" Soon the army came and rescued them. We Christians are being asked to surrender to the world in these last days, but God sends us this message, "Hold on! I am coming soon!" This is the meaning of those great words uttered by our Lord when He said, "OCCUPY TILL I COME." Can He count on you?

Looking Back
Luke 9:62

The Bible says: "AND JESUS SAID UNTO HIM, NO MAN, HAVING PUT HIS HAND TO THE PLOUGH, AND LOOKING BACK, IS FIT FOR THE KINGDOM OF GOD." The Christian life is a warfare and Satan, through various circumstances seeks to get the believer to turn back, but Christ encourages him on. Dr. Jeff D. Ray used to stand before his seminary class with tears streaming down his face and repeat this old poem:

> I want to let go, but I won't let go,
> There are battles to fight by day and by night
> For God and the right,
> And I'll not let go.
>
> I want to let go, but I won't let go
> I'm sick 'tis true and worried and blue
> And worn through and through,
> But I'll not let go.
>
> I want to let go, but I won't let go,
> What? Lie down on the field and surrender my shield?
> I'll never yield
> And I'll never let go.
>
> I want to let go, but I won't let go,
> May this be my song 'mid legions of wrong,
> Oh God keep me strong, So I'll never let go.

Make this your prayer today and keep on keeping on.

Bread On The Water
Ecclesiastes 11:1

The Bible says: "CAST THY BREAD UPON THE WATERS: FOR THOU SHALT FIND IT AFTER MANY DAYS." Many years ago as a young Scotsman was returning from work he saw a young lad caught in quicksand, and at the risk of his own life, he saved the boy from a perilous death. The father of the young boy wanted to reward him, but he refused. Finally however, the Scotsman allowed him to take his son and send him to college where he studied medicine. The name of this young man who was educated as a result of his father's bravery was Walter Fleming, the discoverer of Penicillin. The story does not end there, however, because the son of the wealthy man who had been rescued from the quicksand grew up and went off to war, to die. But because of a vaccine given him, he lived. The vaccine was penicillin. That young man's name was Winston Churchill! Soloman said, "Cast thy bread upon the waters; for thou shalt find it after many days."

The Way To Greatness
Matthew 20:26-27

The Bible says: "... BUT WHOSOEVER WILL BE GREAT AMONG YOU, LET HIM BE YOUR MINISTER; AND WHOSOEVER WILL BE CHIEF AMONG YOU, LET HIM BE YOUR SERVANT." Some people in their craze for greatness think nothing of stepping on others in order to achieve their goals, but that by no means is the sign of a truly great person. Sometime ago I heard Miss Ethel Merman as she was being interviewed on television. She said that as she was just beginning her career, she was privileged to audition before the great composer, Mr. George Gershwin. He handed her one of the compositions that he had laboured over and said, "Miss Merman, I will be happy to change any of this if it does not meet with your approval." Ethel Merman was so encouraged and astonished by the words of this truly great man that it gave her the impetus needed to begin her Broadway career. George Gershwin truly illustrated the words of Jesus when He said, "...AND WHOSOEVER WILL BE CHIEF AMONG YOU, LET HIM BE YOUR SERVANT."

The Light Of The World
Matthew 5:14

The Bible says: "YE ARE THE LIGHT OF THE WORLD. A CITY THAT IS SET ON A HILL CANNOT BE HID." God uses many words to describe Christians or believers. They are described as disciples, sons of God, children of God, but here Jesus Himself describes them as the light of the world. He uses physical words to describe the spiritual function of believers. When we understand what light is physically, then we can understand what, we as believers are to be spiritually. As light, we are to point the way to Jesus. Years ago, a church off the coast of England was levelled by bombs during one of the wars. The people determined they could not rebuild, but an admiral in the British Navy said, "You must rebuild for our ships look for light from your steeple and listen for the sound of the bell from the bell tower." Does your life mean this to men seeking their way in this dark and sin filled world?

Him
John 1:4

The Bible says: "IN HIM WAS LIFE; AND THE LIFE WAS THE LIGHT OF MEN." Men attempt to seek life or salvation in baptism, in the church, or in good works, but God's word says "IN HIM WAS LIFE . . . ." Dr. S.D. Gordon used to tell the story of an old Christian saint who had been an ardent student of God's word, but with the coming of age her mind began to fail her. However, there was one verse that remained with her. She would often quote, "I KNOW WHOM I HAVE BELIEVED AND AM PERSUADED THAT HE IS ABLE TO KEEP THAT WHICH I HAVE COMMITTED UNTO HIM AGAINST THAT DAY." Just before the end of her life she was heard repeating over and over to herself "HIM, HIM, HIM." Dr. Gordon in telling the story often said, "She had lost all the Bible except one word, but in that one word she had all the Bible." If you have tried all else and it has failed, why not TRUST HIM WHO NEVER FAILS.

The Task Of The Minister
II Timothy 4:2

The Bible says: "PREACH THE WORD; BE INSTANT IN SEASON, OUT OF SEASON; REPROVE, REBUKE, EXHORT WITH ALL LONGSUFFERING AND DOCTRINE." A little boy wrote a four sentence essay on Socrates. "Socrates was a Greek. Socrates was a great man. Socrates told people how to live their lives. They poisoned Socrates." Telling other people how to live is hazardous work. Yet this is precisely the task of every minister. The pastor is a God-appointed man to proclaim a God-given message to the world. He is not supposed to tell people what they want to hear, but what they need to hear. His task is one that is difficult. Dr. John F. Anderson suggests four things you should do for your pastor: 1) HELP HIM, don't hound him; 2) HEAR HIM OUT, don't hush him up; 3) HUG HIM, but don't hurt him; 4) HOLD HIM UP, but don't hollow him out. Many preachers give empty messages because they have been drained dry and no one has manned the spiritual pump of prayer. What are you doing to help your preacher fulfill his calling.

Chapter 9
Conquering Circumstances

Tempered Trials
I Corinthians 10:13

The Bible says: "THERE HATH NO TEMPTATION TAKEN YOU BUT SUCH AS IS COMMON TO MAN: BUT GOD IS FAITHFUL, WHO WILL NOT SUFFER YOU TO BE TEMPTED ABOVE THAT YE ARE ABLE..." Sometimes, we feel our trials and troubles are more than we can bear, but God in His Bible promises us that while He permits or orders our trials that He also regulates them. Our trials are so timed that they never come rushing in when we are too weak to bear them. Each test is tempered by His grace and controlled by His wisdom. John Bradford, the famous martyr, was plagued by aches and pains and an unexplainable feeling of sadness, but while confined in a damp dungeon, he wrote, "It is an amazing thing that ever since I have been in this prison and have had other trials to bear, I have had no touch of my rheumatism or my depression of spirit." This is what John Bunyan had in mind when he said, "In times of affliction, we commonly meet the sweetest experience of the love of God." God will not permit us to be tempted above what we are able to bear.

Working Together For Good
Romans 8:28

The Bible says: "AND WE KNOW THAT ALL THINGS WORK TOGETHER FOR GOOD TO THEM THAT LOVE GOD, TO THEM WHO ARE THE CALLED ACCORDING TO HIS PURPOSE." God never has promised that all things that happen are good, but to those who love God and who are divinely called by Him, He promises to bring good out of the bad that may come our way. The story is told of the poet Cowper who was subject to fits of great depression. One day he ordered a cab to drive him to London Bridge. The cab driver lost his way in the fog and finally wound up back at Cowper's home. When Cowper offered to pay him he refused. Yet Cowper said to the cabbie, "You have saved my life. I was on my way to throw myself off London Bridge." He gave him double the usual and went home and wrote the hymn, "GOD MOVES IN MYSTERIOUS WAYS, HIS WONDERS TO PERFORM, HE PLANTS HIS FOOTSTEPS ON THE SEA AND RIDES UPON THE STORM." Yes, dear friends, through faith we do know that all things work together to good to them that love God.

Refiner's Fire
Malachi 3:2-3

The Bible says: "BUT WHO MAY ABIDE THE DAY OF HIS COMING? AND WHO SHALL STAND WHEN HE APPEARETH? FOR HE IS LIKE A REFINER'S FIRE, AND LIKE FULLERS' SOAP: AND HE SHALL SIT AS A REFINER AND PURIFIER OF SILVER: AND HE SHALL PURIFY THE SONS OF LEVI . . ." The Bible presents the Lord as a refiner who is refining and purifying our lives. Whatever method He uses to purify us, we must submit. We cannot become greater or better than what we allow God to do in us or through us. God cannot get depth out of a shallow life. Gold cannot be had except by fire. Sap cannot flow except by a wound. One cannot drink grapes. Oswald Chambers says, "God can never make us wine if we object to the fingers He uses to crush us. However, when He uses someone whom we dislike, or some set of circumstances to which we said we would never submit we object. If we are going to be wine to drink, we will have to be crushed." God is a refiner and purifier of men.

Temptation
James 1:2-3

The Bible says: "MY BRETHREN, COUNT IT ALL JOY WHEN YE FALL INTO DIVERS TEMPTATIONS; KNOWING THIS, THAT THE TRYING OF YOUR FAITH WORKETH PATIENCE." David Wilkerson in a little book entitled, *I'm Not Mad At God*, tells of how he interpreted all the bad things that happened to him in terms of judgment, until one day it was revealed to him by the Spirit that this was a trick of Satan to get him to disbelieve God. James says tribulation brings patience. The poet said: "God hath not promised skies always blue, flower-strewn pathways all our lives through, God hath not promised sun without rain, joy without sorrow, peace without pain. God hath not promised we shall not know toil and temptation, trouble and woe. He hath not told us we shall not bear, many a burden, many a care. But God hath promised strength for the day, rest for the laborer, light for the way, grace for the trials, help from above, unveiling sympathy, undying love." Because I know this I too can say, "I'M NOT MAD AT GOD."

God's Threshing Instrument
Romans 5:3

The Bible says: "TRIBULATION WORKETH PATIENCE; AND PATIENCE, EXPERIENCE..." Have you ever wondered why you have to go through such tribulations as you often go through? An understanding of the word "TRIBULATION" will help you. The word tribulation comes from a Latin word meaning "Tribulum," which was the threshing instrument the Roman farmer used to separate the grain from the husks. When we seek to understand our trials and tribulations in light of this, we will suddenly discover that tribulation is but a divine instrument that God uses to purify His children by extracting the impurities of their lives. The Bible says that "TRIBULATION WORKETH." Tribulation works out what God works in. God has given His children a new character, and tribulation proves our conduct. It is through the trials and tribulations of life that God's love, concern and compassion for mankind are fully revealed through us.

From Where I Sit
Ezekiel 3:15

The Bible says: "THEN I CAME TO THEM OF THE CAPTIVITY OF TEL-ABIB, THAT DWELT BY THE RIVER OF CHEBAR, AND I SAT WHERE THEY SAT, AND REMAINED THERE ASTONISHED AMONG THEM SEVEN DAYS." Recently I read an article entitled, "From Where I Sit." It was the story of a woman who, being restricted to a wheelchair, interpreted life literally from where she sat. When I read this article I thought of the many people who are constantly trying to provide and interpret programs for the lonely, the poverty stricken, the homeless, the jobless and yet they have never sat where they sat. This thought gripped the Prophet Ezekiel so much that he went and sat where the people sat. An understanding of this principle will help us to respond to our trials and sufferings in a Christian attitude. Let us remember that when we are passing through trials that God is only enabling us to sit where others sit. We will then be better able to understand them and minister to them as we become an extension of the life of Christ.

The Faith That Never Falters
Daniel 3:17-18

The Bible says: "IF IT BE SO, OUR GOD WHOM WE SERVE IS ABLE TO DELIVER US FROM THE FIERY FURNACE, AND HE WILL DELIVER US OUT OF THINE HAND, O KING. BUT IF NOT, BE IT KNOWN UNTO THEE, O KING, THAT WE WILL NOT SERVE THY GODS . . . ." Several years ago I was visiting in a hospital when I met a lady whose husband had gone through several crises and was at the very point of death. I shall never forget hearing her say that day, "If God lets him die I will never trust Him again." How sad it is that some people who feel that way look upon trials and troubles as an indication that God is mad at them or punishing them. They fail to see the love of God and the purpose of God in them. Through our fiery furnaces, God is wanting to reveal Himself to us as He did to the three Jews in our text today. He is wanting us to learn the value of trusting Him supremely and resting in Him serenely. This is the way the three Jews responded. They said, "We believe God can deliver us . . . that God will deliver us . . . but if not we will trust Him anyway . . . ." How far can you trust God?

Know Your Pilot
Hebrews 2:18

The Bible says: "FOR IN THAT HE HIMSELF HATH SUFFERED BEING TEMPTED, HE IS ABLE TO SUCCOUR THEM THAT ARE TEMPTED." Sometime ago my wife, Gay, and I boarded a jet in Dallas to fly to New York and on to Israel. On the flight from Dallas to New York we sat beside a man, whom we later learned to be Captain Pollard, a 747 jet pilot, who that day was a passenger. During the course of our conversation, I asked Captain Pollard if the other pilots made him nervous when he was just traveling as a passenger. I shall never forget his answer! He said, "No sir, because I know what they had to go through in order to get in that cockpit." You know, friend, sometimes when we begin to murmur and question whether the Lord really understands our own situations and problems, we need to remember the words of this pilot. You see the Lord was tempted and tried in all points like we are, and because of that He is able to help us. As our pilot, He gives our lives the directions they need. Maybe what you need to do is just get to know your pilot. The Bible can help you do that.

Things That Work For Good
Romans 8:28

The Bible says: "AND WE KNOW THAT ALL THINGS WORK TOGETHER FOR GOOD TO THEM THAT LOVE GOD, TO THEM WHO ARE THE CALLED ACCORDING TO HIS PURPOSE." Here is one of the most tremendous promises in God's Word. God does not promise us that all things that happen to us are good, but He does promise that all things work together for good. The phrase "WORK TOGETHER" is a medical term and refers to medicine and speaks of several ingredients being put together by an Apothecary for the purpose of working together for the good of the patient. We are not told that "some things" but "all things" work together for good. We are not told that they might work together for good. This promise is not to all, but for those first of all who "LOVE GOD," secondly "TO THEM WHO ARE THE CALLED ACCORDING TO HIS PURPOSE." Thus, this promise is given to those who have truly repented of their sins and been born again.

Triumph In The Hour Of Trouble
Psalm 50:15

The Bible says: "AND CALL UPON ME IN THE DAY OF TROUBLE: I WILL DELIVER THEE, AND THOU SHALT GLORIFY ME." An artist once painted an impressive picture of a boat loaded with cattle, crossing a turbulent river. The lightning was flashing, the thunder rolling, and the waves were dashing against the boat. Awful fright was stamped on the faces of the cattle, but underneath were the words, "Just changing pastures." Sorrow and suffering, trials and tribulations are often but instruments that God uses to move us to higher ground. They only serve as heaven's mechanics in the garage of life to tune the motor for the journey ahead. No wonder then that the Apostle James tells us to count it all joy when we enter into divers temptations or trials. We can rejoice, not because of the trials, but because of what we discover through them. Maybe we too are just changing pastures.

Keeping Your Eyes On Jesus
Isaiah 26:3-4

The Bible says: "THOU WILT KEEP HIM IN PERFECT PEACE, WHOSE MIND IS STAYED ON THEE: BECAUSE HE TRUSTETH IN THEE. TRUST YE IN THE LORD FOR EVER: FOR IN THE LORD JEHOVAH IS EVERLASTING STRENGTH." How often it is in life that we get into serious difficulty because we begin to look to self and others and get our eyes off of Jesus. I am reminded of a little boy who begged his father to let him climb a ladder up to a housetop where the father was repairing the roof. Finally the father agreed to let him come up, but he said to him, "Just climb up the ladder and look straight at me and everything will be all right." The little boy started up the ladder, but halfway up he looked down and seeing how far he was from the ground became afraid and began to cry. The father cried out, "Don't look down, son, look up at me and keep climbing." So he looked into his father's face, kept climbing and in a few minutes was in the safety of his father's arms. When trouble surrounds you, remember to look up.

Songs In The Night
Job 35:10

The Bible says: "BUT NONE SAITH, WHERE IS GOD MY MAKER, WHO GIVETH SONGS IN THE NIGHT." Life, not even for the Christian, is always at its best. There are trials and troubles, but God promises to give us a song even in life's darkest hour. Years ago the English steamer, STELLA, was wrecked on a rocky coast. Twelve women were put into a lifeboat, but the boisterous sea immediately carried them away. Having no oars, they were at the mercy of the winds and waves, and probably would have lost hope except for one lady, Margaret Williams, who was well known for her sacred Oratorios. Calmly, she prayed aloud for divine protection, and encouraged her companions by singing hymns of comfort. Early the next morning, a small craft searching for survivors, midst the thick fog, heard Miss Williams singing , and steering in the direction of her strong voice, soon spotted the drifting lifeboat and rescued the ladies. Our victory over life's dark moments rest in our faith in Him who gives us a song in the night.

The Blessings Of The Unoffended
Matthew 11:6

The Bible says: "AND BLESSED IS HE, WHOSOEVER SHALL NOT BE OFFENDED IN ME." Do you sometimes feel that God is unfair to you? Do you resent the trials that come your way? Do you question His dealing with you? Dear friend if you do, then pray and ask God to help you overcome that because He promises to bless those who place their faith in Him and refuse to be offended by trying circumstances. John the Baptist found this out in prison. He knew that his life was about over, and he sent two men to ask Jesus if He was the Messiah or if they should look for another. Jesus demonstrated His power and then sent John the message: "BLESSED IS HE, WHOSOEVER SHALL NOT BE OFFENDED IN ME." John knew He had the power to deliver him but was not offended when He did not. He sealed his testimony with his life. Remember this promise when you find yourself in the midst of difficulty.

Testifying Through Trials
Luke 21:12-13

The Bible says: "BUT BEFORE ALL THESE, THEY SHALL LAY THEIR HANDS ON YOU, AND PERSECUTE YOU, DELIVERING YOU UP TO THE SYNAGOGUES, AND INTO PRISONS, BEING BROUGHT BEFORE KINGS AND RULERS FOR MY NAME'S SAKE. AND IT SHALL TURN TO YOU FOR A TESTIMONY." We often hear of how we are to witness for our Lord, but seldom do we realize that the trials and troubles that come our way are but opportunities for us to do that very thing. The attitude we have during the trials determines how potent our testimony will be for Christ. Henry Ward Beecher said, "It is a trial that proves one thing weak and another strong. A house built on the sand is in fair weather just as good as if built on the rock; a cobweb is as good as the mightiest cable when there is no strain upon it." God's children should thank Him for their trials; it is through them that they give testimony of God's power to change lives.

Divine Woodcutters
Philippians 1:12

The Bible says: "BUT I WOULD YE SHOULD UNDERSTAND, BRETHREN, THAT THE THINGS WHICH HAPPENED UNTO ME HAVE FALLEN OUT RATHER UNTO THE FURTHERANCE OF THE GOSPEL." Paul was in prison, and some of his friends felt this would hurt his ministry and curtail his work. He wrote to inform them that the opposite was true and that what had happened to him had "FALLEN OUT UNTO THE FURTHERANCE OF THE GOSPEL." The word "fallen out" means "to come as the result of." It was a word used to describe the men who went before the Roman Army, clearing out the forest and making way for the army to advance into areas not previously accessible. Sometimes the trials and troubles that befall us are not intended to HURT us but to HELP us. As Christians we are divine woodcutters, and we must see that often the things that happen to us only cut the way for the Gospel to enter where it could not have entered otherwise.

Forgetting The Past
Philippians 3:13-14

The Bible says: "BRETHREN, I COUNT NOT MYSELF TO HAVE APPREHENDED: BUT THIS ONE THING I DO, FORGETTING THOSE THINGS WHICH ARE BEHIND, AND REACHING FORTH UNTO THOSE THINGS WHICH ARE BEFORE, I PRESS TOWARD THE MARK FOR THE PRIZE OF THE HIGH CALLING OF GOD IN CHRIST JESUS." While one may look at the past for instruction, he must not live there. Living in the past can be both distressing and depressing. The great preacher, Watkinson, once took his grandson for a walk by the seaside and while there they met an old man very disgruntled, who was suffering from a slight sunstroke. The little boy had not heard all the conversation correctly, and when they left the grumbling complaints of the old man, he turned to his grandfather and said, "Granddad I hope that you never suffer from a sunset." The Christian march is on, not to a sunset but a sunrise. The Christian's watch word is not backward but forward.

Tribulation
Romans 5:3

The Bible says in Romans 5:3: "... BUT WE GLORY IN TRIBULATIONS ALSO: KNOWING THAT TRIBULATIONS WORKETH PATIENCE." In this verse God tells us how that we can rejoice through troubles and trials and the reverses of life. We understand it by understanding the meaning of tribulation. Tribulation is a Latin word meaning, "TRIBULUM," which was a threshing instrument used by the Roman farmer. In this sense tribulation becomes God's threshing instrument. Tribulation works out what God has worked in. God has given every believer a new character. Tribulation proves our conduct and demonstrates that character. Tribulation may come upon us with great pressure, but remember that out of pressure comes power for great engines and out of pressure comes sweet perfume from the crushed flowers. Understanding this we can rejoice in tribulation when it comes our way.

Purpose Of Sickness
John 9:1-3

The Bible says: "AND AS JESUS PASSED BY, HE SAW A MAN WHICH WAS BLIND FROM HIS BIRTH. AND HIS DISCIPLES ASKED HIM, SAYING, MASTER, WHO DID SIN, THIS MAN, OR HIS PARENTS, THAT HE WAS BORN BLIND? JESUS ANSWERED, NEITHER HATH THIS MAN SINNED, NOR HIS PARENTS: BUT THAT THE WORKS OF GOD SHOULD BE MADE MANIFEST IN HIM." Recently I was introduced to a young dedicated Christian man of twenty-three years of age who has an incurable disease and is at the point of death. The strange thing, however, about this young man and his family is that instead of them being in a constant state of sadness and sorrow, they seem to be praising God every time one goes into the room. The doctors and nurses have been literally amazed at their faith and courage. As I left his room recently, I thought, "Well, that is the purpose of sickness; that the Christian through his troubles might have opportunity to express and demonstrate his faith." Through sickness a man is either proved as was Job, or he is reproved as was the servant of Naiman, or he is approved as was the case of the blind man. Let your sickness praise the Lord.

Fruitfulness
John 15:8

The Bible says in John 15:8: "HEREIN IS MY FATHER GLORIFIED, THAT YE BEAR MUCH FRUIT; SO SHALL YE BE MY DISCIPLES." I remember early in my ministry, hearing the late Dr. Moses P. Timms speak about fruitbearing. He recalled the days when he lived in Whichita Falls, Texas. Brother Timms related that in front of his house he had several pecan trees. Each year when the pecan trees would begin to bear he would come home from revival meetings and find sticks and rocks under the trees. He said the old pecan trees would say, "MASTER DON'T LEAVE ME ANY MORE BECAUSE WHEN YOU ARE GONE PEOPLE COME AND THROW ROCKS AND STICKS AT ME AND BREAK MY LIMBS." Brother Timms said he would say to the pecan trees, "MR. PECAN TREE, DO YOU SEE THOSE MESQUITE TREES OUT YONDER? THE REASON YOU DON'T SEE ANY STICKS UNDER THEM IS BECAUSE THEY DON'T BEAR FRUIT. NOW DO YOU WANT TO BE LIKE THEM?" The pecan tree would say, "MASTER JUST LET THEM KEEP THROWING." A Christian can't bear fruit without having the devil throw rocks at him.

Spiritual Depression
Psalm 42:5

The Bible says: "WHY ARE THOU CAST DOWN, O MY SOUL? AND WHY ART THOU DISQUIETED IN ME? HOPE THOU IN GOD: . . ." Perhaps there is no problem man has to face more often than that of depression. In the Bible, Sampson, Elijah, Rachael, and Baalim were among those who became so depressed that they said to god, "LET ME DIE." David was suffering from depression when he wrote Psalm 42. Depression can be psychological, physical, or spiritual. Should one be depressed because of psychological reasons, they need to see a counselor; if it is physical they need to see a doctor; if it is spiritual they need to see a preacher. In Psalm 42, David's depression was the result of a spiritual problem. He had lost the reality of God's presence. This happened to Job. Job 3:3 says, "LET THE DAY PERISH WHEREIN I WAS BORN," but when his faith was restored he says in Job 19:25, "I KNOW THAT MY REDEEMER LIVETH." Faith in God usually corrects one's depression immediately.

The Good That Comes From Evil
Genesis 50:20

The Bible says: "BUT AS FOR YOU, YE THOUGHT EVIL AGAINST ME; BUT GOD MEANT IT UNTO GOOD . . ." These are the words that Joseph spoke to his brothers who had sold him into slavery when they came seeking food from him in Egypt. We, like Joseph, often find out in life that the evil that men would do to us often turns to good. I heard a story recently that illustrates this. A Danish sculptor went to Rome, produced some great works and shipped them back home. He had some servants who were resentful and as they uncrated the statues, they took the straw they were packed in and scattered it over the well-tilled garden hoping they would take root in the soil. Instead, exotic plants, native to Rome sprang up, and today they are some of Copenhagen's most beautiful flowers. When distressing circumstances come your way in life trust the Lord to bring good out of the evil.

Affliction
Hosea 5:15

The Bible says: "I WILL GO AND RETURN TO MY PLACE, TILL THEY ACKNOWLEDGE THEIR OFFENCE, AND SEEK MY FACE: IN THEIR AFFLICTION THEY WILL SEEK ME EARLY." There are many things that cause a person to seek the Lord. Some seek the lord as the result of a revelation of the love of God; others as the result of a deep hatred that they sense that God has against sin; others as the result of a conscious guilt of sin in their life. However, often people seek the Lord as the direct result of affliction that comes upon them. It is strange that affliction, trouble, and heartache have to come to get a person to see their need of the Lord, and yet this is often the case. This is what Stuart Hamblin meant when he said in giving his testimony, "That it's hard to sell Christ to a man who has a good job, money in his pocket, good health and a fine family." Could it be that your present affliction is but an effort of the Saviour to get you to seek Him?

Knowing The Voice Of God
John 10:27

The Bible says: "MY SHEEP HEAR MY VOICE, AND I KNOW THEM. AND THEY FOLLOW ME." The fact that God speaks and that men hear Him when He speaks is a truth often asserted by Christ Himself. The question is, how does God speak to us? In the Bible we discover that God through the ages has spoken to man through dreams, through the prophets, through the apostles and preachers, through the Bible, the Word of God itself and yes, even often through troubles that come upon us. I read once of a man who worked at an ice plant and who lost his watch in the saw dust. He sought to find it but couldn't. Finally he gave up and went to lunch. Later, after returning, he discovered that a young boy who worked at the ice plant had found it. He asked the lad how he found it. The lad replied, "I just laid down in the sawdust and listened for the tick. May the Lord help us amidst all of our troubles to listen to His voice and hear what He is saying to us.

Listening To God
Isaiah 55:3

The Bible says: "INCLINE YOUR EAR, AND COME UNTO ME: HEAR, AND YOUR SOUL SHALL LIVE; AND I WILL MAKE AN EVERLASTING COVENANT WITH YOU, EVEN THE SURE MERCIES OF DAVID." Jeannette Clift George, who played the role of Corrie Ten Boone in the movie, "THE HIDING PLACE," tells of how the pilot of the plane on which she was aboard, came on the intercom to announce that he had been informed that a bomb had been placed on their plane. She told of the fear that gripped her, along with many other passengers, and the pandemonium that broke out. However, sitting next to her was a man who never stopped reading his book. He remained completely at ease through the entire ordeal. When the plane finally landed safely, Jeannette Clift George thanked the man for the lesson of patience and faith he had taught her through the ordeal. He replied, "it's all part of traveling," and then he asked, "Incidentally, what did the pilot say when he came on the intercom?" It is often in life that God speaks to men, but they are too preoccupied to hear Him. The Bible says: "HEAR AND THY SOUL SHALL LIVE."

Patience
James 1:2-3

The Bible says: "MY BRETHREN, COUNT IT ALL JOY WHEN YE FALL INTO DIVERS TEMPTATIONS; KNOWING THIS, THAT THE TRYING OF YOUR FAITH WORKETH PATIENCE." G. Coleman Luck, in a little book of his, tells how a young minister who was lacking in patience once asked an older preacher to pray that he might have more patience. The old preacher got on his knees and began to pray that God would send troubles and difficulties upon the young preacher. As he was praying the young preacher tapped him on the shoulder and said, "You have misunderstood me. I asked you to pray that I might have more patience, not trouble." The older preacher replied, "The scripture says: 'Tribulation worketh patience.' That's the only way." If you are going through trouble remember that God may be working patience in your life.

Bibliography

Barclay, William. *The Letter to the Galatians and Ephesians.* Philadelphia: The Westminster Press, 1954.

Barclay, William. *The Letter to the Romans.* Philadelphia: The Westminster Press, 1955.

Blackstone, W. E. *Jesus Is Coming,* Old Tappan, New Jersey: Flemming H. Revell Co,. 1898.

Broadus, John A. *On The Preparation and Delivery of Sermons.* San Francisco: Harper and Row Publishers, 1870.

Brooks, Phillips. *Lectures on Preaching.* Grand Rapids, Michigan: Baker Book House, 1969.

Criswell, W. A. *Did Man Just Happen?* Grand Rapids, Michigan: Zondervan Publishing House, 1957.

Fromke, DeVern. *The Ultimate Intention.* Cloverdale, Indiana: Sure Foundation, 1963.

Jones, Ilion T. *Principles and Practice of Preaching.* Nashville: Abindon Press, 1956.

Knight, Walter B. *3000 Illustrations For Christian Service.* Grand Rapids, Michigan: Wm. B. Eerdmans Publishing Co., 1954.

Laurin, Roy L. *Philippians, Where Life Advances.* Findlay, Ohio: Dunham Publishing Co., 1948.

Laurin, Roy L. *Romans, Where Life Begins.* Findlay, Ohio: Dunham Publishing Co., 1948.

Lee, Robert G. *Payday Someday.* Grand Rapids, Michigan: Zondervan Publishing House, 1957.

McMillen, S. I. *None of These Diseases.* Old Tappan, New Jersey: Flemming H. Revell Co., 1971.

Maurer, B. A. *The Ten Commandments Will Not Budge.* Saint Louis, Missouri: Concordia Publishing House, 1951.

Oursler, Fulton. *Why I Know There Is A God.* Garden City, New York: Permabooks, 1954.

Perry, Lloyd M. *Biblical Preaching For Today's World.* Chicago: Moody Press, 1973.

Robinson, Haddon W. *Biblical Preaching.* Grand Rapids, Michigan: Baker Book House, 1980.

Sunday, Billy. *Wonderful And Other Sermons.* Grand Rapids, Michigan: Zondervan Publishing House.

Wagner, C. Peter. *A Turned On Church In an Uptight World.* Grand Rapids, Michigan: Zondervan Publishing House, 1971.

Wilkerson, David. *I'm Not Mad At God.* Minneapolis, Minnesota: Bethany Fellowship Inc., 1967.

Wuest, Kenneth S. *Golden Nuggets From The Greek New Testament.* Grand Rapids, Michigan: Wm. B. Eerdmans Publishing Co., 1940.

Wuest, Kenneth S. *Studies In The Vocabulary Of The Greek New Testament.* Grand Rapids, Michigan: Wm. B. Eerdmans Publishing Co., 1945.

INDEX

A Christian Home, 155
A Comforting Promise, 28
A Good Name, 118
A Mother's Influence, 158
A Sinning Brother, 149
A Son's World In His Father's Hand, 162
A Testimony From The Grave, 41
The Absurdity Of Excuses, 57
Abundant Life, 60
Acceptance Of Self, 18
Adultery, 160
Affiction, 204
Alcohol, 120
Almost But Lost, 48
The Anchor Of Hope, 178
Assurance, 176
Assurance Of Salvation, 176
Atheism, 69
The Atonement, 39
Attitudes, 102
Be Filled With The Spirit, 80
Be Still And Know, 95
Beautiful Feet, 188
Beholding Christ, 22
Being, 91
Believing, 41
Believing God, 39
Believing Is Seeing, 10
The Benefits Of Dying, 133
Besetting Sins, 86
The Blessing Of Believing, 168
The Blessings Of The Unoffended, 200
The Blood Of Christ, 61
The Book That Changes Lives, 3
The Book That Won't Burn, 4
The Book You Can Trust, 4
The Bread Of Life, 71
Bread On The Water, 190
Broken Cisterns, 56
Brokenness, 173
Building Faith In Others, 8
Building On Proper Foundations, 3
Carriers, 146
Checkpoints For Christians, 122
The Christ Who Dwells Within, 7
Christian Commitment, 164
Christian Example, 33
The Christian's Power, 88
The Christians Benefits, 76
Church Attendance, 147
The Church, Love It, 31
Cleaning Out The Well, 89
Coming Again, 28
Coming To Christ, 59
Consecration, 78
Conviction, 144
The Correction For Deception, 115
Counseling, 170
Counting The Cost, 46
Covering Sin, 127
Creation, 13
Criticism, 123
The Cross Of Christ, 61

Crossing The Branch, 129
Danger Of Boasting, 135
Danger Of Delay, 122
The Dead Give-Away, 117
Dead Men Talk, 138
Dead Or Alive, 91
Deadly Defiance, 135
Dealing With Delinquency, 162
Dealing With Our Past, 93
Death, Preparing To Meet God, 129
Defiled Hearts, 52
Denying The Flesh, 121
Depravity, 43
The Difference Christ Makes, 25
Discipline, 89
Discouragement, 185
Discovering The Reality Of Christ, 21
Divine Confidence, 184
Divine Direction, 82
Divine Guidance, 87
Divine Woodcutters, 201
Doctrine, 2
Don't Defile The Temple, 116
Don't Sell Out Too Cheaply, 53
Don't Waste Your Life – A Loss You Cannot Afford, 36
Drinking, 118
Empty Hands, 73
Enemies Of The Cross, 145
Enternal Separation, 156
Entertaining Angels, 23
Escaping God, 11
Eternal Darkness, 74
Everlasting Life, 48
Every Man Counts With God, 19
Excess Baggage, 94
Excuses, 113
The Eyes Of The Lord, 107
The Face Of The Lord, 168
Facing Evidence, 9
Facing The Future, 51
Failure Is Not Final, 185
Faith, 40
The Faith That Never Falters, 197
Falling Leaves And A Coming King, 29
False Gods, 16
False Prophets, 186
Famine, 30
Fault Finding, 109
Fear Of Death, 130
Fearing God, 15
Following A Father's Footprints, 157
Following Through, 79
Fools, 70
Fools For Christ's Sake, 186
Forgetting The Past, 201
Forgive And Forget, 114
Forgiveness, 124
The Forgiving Father, 180
Forms Of Religion, 12
Forsaking The World, 47
Free Homes, 74
From Where I Sit, 196
The Fruit Of A Father's Sin, 161

Fruitfulness, 203
Fruits Of Repentance, 100
Garbage Dump Thinking, 102
Getting Rid Of Jesus, 20
Giving, 32
God Cares, 166
God's Ability, 184
God's Answer For Hopeless Situations, 175
God's Cure For Tugging, 83
God's Grace Is Sufficient, 178
God's Judgement, 134
God's Law, 92
God's Love Demonstrated, 25
God's Plan For Happiness, 121
God's Principle For Receiving, 152
God's Promise Of The Rainbow, 166
God's Purchased Possession, 63
God's Response To His Enemies, 151
God's Standard For Judgement, 119
God's Threshing Instrument, 196
God's Unchanging Hand, 132
God's Wrath, 58
Good For Nothing Christians, 97
The Good That Comes From Evil, 204
The Great Blackout, 71
The Great Deceiver, 114
The Great Exposure, 151
The Greater One, 183
The Greatest Desire Of Men, 146
The Greatest Thief Of All, 64
Hand-Me-Down Religion, 182
Have Faith In God, 8
Heaven, 125
Heavenly Aspirations, 126
Helping The Weak, 141
Heritage, 177
High Cost Of Low Living, 65
Him, 192
History's Greatest Failure, 11
Holders On, 179
Home, 156
Hope, 72
Hope Of Life After Death, 137
How God Sees Us, 99
How To Face Death, 134
How To Hang On To Life, 140
How To Have A Good Day, 111
How To Hear God, 81
How To Love And Be Loved, 124
How To Take It With You, 64
How To Understand The Bible, 5
I Am Not Ashamed, 62
Immortality, 131
Impossibilities, 187
In The Image Of God, 13
The Indwelling Christ, 79
Is Death All?, 27
It Starts In The Heart, 188
Jesus Our Mediator, 66
Joy In The Lord, 169
The Joy Of Thankfulness, 175
The Judgment Of God, 52
Just As You Are, 38
Keeping Your Eyes On Jesus, 199
Know Your Pilot, 197
Knowing Christ, 67

Knowing Christ Personally, 24
Knowing God, 67
Knowing The Voice Of God, 205
Laborers Together, 148
The Lamb's Book Of Life, 73
Lamps Without Light, 68
The Last Days, 57
Laziness, 117
Learning To Love Oneself, 126
Leftovers, 115
Let Me Die, 136
Let Your Light Shine, 150
Let's Go Back, 181
Letting Your Influence Count, 155
Life After Death, 138
Life At Its Best, 98
Life's Contrast, 72
Life's Great Change, 133
Life's Great Choice, 50
The Light Of Jesus, 49
The Light Of The World, 191
The Light Still Shines, 22
Listening To God, 205
Living By Love, 152
Living By The Sword, 112
Living Dangerously, 123
Living Letters, 181
Living The Risen Life, 84
Locked Out, 69
Looking Back, 190
The Love Of God, 42
Making The Church, 32
Making Vows To God, 17
The Man Who Might Have Been, 159
Man's Worth To God, 42
Marriage, 157
Missions, 143
Moral Decay, 34
Motives For Giving, 98
Motives For Service, 141
Moving Mountains, 103
Much More, 77
The Name Of God, 17
The Name That Saves, 43
Narrowness, 63
Nature And God, 14
Neglect, 163
Neglected Vineyards, 96
The New Birth, 45
No Double Standards Please, 161
No Room In The Inn, 26
Nothing But Leaves, 90
Overcoming Evil, 109
Overcomming Fear, 174
Patience, 206
Peace, 110
Peace At Last, 111
Peace With God, 54
The Peculiar People Of God, 179
The Peril Of Working Mothers, 158
Pleasing God, 171
Possessing The Mind Of Christ, 85
The Power Of A Changed Life, 160
The Power Of God's Word, 169
The Power Of Influence, 150
The Power Of Living With Others, 153

The Power Of The Holy Spirit, 86
The Power Of The Spoken Word, 167
Prayer, 92
Predestination, 19
Preparing For The Final Event, 29
Pressing Onward, 88
Pretence, 110
The Price Of Following Christ, 183
Pride, 112
Prosperous But Perishing, 113
Purpose Of Sickness, 202
Pursuing Peace, 125
Put That On My Account, 40
Real Love, 15
The Reality Of Sin, 37
Reaping Where We Have Not Sown, 173
Redeeming The Time, 143
Redemption, 51
Refiner's Fire, 195
Repentance, 171
Revealed By Fire, 46
Revenge, 108
Reviling, 104
Revival, 127
The Right Way To Give, 159
The Risen Christ, 26
The Risen Life, 84
The Robe Of Righteousness, 172
Roll Call In Heaven, 136
Safe And Secure In Christ, 177
Saints, 148
The Salt Of The Earth, 144
Salvation, 68
Sanctification, 5
Satan's Lie, 76
Saving Faith, 93
The Second Coming Of Christ, 167
Second Hand Religion, 47
The Secret Of Obedience, 147
The Security Of The Saved, 170
Seizing Our Opportunities, 189
Self Examination, 99
Self Sufficiency, 12
Selling Out, 119
Seriousness Of Hell, 70
Service, 83
Shooting Holes In Darkness, 53
Short Beds And Narrow Cover, 37
Showing Our Gratitude, 142
The Shut Door, 49
The Signs Of The Times, 30
Sin And Prayer Or Unanswered Prayers, 96
Sin In The Believer, 85
Sin Of Omission, 106
Sin's Finished Product, 62
Sincerity, 180
Songs In The Night, 199
The Soul Of Man, 14
Soul Winning, 140
Sowing And Reaping, 107
Spirit Controlled Life, 80
Spiritual Castaways, 33
Spiritual Death, 59
Spiritual Depression, 203
Spiritual Handicaps, 78
Spiritual Mirages, 2

Spiritual Values, 55
Steadfastness, 189
Steps To Spiritual Power, 87
The Sting Of Death, 130
The Sting Of Sin, 142
The Strength Of Ignorance, 81
Subject For The Kingdom, 104
Subjects Of The Kingdom, 172
The Task Of The Minister, 192
Telling Someone How To Die, 137
Tempered Trials, 194
Temptation, 195
The Ten Commandments, 6
Testifying Through Trials, 200
Thankfulness, 106
Things That Work For Good, 198
Things To Think On, 105
Those Whom God Uses, 174
The Three Men In The Bible, 77
Too Late, 45
The Tragedy Of An Incomplete Life, 97
Tribulation, 202
Triumph In The Hour Of Trouble, 198
The True Way Proverbs, 65
The Ultimate Purpose Of God, 20
The Umpire Of Peace, 108
Understanding The Bible, 6
The Unspeakable Gift, 24
Unused Power, 90
Urgency Of Salvation, 50
Vengeance, 103
Walking By Faith, 182
Walking In The Light, 95
The Way Of The Cross Leads Home, 131
The Way To Greatness, 191
The Way To Happiness, 120
The Way To Life, 44
Wells Without Water, 149
What God Does With Our Sins, 38
What Is A Christian, 58
What's Right And What's Wrong, 105
What's Right With The Church?, 31
What's Wrong With The World, 163
When A Nation Forgets God, 16
When Death Becomes Invisible, 132
When God's Law Is Broken, 94
When Jesus Wiped The Mud Off, 55
When Love Grows Cold, 164
Where Is Christ, 27
Where Is God, 21
Who Is Worse, 9
Why Have The Showers Been Withheld?, 82
The Winning Choice, 60
The Wise Men, 23
Without Excuse, 44
Witnesses Of His Grace, 10
The Word Of God, 54
Working Together For God, 194
World Destruction, 56
The World's Greatest Banquet, 66
Worldly Affection, 187
Worship, 7
Worthy Of Praise, 18
Ye Are The Light Of The World, 145
You Have The Key To Life Or Death, 36
Zeal Without Knowledge, 116